Quitting Smoking
FOR
DUMMIES®

by David Brizer, MD

WILEY

Wiley Publishing, Inc.

Quitting Smoking For Dummies®

Published by
Wiley Publishing, Inc.
111 River St.
Hoboken, NJ 07030
www.wiley.com

About the Author

David Brizer, MD, chairman of psychiatry at Norwalk Hospital in Norwalk, Connecticut, has written half a dozen books on addiction, healthcare, and psychiatry. Dr. Brizer received his MD degree from the Albert Einstein College of Medicine and his psychiatry training at the Payne Whitney Clinic in New York. He has been treating people with addictive disorders for two decades. Dr. Brizer also serves as medical editor of *Mental Health News* and publishes numerous articles, papers, and chapters in the field. He is currently at work on a book called *Medical Kabbalah: The Ten Commandments, the Divine Comedy, and the Work of Dutch Schultz.*

Dedication

This book is dedicated to every person who wants something better in life — to every hero who has or will quit smoking.

Author's Acknowledgments

The following people have inspired me by their example, their support, and their wisdom:

Carol Bauer
George Bauer
Alex Brizer
Max Brizer
Ricardo Castaneda, MD
Frank di Costanzo
Philip di Costanzo
Helen Klisser During
Max Ernst
Marc Estrin
Jonathan Fine, MD
Claudia Fletcher
Peter Green
Margaret Haggerty, APRN
Joris-Karl Huysmans
Alfred Jarry
Amy Levin
Barbara McCormick
Harry de Meo, MD
Harry Mathews
Solomon Moses
Paul Nurick
David Osborne
Whitney Pastorek
Professor Tammy
Robert Ready
Maura Romaine
Raymond Roussel
Gustav Vintas
Marianne Williamson
Stephen Winter, MD

Publisher's Acknowledgments

We're proud of this book; please send us your comments through our Dummies online registration form located at www.dummies.com/register/.

Some of the people who helped bring this book to market include the following:

Acquisitions, Editorial, and Media Development

Editors: Pam Mourouzis, Kelly Ewing

Acquisitions Editor: Natasha Graf

Acquisitions Coordinator: Holly Gastineau-Grimes

Technical Editor: Ricardo Castaneda, MD

Editorial Manager: Michelle Hacker

Editorial Assistant: Elizabeth Rea

Cover Photos: © Pulse Productions/ Superstock/PictureQuest

Cartoons: Rich Tennant, www.the5thwave.com

Production

Project Coordinator: Kristie Rees

Layout and Graphics: Seth Conley, Joyce Haughey, LeAndra Hosier, Stephanie D. Jumper, Jacque Schneider, Shae Wilson

Special Art: Kathyrn Born

Proofreaders: Laura Albert, Brian H. Walls, TECHBOOKS Production Services

Indexer: TECHBOOKS Production Services

Publishing and Editorial for Consumer Dummies

> **Diane Graves Steele,** Vice President and Publisher, Consumer Dummies
>
> **Joyce Pepple,** Acquisitions Director, Consumer Dummies
>
> **Kristin A. Cocks,** Product Development Director, Consumer Dummies
>
> **Michael Spring,** Vice President and Publisher, Travel
>
> **Brice Gosnell,** Associate Publisher, Travel
>
> **Kelly Regan,** Editorial Director, Travel

Publishing for Technology Dummies

> **Andy Cummings,** Vice President and Publisher, Dummies Technology/General User

Composition Services

> **Gerry Fahey,** Vice President of Production Services
>
> **Debbie Stailey,** Director of Composition Services

Contents at a Glance

Table of Contents

Introduction

*L*ong before medical science came up with sophisticated explanations for addiction, people were using tobacco. Evidence suggests that the leaf was grown and used for both medicinal and nonmedicinal purposes on the American continents before it was introduced in Europe. Once tobacco made the transatlantic voyage, its popularity mushroomed. In 18th-century Europe, outbursts of enthusiasm and consumption quickly followed. Just as quickly, church and state efforts to suppress its spread got underway.

Tobacco in all its forms has gone in and out of favor over the years. In the 20th century, cigarette smoking in western nations became pandemic. Reaching for a cigarette — after a meal, at the office, in the theater, or on a plane — became as normal as chewing a stick of gum. Only more recently has a harsher light been shed on smoking. A mountain of irrefutable evidence has indicted tobacco as the culprit in unspeakable amounts of suffering and loss. The sooner you stop smoking, the better your chances of avoiding some of the unwelcome consequences. Your body and brain begin to recover almost immediately. Cigarette cravings aside, your body *wants* to stop smoking, and the moment you cut the smokes loose, your respiratory system begins to clear itself out.

The decision to quit smoking is far from a casual one. Quitting smoking involves your complete commitment. It must become your (not your spouse's or your best friend's) number-one priority. If it isn't, now may not be the right time to quit. Mustering all the support you can get, you need to decide to turn up the flame of your survival instinct, your belief in a healthy future, and your will power and believe that you can and will quit.

Throughout this book, I describe strategies, tools, and action plans in great detail. Although quitting smoking hasn't yet reached the stage of hard science, it is clear that the more energy and purpose you devote to quitting, the better your chances of success. Consulting with your doctor, attending workshops and support groups, and improving your lifestyle (including making exercise and dietary changes) work together to make your decision to quit an effective and lasting one.

You can approach quitting smoking as a singular lifestyle change or as a springboard for all kinds of self-transformation. Quitting smoking means refining your relationship with yourself. When you succeed, you show yourself that you have control over what you do, think, and feel. Being able to call the shots more often is intensely gratifying.

Paraphrasing another writer, the author Paul Auster said, "Write only that which gives you great pleasure." This advice applies to breathing and living as well. Smoking yields immediate pleasure but also delivers withdrawal symptoms, low self-regard, illness, and feelings of guilt and helplessness. Who needs that?

About This Book

You don't need to know much about medicine or chemistry to find this book useful. *Quitting Smoking For Dummies* covers a lot of ground, but it does so in a friendly, accessible, and nonacademic way. The last thing you need at this great milestone in your life (the milestone of quitting smoking, that is) is an unsympathetic voice from the ivory tower. At the same time, I've tried to give you the latest, most useful, and most accurate health-related information available today. Medical science gets a great deal of attention these days, and I'm sad to say that there's a great deal of hype out there. My approach is that you are an intelligent person who is capable of and interested in making the best possible choices for yourself.

You'll also find that the book does not toe a party line. You may be familiar with smoking and other addiction interventions that are very doctrinaire and rigid. Your assignment, should you choose to accept it, is to review the many options described in this book and pick the ones that work for you. Millions of people have quit smoking by using many different methods; there is no single formula for success.

Many of the chapters in this book are broad in scope, while other chapters are quite focused. The modular approach of the book, whereby each chapter stands on its own without demanding that you read everything that precedes it first, lets you "pick the best and leave the rest." You don't have to memorize anything, either; feel free to reference sections as often as you need to. This book isn't a didactic tutorial, but a useful reference tool that's meant to be used again and again.

Conventions Used in This Book

Like all the books in the *For Dummies* series, *Quitting Smoking For Dummies* is highly structured. You can skip to any section that appeals to you and dive into the chapters and sections at will — you're free to use this book in the ways that make it most useful to you. The headings are very visible. Sidebars complement the main text and contain information that may be of particular interest to you, although you can skip over them without missing any critical points.

The absence of citations (footnotes) is intentional. I've adjusted the pacing so that you can sail from one topic of interest to the next. Despite the absence of footnotes, the book makes many references to both printed and electronic matter that you can easily access if you want more information about a given topic.

I've also included illustrations and tables, which are intended to enlist greater involvement on your part. This is your book, so please fill in the interactive tables and even make notes to yourself in the margins if you feel that doing so will be useful in your effort to quit smoking or help someone else kick the habit.

Foolish Assumptions

If you're quitting for the first time, this book is for you. If you've tried to quit before, this book is for you. If you aren't a smoker yourself, but you care deeply about someone who is, this book is for you. In writing this book, I have assumed that either you're interested enough in quitting smoking to take the time to read at least selected parts of this book, or you know and care about someone who smokes and you want to help that person quit. I've also assumed that

- ✔ You will take this book's suggestions within the larger context of your personal health. If you have one or more medical conditions, you will discuss the pros and cons of nicotine replacement therapies or other interventions mentioned in this book with your doctor.

- ✔ You don't just live for the moment. You believe in and plan for the future and care about your health and well-being.

One assumption I'd like *you* to make is that my advice is solid, but should be seconded by your doctor before you proceed. Every smoker is different, so it's best to consult a medical professional who knows your personal situation before you make lifestyle changes that involve your health.

How This Book Is Organized

This book is organized into five parts, each of which covers a major area of quitting smoking. Each part is then divided into chapters that give you the extra focus you need to quit for good. The following sections provide a summary of each part.

Part I: Taking Stock: Your Decision to Quit

Your decision to quit smoking is great! This milestone deserves as much attention as you can muster. This part of the book helps you analyze where you're coming from — why you started smoking in the first place and why you continue to smoke today — and define where you want to go. You may or may not be ready to stop smoking right away. As you become more familiar with both the personal and the wider effects of tobacco use, I hope that your incentive to quit will grow.

Part I also gives you a great deal of information about addiction in general and tobacco addiction in particular, as well as the risks that you pose to your health every time you light up. As you evaluate the downsides of smoking, your motivation to cast smoking aside likely will become even stronger.

Part II: Packing It In: Taking the Leap

The best quitter is usually an informed quitter. In this part, you arm yourself with the information you need to make well-informed decisions about the many alternatives to smoking, such as the nicotine patch and nicotine gum. I also talk about alternative methods that smokers often try in an effort to rid themselves of their habit, such as meditation and hypnosis. In addition, this section of the book helps you create a specific and detailed plan about how you will quit: what lifestyle alterations you'll make, how you'll change your eating and exercise habits, and so on. Most people find that having a plan makes it easier to stay focused on the task at hand.

Part III: Sticking with Quitting

Once you've gathered the knowledge and determination you need to quit smoking, your next logical goal is to *stay* quit. This part answers common questions about getting through the first days and weeks of quitting. The changes in the way you feel, think, and behave are significant but not incapacitating. This part also gives you the tools you need to quash rationalizations and other infamous delay tactics that can get between you and your target. If you look at smoking as a behavior and a lifestyle that's triggered by recognizable causes, conquering those cravings becomes that much easier. Support groups, quit-smoking programs, and educational resources such as community agencies and quit-smoking Web sites are also very useful as you move ahead with your quit plan. This part provides a number of resources that you can turn to.

Part IV: Looking at Special Groups

You don't have to belong to any particular group or demographic to get some mileage out of this part. These chapters focus on smoking and quitting during pregnancy and during the teen years, as well as smoking's effects on male and female fertility and on children. The part also contains a chapter about relating to someone you care about who is caught up in smoking. The information that this section offers will keep you feeling supported as you work toward freeing yourself from the stranglehold of smoking. It's hard to change another person's habits and behavior; the best place to start is by working on yourself.

Part V: The Part of Tens

The Part of Tens is an essential part of every *For Dummies* book — it provides quick and dirty lists of key points. This book contains four of these "shortcut" chapters.

How do you know when you're ready to quit? The first chapter in this part is a kind of personal prompter, offering you a number of familiar and perhaps not-so-familiar smoking scenarios. I hope that you can relate to many of them. The subsequent chapters talk about rationalizations and alternatives to smoking. The money you save by not smoking adds up quickly. Perhaps you've already thought of many things you can do with the money you save by quitting. If you need additional suggestions, read the final chapter in this part.

Icons Used in This Book

This book contains *icons* — little picture prompts that act as idea boosters for your voyage to health. The icons are strategically placed to reinforce the most important information in the book. Here's what the icons mean:

This icon highlights better, faster, and easier ways to approach various aspects of quitting smoking.

This icon draws your attention to areas of particular caution — traps and triggers that often cause quitters to relapse or keep smokers from attempting to quit in the first place.

This icon points to words of wisdom that are worth remembering over the long haul. If you wanted a quick summary of the essential information in this book, you could read just the Remember sections.

Many smokers who are in the process of quitting find it useful to hear others' stories, whether they are success stories, stories about what finally made them kick the habit, or stories of regret that they never did quit. This icon marks this book's true stories from the trenches (including my own!).

Where to Go from Here

Where you go from here depends on where you are in your journey to quit smoking. The information in this book is intended to be as accessible and immediate as possible. When you want to find out about a particular topic, feel free to go to the chapter that discusses that topic. The table of contents at the front of the book and the index at the back can help you find your way.

Because I can't cover everything about the complex worlds of addiction and medical science, you may want to boost your knowledge by surfing the Internet (see Chapter 13 for some Web sites to check out) or the stacks of your local library. The learning process is lifelong, and quitting smoking may be the launching pad for a lifetime's journey of increasing awareness of and insight into health, vitality, and well-being.

Part I
Taking Stock: Your Decision to Quit

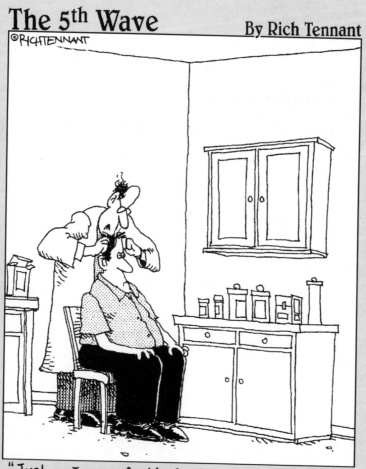

The 5th Wave   By Rich Tennant

"Just as I was afraid of. The years of smoking have begun to take their toll. This bump on your head, Mr. Mundt, it appears to be the beginnings of a chimney."

In this part . . .

Smoking is an addiction, a compulsion, and an appetite that takes on a life of its own. Deciding to quit smoking is a major life step that requires understanding, knowledge, and courage. Knowing the facts — about the consequences of smoking, about the roots of your habit, about the realities of addiction, and about your readiness to quit — makes the decision easier to stand by. This part's puff-by-puff guide to evaluating your habit, understanding who smokes and why, and appreciating the impact that smoking has on those around you clears the air. The more information you have, the better equipped you are to succeed.

Chapter 1

Calling It Quits

. . . .

In This Chapter

▶ Approaching the idea of quitting in the right frame of mind

▶ Looking forward to life after quitting

▶ Admitting that you are addicted to tobacco

▶ Knowing when you're ready to quit

▶ Tooling up for quitting success

▶ Finding the support you need to make quitting last

. . . .

Quitting smoking is a major commitment — and an enormously positive life step. If you're like most smokers, you've tried to quit before. You probably appreciate the difficulty and some of the complexities involved in kicking the habit. This chapter discusses the major issues involved in quitting smoking. It also helps you flesh out your decision to stop smoking by directing you to the tools you need to make this attempt to quit a lasting success.

Making the Call

Ever want to call it quits? Ever feel like you've just had enough (cigarettes, I mean)? If so, welcome to the crowd. Millions of people have been through this experience, and millions of people have succeeded at quitting. Millions of others, through education and the media, have gotten the message never to pick up.

If you're like most smokers who are thinking about quitting, it's very likely that you've tried to quit before. Those who do quit often make up to half a dozen attempts before succeeding. This book is your guide through the process. It is a friend, a tool, a source of information, and a weapon.

Quitting smoking is one of the best and most important things you can do for yourself. As you read this book, you will find that the best way to do it is to do it comprehensively. This book arms and fortifies you not only with the facts, but also with self-knowledge and with commitment on an intellectual, emotional, and perhaps even spiritual level.

Why do you want to quit?

- ✔ Maybe you think you need to, although you would prefer to smoke forever. (If there were a way to make cigarettes harmless, it would have been done. The tobacco companies have spent millions on research, and cigarettes are as deadly today as they've always been.)

- ✔ Maybe you've been asked or told by friends and family that you really should cut it loose. There's that nagging cough, that telltale odor on your clothes, in your house, and in your car. Your kids, if you have kids, can't be happy about your habit unless they smoke, too. People around you want you to succeed. They want you to live and be well.

- ✔ Or maybe it's the idea of being addicted to anything. Ever got caught in the course of a day or evening without a smoke — when you just had to have one? Ever had the experience of running out of the house in the middle of the night to find a convenience store that could service your need?

When you think about it, smoking is a gruesome process. The ingredients of tobacco smoke (or chew, or dip) are no better than what comes pouring out the chimneys of factories or out of a car's exhaust pipe. Along with nicotine, the fumes contain carbon monoxide, tar, and literally thousands of other chemicals, dozens of which are known to harm the body.

Part of what I do in this book is to present information. I also ask you to contribute to the book by responding to questions that draw on your life and experience. Learning involves repetition, so as you go along, you'll find that certain areas and items come up more than once.

Visualizing the New, Healthy You

Who is the person staring back at you in the mirror each day? Do you like that person? Do you respect that person? Or does the person in the glass look tired, hassled, and burned out?

Whomever you see, you see that person through a haze of smoke. Like all *psychoactive drugs* (drugs that have an effect on the psyche), nicotine changes the way you feel momentarily and then puts you in a state of withdrawal until the next smoke. When you look in the mirror, you see a person who is getting doused in nicotine many times a day. The smoke percolates through your lungs into your bloodstream and from there to every part of your body. Even if everything else in your life is on an even keel, why surrender any personal options to tobacco? Feeling helpless and even hopeless is not fun!

You bought this book because you're ready to clear the air — you're seriously interested in quitting smoking for good (or someone who really cares about you wants you to quit). You're probably feeling frustrated and angry about the difficulties involved in quitting. If you're like most quitters, you've tried before and failed.

The most important step is to make the decision to quit.

Once you decide that you want to quit, you take it from there. Imagine how you will look and feel, and how things will taste and smell, once the haze has lifted. The ripple effects of quitting are tremendous, almost beyond imagination. The moment you stop, your body's cells and airways begin healing, cleaning themselves out. Yes, the first few days may be rough going, but even during that time you start to experience a physical, mental, and even spiritual renewal.

What I'm telling you may sound too good to be true. Or it may sound like hogwash. It isn't. Take it from someone who's been through the mill. I smoked a pack a day for more than ten years. Like many other smokers, I had a love affair with cigarettes. At times they were my constant companion, my solace, my sustenance. The act of lighting up was filled with meaning for me. Lighting up meant doing something; it made me feel young, sexy, and alive; and it gave me something to do with my hands and mouth.

And then there was the downside. I had sore throats, congested lungs, and a persistent cough. The rank and acrid taste of tobacco that lingered in my mouth the morning after a smoking binge made me gag. Along with all that unpleasantness, there were the decades of health warnings and the deaths of many others from lung cancer that I tried to store away in a faraway corner of my mind.

You get to a point where you've had enough. Just because the damage is internal doesn't mean that it's invisible. You *know* that you're harming yourself. After a while, I realized that I wanted something better for myself. I wanted to be able to jog around the reservoir without looking forward to the reward of a smoke. I wanted clean, kissable breath and an unburdened conscience. As the saying goes, the parts are related to the whole. If I insisted on using my lungs as a garbage dump for tar and nicotine, then that choice would somehow show up in my appearance: a cough, smoker's breath, stained fingertips. Clearing the body is clearing the conscience. When you feel better, you look better, too.

As an ex-smoker, how will you look? Visualize your renewed, healthy self, and describe what you see in Table 1-1. Be as specific as possible. For example, under "Exercise habits," document what kind of exercise you can do now and what kind you would like to be able to do after reaching Quit Day 1.

Table 1-1	Life After Quitting: My New, Healthy Self
Category	*What I Want for Myself*
Overall appearance	
Weight	
Food preferences	
Exercise habits	
Fitness level	
Clothing	
Other	

Visualization is an incredibly powerful tool. The more you see yourself this way, the closer you'll come to achieving your goals.

Getting a Fresh Start

Rebirth is one of humanity's major spiritual themes. One of the reasons rebirth is a central belief in many of the world's major religions is that the cycle of death and renewal occurs constantly throughout nature. For example, autumn transforms the color of foliage; winter whisks the brown, shriveled leaves away; and then everything turns green again when spring rolls around.

The concept of renewal is a terrific metaphor for starting fresh. Whether you struggle with your appearance, your self-esteem, or a habit that you want to cut loose, each and every moment of each and every day presents you with a new opportunity to say, "I'm going to do it differently this time. This time, I'm taking the high road."

The first step in your "rebirth" is to decide what shape your phoenix will take as it rises from the ashes. (Speaking of ashes: Get rid of your ashtrays, to start!) Now is a great time to take a detailed, point-by-point inventory of what you want your life to be like after you quit smoking. Flesh out the particulars in Table 1-2.

Table 1-2	Life after Quitting: Who I Want to Be
Category	*What I Want for Myself*
Career goals	
Educational goals	
Non-work/school-related activities	
Financial goals	
Emotional goals	
Spiritual goals	
Other goals	
Goals for the coming month	
Goals for the coming year	
Goals for the long-term	

Feel like you're biting off more than you can chew? *You aren't.* Does thinking about the future in this way seem way too ambitious? *It isn't.* If you can quit smoking (and you can!), you can set goals and achieve more, using the same tools, energy, and commitment that will work for you in your effort to quit.

After you fill out Table 1-2, go through your personal goals again in Table 1-3, this time identifying exactly what steps you will need to take to accomplish them.

Table 1-3	Who I Will Be After Quitting: Action Plan
Category	*Steps I Need to Take to Achieve My Goals*
Career goals	
Educational goals	
Non-work/school-related activities	
Financial goals	
Emotional goals	
Spiritual goals	
Other goals	
Goals for the coming month	
Goals for the coming year	
Goals for the long-term	

Having put your goals in writing, you may have a much stronger reason to believe that there is life after cigarettes. And the life you have after cigarettes, just like the life you've had while smoking, is in large part shaped by the decisions you make.

Some people may argue that I'm making too much of this process — that the point is "simply" to stop smoking. But, as I hope this book demonstrates, quitting is not a simple act. Because smoking has played so many pivotal roles in your life, quitting is a highly complex process. When you give up such an important part of your life, you need to replace it with something as compelling and powerful. Being a healthier (or smarter, or more energetic, or more loving, or more effective — you decide) person is the real payoff for quitting.

Coming to Terms with Your Addiction

You may feel that you can handle smoking. You may feel that smoking is not a problem for you. How do you know when you need to quit?

Why did you buy this book? You may know people who have been harmed by smoking and have become ill, either acutely or chronically. Friends or relatives may have suggested or hinted that it might be a good idea for you to cut back on cigarettes or to quit altogether. Do these hints anger you? Do you worry about the effects of smoking on your health, your appearance, and your wallet? Do you ever feel like smoking is cramping your style — you resent always having to make allowances, find excuses, and look for opportunities to get outside to find a private spot to light up?

Ask yourself whether smoking is making problems for you. And answer as honestly as you can. Once you have a crystal clear understanding of the actual and potential damage that smoking causes, you will feel less doubtful and more committed than ever to quitting smoking.

Tobacco toxicity comes in many forms. Tobacco and the chemicals and additives it contains are physically harmful, have powerful effects on behavior and the nervous system, and have widespread negative impact on public health as well.

Your decision to quit smoking is based on personal motivations. You may want a healthier body, you may want greater stamina, or you may be sick and tired of feeling sick and tired. Smoking has been shown to cause breathing and other kinds of problems in both smokers and in people who inhale secondhand smoke (smoke exhaled by others or given off by lit cigars, pipes, and cigarettes).

Whatever your reason to quit, bulk it up by understanding as much as possible about the intermediate and long-term consequences of smoking. You'll get to a point where justifying more smoking is no longer possible. (Chapters 5 and 6 give you a clear picture of smoking's many negative consequences.)

The most direct approach to coming to terms with smoking is to ask yourself whether smoking is a problem for you. Remember that problems can be in the future as well as the present. (For example, if your favorite food is peanut butter sandwiches and you know that you will run out of peanut butter next week, you will have a problem.) Burying your head in the sand and denying what the future is likely to bring can be a problem, too.

You need to come to terms with your level of tobacco use in order to become ready to quit. You may have a problem with the word *addiction*. You might so dislike the entire concept that you either completely abandon the pursuit of quitting . . . or you might quit.

If you think that smoking isn't a problem for you, you're unlikely to dedicate yourself heart and soul to quitting. On the other hand, if you take an honest self-inventory of your commitment to smoking, you may want to quit . . . yesterday!

One sure sign that you're really hooked, and that you may want to cut tobacco loose, is the presence of nicotine withdrawal symptoms. These highly unpleasant sensations arise within one or two hours of your last cigarette and include

- ✔ Irritability
- ✔ Fatigue
- ✔ Mood swings
- ✔ Insomnia (inability to sleep) or hypersomnia (too much sleep)
- ✔ Trouble concentrating
- ✔ Headaches
- ✔ Increased appetite
- ✔ Anxiety
- ✔ Depression
- ✔ Shifting energy levels

These withdrawal symptoms naturally lead to cravings for tobacco.

As you think about quitting, consider how powerful a hold nicotine has on you. Anything that can cause withdrawal symptoms like these is powerful and ultimately toxic. Do you really want to be a slave to something so terrible for you?

As you come to understand the impact that smoking has had on your life — particularly if you've had some health problems as a result — you may feel slightly or even more than slightly overwhelmed. How can you have done this to yourself? Fortunately, you get lots of chances in life, including the chance to quit smoking and recapture part or all of your physical health.

Many people have made bad decisions, such as starting to smoke. The challenge is to see where you've been *and to make a conscious decision about exactly where you want to go from here.* If you've been in the habit of saving or investing money, for example, you know that the amount you have continues to grow. The same applies to forward-looking acts of goodwill and kindness toward yourself — including quitting smoking. The self-denial that you practice now will pay off enormous dividends in just a short time. One clean, smoke-free breath leads to another . . . and successive ones feel better and better.

Knowing When You're Ready to Stop

You're ready to stop smoking when

- ✔ You've decided that quitting smoking is the most important goal in your life.

- ✔ You accept the fact that in order to get ahead and get more of the things you want, such as health, well-being, and self-respect, you have to make sacrifices.

- ✔ You know in your heart that the future is real, and that the ribbon of time continues to unfurl regardless of how you try to escape it.

- ✔ You feel a sense of responsibility not only toward yourself but toward your family, your friends, and even your pets. A great, mysterious web of life hovers around you. Your decision to quit smoking is a choice to remain a living, breathing participant in this incredible dance.

You can look at this move in many ways. I hope that you see your decision to quit as positive, life-affirming, and absolutely necessary. It's regrettable that some of the pleasures in life are as harmful as they are. It's also regrettable that you have to give up certain pleasures for your own good. Growth is like that. Imagine what life would be like if you'd never learned how to walk or dress yourself. Quitting smoking feels like deprivation, like a wicked, deep loss. There's no getting around it: It *is* a loss. But it's a loss that brings you a great deal of gain at the same time.

Finding Quitting Aids to Help You

A dedicated quitter — you! — must be prepared to face both the physical and psychological manifestations of nicotine withdrawal. When you smoke, chew, or inhale snuff, your blood level of nicotine jumps. The nicotine in the blood passes through every part of the body. In the brain, nicotine triggers different receptors, and the receptors get used to your customary blood nicotine level. When that level drops — for example, after a night's sleep — your brain wants more nicotine, *now.*

Quitting smoking is war. The more weapons you have to fight with, the better your chances of quitting for good. That's why a combination of strategies works best for many people. A *nicotine replacement therapy,* such as the patch or nicotine gum, plus a smoking cessation program that involves behavioral changes can significantly increase the likelihood of success.

Nicotine replacement therapies (NRTs) are a reasonable way to substitute plain old nicotine for smoking, which comes with a host of other poisons that your body doesn't need. The idea is to wean you off tobacco at the same time that withdrawal symptoms are prevented from developing. Figure 1-1 depicts some common NRTs.

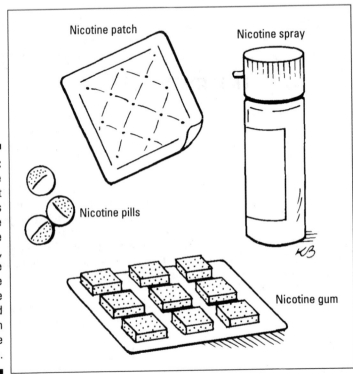

Figure 1-1: Nicotine replacement therapies include nicotine gum, nicotine sprays, the nicotine patch, and prescription drugs like Zyban.

Smoking cessation programs take many forms. Areas that contain one or more medical centers or healthcare practices offer a choice of programs. You need to be a smart shopper when it comes to picking a smoking cessation program — but not too smart. You don't want to think yourself into a state of inaction.

At our medical center, patients visit with respiratory therapists, smoking cessation counselors, and pulmonologists. The approach is multidisciplinary and aims to give patients as much information and support as is currently available. Dr. Stephen Winter, chief of pulmonary medicine at Norwalk Hospital in Connecticut, advocates this intensive approach to quitting smoking. He is also impressed with the effectiveness of Zyban, the antitobacco medication, in some patients. (See Chapter 13 for information about support groups and smoking cessation programs.)

Sixty to seventy percent of would-be quitters fail on their first attempt. Most of these people would readily acknowledge that they relapsed because of severe, persistent cravings and withdrawal symptoms. Use the tools that are available to fight back!

Prescription and over-the-counter nicotine replacement therapies (NRTs)

Most nicotine replacement therapies, with the exception of the nasal inhaler, are available over the counter. How will you choose your weapon? What will work best for you? Your doctor can help you find the optimal therapy for your personal situation.

Chewing gum may be the answer if you need some kind of substitute oral gratification. Or maybe the convenience of the patch makes it the optimal NRT for you. Are you looking for rapidity of action? Then nicotine nasal spray may be the solution that works for you. Do you miss the feel of the cigarette in your hand? Consider using a nicotine inhaler. Following is some basic information about the NRTs that are available — see Chapter 9 for details about these quitting aids.

- **The nicotine patch:** The patch, available in both over-the-counter and by prescription, delivers nicotine to your system through your skin. You use patches of decreasing strength until your body no longer craves nicotine.

- **Nicotine gum:** This NRT, an over-the-counter product, works similarly to the patch. The gum delivers nicotine to your body, and you wean yourself off by chewing less and less.

- **Nicotine nasal spray:** With this NRT, available by prescription only, a spray that you inhale through your nose delivers nicotine to your system quickly. It provides almost instantaneous relief of cravings and other nicotine withdrawal symptoms.

- **Nicotine inhalers:** Nicotine inhalers became available in recent years and are available only by prescription. The device is a typical inhaler that delivers a fine mist containing nicotine to the lining of the mouth. This method gives the user more of an oral feel, which many smokers miss when they try to quit.

- **Nicotine lozenges:** Nicotine lozenges are like throat lozenges, except that instead of soothing a sore throat, they reduce nicotine cravings by supplying the body with nicotine. Like the other NRTs, you taper the number and strength of the lozenges you use as you break your nicotine habit.

✔ **Zyban:** Zyban (chemical name buproprion, also known as Wellbutrin) is an antidepressant that's been found to be useful in reducing nicotine cravings and other withdrawal symptoms. It can be used alone or in combination with one of the other NRTs. Only a doctor can prescribe it.

According to a handful of studies published in medical journals, about 25 to 35 percent of those who use Zyban or a nicotine replacement therapy remain smoke-free for at least six months. Combining Zyban and an NRT may be even more effective than either approach by itself. By way of comparison, about one person in ten is able to quit for at least six months without the support of any medication.

Alternative quitting methods

NRTs and/or Zyban alone may not be enough support for you — or you may prefer not to continue to take in nicotine, even without the accompanying smoke. A wide variety of alternative quitting methods are available:

✔ **Quitlines:** Telephone counselors are available in most states to help you design a customized quit strategy and support your adherence to it. Data show that people who use quitlines succeed at twice the rate of those who don't. You can find your local quitline by calling the American Cancer Society at 800-ACS-2345.

✔ **Support groups:** Evidence shows that having a network of friends and family to provide emotional support as you quit smoking increases your likelihood of staying quit. Other people, particularly those who have quit themselves, can offer empathy, boost your morale, and keep you moving in the right direction even when you're feeling shaky. *Network therapy* is the name that's been given to this approach in the treatment of substance addiction. Having a caring person on the other end of the phone line, or in a group meeting, is sometimes all you need to steer clear of that next cigarette.

✔ **Quit-smoking programs:** These programs include Nicotine Anonymous and locally based programs from the American Lung Association and the American Cancer Society. Many quit-smoking programs feature classes or workshops that charge a fee. If the program has helped others, it may help you — and the long-term benefit will almost surely outweigh the present cost.

✔ **Acupuncture:** Acupuncture is an ancient Chinese technique that involves the placement of small needles at strategic points on the body. Although its capability to make quitting smoking easier has not been scientifically proven, some people swear by acupuncture (for help with quitting smoking as well as with a host of other problems).

These methods can be used to complement rather than substitute for nicotine replacement therapies. Chapter 10 goes into much more detail on alternative quitting methods.

The more strategies and tactics you use, the more likely you are to succeed at quitting. Do whatever it takes to quit and stay quit!

Chapter 2

Filtering Out the Many Forms of Tobacco

Tobacco, a plant, comes in many forms. Although the cigarette is the most familiar "nicotine delivery system," plenty of other "vehicles" cleverly and efficiently get that nicotine into the body. This chapter discusses the different tobacco products such as cigars, pipes, snuff, and chew, which have more in common than you may think.

Whatever form they take, tobacco products exert similar harmful effects on health. In this chapter, I talk about some of the health hazards associated with each form of tobacco and debunk the myths surrounding the supposed greater safety of smokeless tobacco and low-tar and low-nicotine cigarettes.

Naming Your Poison: Different Smokes for Different Folks

Whether you chew it, sniff it, or smoke it, tobacco smoke contains hundreds of chemical compounds that are *not* your friends (although the tobacco companies have spent many years trying to convince people otherwise). And it's not just tobacco *smoke* that's dangerous. Tobacco itself contains many toxic chemical compounds. This section gives you the straight dope on the various forms of tobacco.

Cigarettes

Cigarettes are as common as windows, as ubiquitous as cats and dogs. They are not man's best friend, however. Cigarette smoke contains the combusted, vaporized form of many chemicals, which have often fatal toxicities. This entire book, including this chapter, raises your awareness of the toxic ingredients that cigarettes contain. The packaging, the neat look of a crisply rolled manufactured cigarette, is misleading. Cigarette smoke can wreak havoc with your health and mess up all the beautifully synchronized movements of the earth's greatest machine: the human body.

Smokeless tobacco

It's interesting how powerful and misleading words can be. A prime example is the term *smokeless tobacco.* For many people, *smokeless tobacco* conjures up visions of a form of tobacco that's safe to use. Nothing could be further from the truth. Smokeless tobacco, whether dry (snuff or dip) or wet (chew), contains as complex and toxic a mix of chemicals as cigarettes, minus the smoke.

The *carcinogens,* or powerful chemicals that cause cancer, known to be in smokeless tobacco include nitrates, nitrites, nitrosamines, and polycyclic hydrocarbons. Laboratory animals given these chemicals in amounts thought to approximate human exposure over a lifetime of smokeless tobacco use have developed a variety of terrible cancers. Smokeless tobacco causes cancer in humans, too.

Chewing tobacco and dip spend a lot of time in your mouth, and the tobacco juices are extremely irritating to the delicate mucous membranes that line the mouth. After a while, the cells of the mouth become chronically inflamed and essentially start to scar over. Some of the cells take on abnormal shapes and growth cycles that can be seen clearly not only under a microscope but sometimes with the naked eye as well. Some smokeless tobacco users develop white patches on the lining of the cheeks or on the tongue — *leukoplakia* — which can lead to oral cancer. Cancer of the mouth, throat, esophagus, stomach, and bladder — all caused by constant and repeated exposure to tobacco — is nasty and difficult to treat and may prove fatal.

If you notice sores, lumps, or white patches in your mouth — on your gums, the lining of your cheeks, or tongue — that persist after a week, have your dentist or doctor check them out. Also see a professional if you have long-lasting difficulty chewing or if you feel like you have a mass in your throat or mouth.

The history of a habit

The tobacco leaf was probably first used by the indigenous people of the Americas, before the arrival of Christopher Columbus. The cultivated leaf was smoked in pipes for ritual and therapeutic purposes. Columbus returned to Europe with some tobacco, but the habit didn't really catch on until the 1600s, when a variety of explorers and men of state popularized its consumption. In Europe, tobacco became known as a cure-all.

Tobacco is first mentioned in English literature in Edmund Spenser's poem *The Faerie Queene*. In that work and others of the era, tobacco is described as a panacea, a miraculous herb that could cure most ailments. According to authorities of that time, tobacco could even prevent the plague!

It didn't take long for tobacco to become the Virginia colony's number-one export in the early 17th century. As demand for the crop grew, so did the demand for slave labor to work the fields.

When tobacco use was introduced in Europe, the gentry and aristocracy were among the first users. Possibly the glamour of the gilded classes added to the leaf's nearly universal appeal. In France, the plant was eventually known as *nicotiane,* named after ambassador Jean Nicot, who brought it to the attention of the French royalty. The plant was known by many other names, but the most widely used to this day is *tobacco,* probably an adaptation of the Native American term *tabaco.*

Following a couple hundred years' use of tobacco for pipe smoking, chewing, and snuff-taking, cigarettes came into their own in the United States following the Civil War. They became ever more popular due to the introduction first of yellow-leaf Bright tobacco, and then of the White Burley leaf. Later in the 19th century, the invention of the cigarette-rolling machine, backed by tobacco giant James Buchanan Duke, gave further impetus to the widespread use and popularity of the leaf. After three centuries of pipe smoking, cigarettes became extremely popular during the period between World War I and World War II. The plant became so popular because its smoke was an immediate and accessible drug that caused a nearly instantaneous mood shift.

Chewing out chew

Chewing tobacco is also called "chaw" or "chew." A large wad of the stuff is placed between the cheek and gum. People chew tobacco, which comes in bricks, packets, and strands, for the same reason they smoke cigarettes. Chewing tobacco is easy to buy, is readily available, is condoned by society, and is relatively inexpensive (compared to a new Jaguar, I guess).

Chewing tobacco also contains up to 2,000 chemicals, many of which are toxic and some of which cause cancer. Sure, baseball players and other athletes may look tough and sexy as they disgorge gobs of dark brown tobacco juice onto the playing field, but they may not look so cool if they're unlucky enough to develop a lesion of the mouth, which can lead to cancer.

Chewing tobacco, just like cigarettes, is a euphoriant. It increases alertness, is addicting, reinforces continued use, and causes brain cells to adapt in such a way that they feel withdrawal after several hours of going without. The brain wants *more!* Chew also causes a host of diseases in addition to cancer, such as high blood pressure, peptic ulcers, and cardiovascular disease.

Have I convinced you to toss your can of chew away? If not, consider this: Other possible consequences of repeated and long-term use of chewing tobacco include bad breath, gingivitis (inflammation of the gums), tooth decay, loss of gum tissue, and wearing down of tooth surfaces.

As with cigarettes, adolescents use chew as a sign of having "arrived." Having the telltale tobacco-can ring imprinted on their rear jeans pocket is a sign of belonging for some teens. As it does with older smokers, tobacco exerts its pull through peer pressure and "cool" appeal.

As if peer pressure weren't enough, chew users who are trying to cut it loose describe how they miss the ritual of opening the can and placing the leaf in their mouth. Chew also contains a great deal of salt, and quitters miss that, too. Giving up chew is tough: You have to give up the ritual, the feeling of belonging to a group, the nicotine addiction, *and* the salt.

Last year, a further disincentive for users of chew and snuff arose in California, which enacted a mammoth tax increase on the products. The retail price of some products went up almost 300 percent. Users of brands like Copenhagen, Skoal, and Red Man tobacco may be drinking Perrier or chewing gum from now on. Additional antichew pressure has arisen in (of all places) California high school rodeo championships, where competitors have been urged to cut the chew loose.

Saying enough about snuff

Snuff is a dried, powdered form of tobacco that's placed between the lower lip and gum. This action is called *dipping.* The grains of tobacco can also be taken in a pinch and inhaled sharply into the nose, resulting in a window-shattering sneeze. The use of snuff, though once considered a refined habit among high society, is a fairly repulsive habit.

Cancer of the mouth is known to occur significantly more often among people who dip than among those who don't use tobacco at all. As if that's not bad enough, the risk of cheek and gum cancer among snuff users can be 50 times that of nonusers. Not only that, but tobacco's repeated contact with the delicate lining of the nostrils (the *mucosa*) is irritating and can lead to sores, respiratory infections, and a general dulling or even total loss of the sense of smell. Smokeless tobacco is addictive, too. It's not something that you can take or leave.

Tobacco toxicity

Tobacco toxicity has a history, too. Early on, the adverse health effects of taking tobacco were not known. Native Americans used the leaf for medicinal purposes. However, by the start of the 20th century, information from health researchers began to appear about tobacco's negative impact on health. As far back as 1930, German researchers noted an association between cancer and smoking. In 1938, a report from a Johns Hopkins doctor stated that smokers had shorter lifespans than nonsmokers did. Not long after, the American Cancer Society was warning people about the possible toxic effects of tobacco.

The ambiguity surrounding the issue of smoking and health — was it dangerous or wasn't it? — was laid to rest (or so one would have hoped) by a 1952 *Reader's Digest* article titled "Cancer by the Carton." The public took note, and many other reports on the negative health effects of smoking began to appear. Cigarette sales declined for the first time in many years.

Big Tobacco — the major tobacco companies — didn't take these developments lying down. The Tobacco Industry Research Council, formed in 1954, began a countercampaign, spreading comforting information (you might consider these myths) about cigarettes. At the same time, filtered and low-tar cigarettes were pushed as solutions to the health worries raised by the "troublemakers."

Comparing smokeless tobacco to cigarettes

You still may be wondering, "Isn't smokeless tobacco healthier than smoking cigarettes?" The answer is *no*. Although the likelihood of getting lung cancer is lower with smokeless tobacco, smokeless tobacco users have an increased chance of developing cancer of the mouth. Oral cancer is deadly, with a five-year survival rate after diagnosis of only about 50 percent. And smokers and smokeless tobacco users end up having about the same overall exposure to nicotine and its damaging effects.

Pipes

Pipes are ornate collectors' items and line many a proud owner's walls, cabinets, and bookshelves. They're made of a variety of materials, from low-end corncob to briar to clay. Pipes are used to smoke not only tobacco but also marijuana, hashish, opium, and other mind- and mood-altering substances.

Aside from its ornamental and ceremonial value, a pipe is built to deliver air-cooled smoke. Some pipes have chambers that are filled with water or other liquids that not only cool the smoke but also flavor it.

If you think that pipe smoking is safe, you're having a pipe dream. Pipe smokers develop cancers of the lip and mouth, among other diseases. While the rate of lung disease among pipe smokers may be lower than that of cigarette smokers, pipe smokers still face a very real risk of becoming seriously ill as a result of their habit.

When you consider the risks involved in smoking a pipe and weigh them against the benefits, your decision to quit should be crystal clear. Like cigarettes and cigars, the perception of pipe smoking has undergone a major shift in recent decades. A smoking pipe clutched in hand used to make people think of scholarly types like Sherlock Holmes. Nowadays, people are more likely to view a pipe as a bad-smelling prosthesis, a personal accoutrement that suggests addiction more than academia.

Cigars

An entire culture surrounds cigar making, tasting, and smoking. For many years, aficionados insisted that the only cigars worth smoking were Cuban. Premium cigar tobaccos thrive in the Caribbean climate; Dominican cigars are also considered to be fine smokes. The cigar leaves are wrapped in a tobacco leaf and usually finished off with a paper band or wrapper displaying the brand name. Cigaroholics compare the burn rate, the length of the lingering ash, and the taste of the remaining butt. The best cigars can cost $20 or more each.

In the last ten years, the number of cigar users has increased by a third. Cigars have become more popular not just among adults but also among the young. According to the Centers for Disease Control (CDC), more high school students in the United States smoke cigars than use smokeless tobacco.

According to the CDC (www.cdc.gov):

 ✔ Almost 5 billion cigars were used in 1996.

 ✔ Cigar production is at its highest levels since the 1980s.

 ✔ About 6 million U.S. teenagers smoked cigars in the last year.

 ✔ Compared to non–cigar smokers, cigar smokers have a 410 times greater chance of developing oral-type cancers.

 ✔ Smoking five or more cigars daily increases the risk of dying from lung cancer by a factor of 23.

The poetry of poison

Those who sought glamour and wished to be considered at the height of fashion in Dutch, French, and English social circles were smokers in the 17th century. Mercenaries were also among the ranks of early smokers. Despite the prohibition of tobacco by King James I, English society of the 18th century adored the use of tobacco. Tobacco use was prominent and played a central role in the ritual and pomp of the gentlemen's club.

The smoking habit historically has cut across all classes of society. Paintings and drawings from the 17th century frequently depicted peasants using tobacco. A poem by George Crabbe, written in 1810, describes a smoking club like this:

A Club there is of Smokers – Dare you come

To that close crowded, hot, narcotic Room?

When midnight past, the very Candles seem

Dying for Air, and give a ghastly Gleam;

When curling Fumes in lazy Wreaths arise, . . .

When but a few are left the House to tire,

And they half sleeping by the sleepy Fire;

Ev'n the poor ventilating Vane that flew

Of late, so fast is now grown drowsy too.

Portraits of sailors throughout the centuries often showed these men of the sea with pipes in hand or mouth. The Spanish and the Dutch came to be especially known as pipe smokers in the early days. Smoking a pipe came to be seen as a sign of detachment or reflection.

The U.S. Surgeon General's reports on the health consequences of smoking did not exempt cigars from the list of harmful tobacco products. Cigars are *not* a safe alternative to cigarettes. Although cigar smokers generally don't inhale the smoke as deeply as cigarette smokers do, cigars contain much more tar and nicotine than cigarettes and come into contact with the mouth for much greater lengths of time. Also, despite the shallower inhalation of cigar fumes, cigar smokers are at a greater risk for developing chronic lung disease, which is often regarded as a cigarette-smokers' disease. Cigar smoking can also cause throat cancer, laryngeal cancer, and esophageal cancer.

Cigars have been popularized, glamorized, and hyped in recent years by prominent citizens and celebrities such as Demi Moore and Arnold Schwarzenegger parading their panatelas. *Cigar Aficionado,* a magazine dedicated to purveying cigars and cigar accessories, offers readers a glorified world in which sexy men and women smoke cigars, swill cognac, and enjoy affluent, exciting lives. But how can you be sexy, how can you enjoy life, if you're suffering from cancer, lung disease, or some other tobacco-related illness? Don't believe the hype.

Cigarillos and *bidis* are miniature cigars. Bidis are particularly popular among young people, who consider their use a sign of sophistication. They, too, are addictive and potentially harmful to your health. Part of their appeal is their different, quasi-exotic look. They also contain much more nicotine than ordinary cigarettes do.

Breathing Deep: The Lowdown on Low-Tar and Low-Nicotine Cigarettes

Despite all the hoopla about "safer" cigarettes — low-tar and low-nicotine cigarettes that are supposed to contain fewer toxic substances — there ain't no such animal. In a study reported last year in the journal *Tobacco Control,* one of these newer, supposedly safer cigarettes actually delivered 25 percent *more* nicotine than the smokers' own brands did. The newfangled cigarette didn't do that well as far as diminishing withdrawal symptoms or cravings, either. Another brand reported on in another study raised smokers' levels of carbon monoxide by 30 percent more than regular cigarettes did.

For many years, people have taken comfort in the fact that they're smoking low-tar or low-nicotine brands. However, years of studies of these "healthier" cigarettes demonstrate that low-tar and low-nicotine-brand smokers smoke more cigarettes and inhale more deeply to compensate for the reduced nicotine per cigarette. Don't be fooled!

A major part of the tobacco addiction game is maintaining a steady level of nicotine in the blood. This is why you think about and reach for a cigarette first thing in the morning. The longer the time between cigarettes, the lower your blood nicotine level dips. You feel this as increasing nicotine withdrawal symptoms. If you smoke a low-nicotine brand, you will either inhale more deeply or smoke more often to equal the amount of nicotine you would be getting from regular cigarettes.

You can get further information about supposedly safer cigarettes and related issues from the Foundation for a Smoke Free America (www.tobaccofree. org) and from Action on Smoking and Health (http://ash.org).

Getting the Effects of Tobacco

Regardless of the type or types of tobacco you use, the take-home message is the same. The stuff kills. This section gives you a quick review of the effects of *any* kind of tobacco on your physical and mental health.

Physical effects

Your body is an incredibly complex orchestra that plays symphonies, concertos, waltzes, tangos, *and* rock-and-roll, depending on your mood, the time of day, and a host of other factors. Your body is an engine that can run at idle, rev up when it needs to, and switch gears from moment to moment. The skeletal system provides the infrastructure and, in the case of the brain, the protective covering. The muscular system moves the whole apparatus around so that you can access food, shelter, a life partner, or a cup of joe. Add to this the incredibly sophisticated circulatory, hormonal, immune, excretory, respiratory, and nervous systems, and you start to appreciate the fantastic complexity of this miraculous machine.

Nicotine and the other ingredients of tobacco wreak royal havoc on these systems. Not a single organ or organ system in your body is unaffected by exposure to smoke — particularly chronic exposure. Don't get your medical education from smoking-related visits to the doctor. Smoking can harm every part of your body.

The cardiovascular system

Repeated doses of nicotine cause a general overload of the nervous and cardiovascular systems. Blood vessels, particularly arteries and smaller arteries called *arterioles,* clamp down in response to this repeated chemical assault. Narrower, constricted blood vessels lead to elevated blood pressure and a greater likelihood of obstructions to circulation. When any kind of pipe becomes too narrow, it's much easier for small particles to become trapped and physically block the flow, eventually leading to permanent obstruction. (See Chapter 14 for a detailed discussion of nicotine's effects on the brain.)

In the human body, dangerous backups, bleeds, hemorrhages, and *infarcts* occur. Infarcts are cell deaths resulting from the cutting off of the blood/ oxygen supply. Long-term constriction of blood vessels and increased blood pressure also lead to increased formation of *atheromas,* which are fatty deposits that form right beneath the delicate inner lining of blood vessels. Atheromas clog the pipes; what starts out as a microscopic bump or hillock may end up as a life-threatening blockage in an artery of the heart or brain.

The immune system

Your body also performs remarkable waste management services 24/7. Defender white blood cells *(macrophages)* continually engulf and gobble up foreign matter such as dust, soot, splinters, and noxious fumes, keeping these toxic particles from further contact with the tissues. Other white blood cells, called *lymphocytes,* recognize foreign matter and fight it with antibodies or other molecules that tag invaders such as viruses as "foreign" and lead to their later ingestion by white blood cells.

The entire process is fantastically complex; medical scientists don't fully understand the immune system yet. As sophisticated as your immune system may be, though — it can even mount a response to a germ it was exposed to decades before — it has its limits. Although it's fully capable of recognizing and fighting off thousands of microorganisms and toxins, your immune system can become overwhelmed. One sign of immune system burnout is frequent or persistent infections, such as upper respiratory infections and colds.

The allergic response is yet another component of the highly intricate immune system. Some people are allergic to components of tobacco and tobacco smoke. The allergic response takes many forms, from a few sneezes to an all-out and potentially life-threatening rash, difficulty breathing, and even systemic shock. If you or anyone you know has a serious allergic response, see a doctor right away.

If you keep exposing your systems to tobacco, you stress your immune response, which should be on guard for other potential invaders such as pollutants in food, water, and air; bacteria; viruses; and other dangerous foreign matter. When you smoke, you put your immune system to work overtime.

The gastrointestinal and genitourinary systems

When you use tobacco, you end up swallowing some of the smoke and/or tobacco and associated particulate matter. Your stomach lining is thereby repeatedly exposed to the harmful ingredients of tobacco. Like the lining (*mucosa*) of your mouth and intestines, the gastric mucosa can react to repeated contact with tobacco carcinogens such as nitrosamines and free radicals by forming mutated (cancerous) cells. In addition, the adrenaline boost that comes with each puff can eventually lead to the breakdown of the gastric lining and to peptic ulcer disease.

The constituents of tobacco smoke that make it from your lungs into your bloodstream pass through your kidneys, which filter the blood and excrete these toxins into the urine. Urine that contains carcinogens sits in the bladder for hours at a time — a setup for bladder cancer.

Had enough? There's more. Your liver, which is the recycling plant of your body, ordinarily breaks down (*metabolizes*) the thousands of chemical compounds, including tobacco compounds, that pass through your gut and bloodstream every day. Complex chemical compounds activate enzymatic "garbage removal" systems in the liver, which makes the liver that much more effective as a waste recycler. One result of this metabolic ramping up is an increased ability to break down other chemical compounds, such as prescribed medications. Smokers often need higher doses of medication than nonsmokers because their livers break medications down more rapidly.

Mental effects

Curiously, the mental effects of tobacco, at least in lower doses, are stimulating. Alerting. Tobacco's stimulating effect explains why many smokers practice *titration,* or blending of sedatives like alcohol with nicotine. They take themselves up with cigarettes and lower themselves back down with drinks. Many people who take tranquilizers for serious mental illness are also heavy smokers. The nicotine boosts the energy level and mood, effectively counteracting the tranquilizer the person is taking.

A curious fact about tobacco, and about stimulants in general, is that the stimulating effects of the drug are real. Scientific studies of behavior that measure levels of alertness and activation document nicotine's mentally invigorating properties.

At higher doses, nicotine acts as a sedative on the central nervous system by occupying and triggering brain receptors (see Figure 2-1). This sedative effect is well borne out by numerous examples of nicotine poisoning, which can lead to nausea, vomiting, convulsions, and even death. These unfortunate events typically occur as accidents, with a child or teenager ingesting too much nicotine in any of its various forms.

Additional mental effects of smoking include the following:

✔ Low self-esteem

✔ Low self-confidence

✔ Feelings of guilt

✔ Feelings of embarrassment

Social effects

The social effects of tobacco are likewise complex. They depend largely on which social group you belong to.

Decades ago, smoking — on the job, at home, in bed, in restaurants, at the theater, or wherever — was a given. Few people gave it any thought.

At other points in history, tobacco use was considered low-class, and people who favored healthy looks and bright white smiles tossed their cigarettes away for good. But smoking as a way of life has continued among certain parts of the population and is still seen, at least in Hollywood and by many kids, as a sign of being cool.

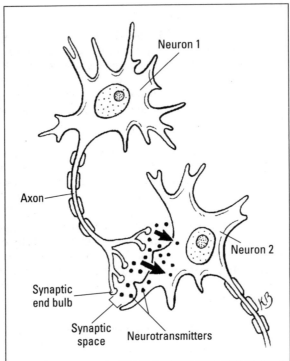

Figure 2-1:
Brain
receptors.

Young people often smoke to act tough, using a cigarette as a calling card for their particular clique. Smoking is often a rite of passage from adolescence to adulthood. It's a gesture that accompanies the movement from your family of origin to college or work or your own place to live.

In most circles, though, smoking brings about negative attention that many people try to avoid. Recently, at a family event, a cousin sidled up to me. Scanning the room for onlookers, she asked in a low voice if I still smoked. I told her I didn't. Her disappointment was obvious. She was looking for someone to join her on her obligatory exodus to the restroom, where she knew she could (and had to) light up.

When you smoke, you are a role model to the people, including any children and teenagers, around you. Your kids, if you have kids, may say, "My mom smokes and so can I." The parental gambit of "Do what I say, not what I do" doesn't carry a lot weight. An adult who does one thing and says another quickly earns a reputation as a hypocrite, a mockery, a caricature.

Financial effects

The financial effects of smoking are both immediate and long-term. Smoking has an enormous detrimental economic impact on the smoker as well as on society as a whole. As a smoker, you may spend $4 or more a day on a habit that you often hate, that pollutes the air, and that may gradually suffocate you or even kill you someday. On a macro level, your health insurance costs keep on climbing — skyrocketing, actually — partly because of the billions of dollars needed for expensive procedures used to diagnose and treat lung disease and other medical complications of tobacco use.

The cost of the long-term care — rehabilitation, nursing homes, hospice settings — for chronically debilitated smokers is practically off the charts. Keeping someone with chronic obstructive pulmonary disease alive costs barrels full of money. Many, if not most, of the afflicted run out of insurance benefits and are forced to rely on Medicare and hospitals' charity care funds, and taxpayers — you and I — end up as the big spenders at the end of the day. The cost of healthcare as we know it is skyrocketing, too. Exorbitant healthcare costs, including hospital stays and chronic care at home or in nursing facilities, is destroying our ability to adequately treat the sick.

See Chapter 6 for much more on the financial costs of tobacco use.

Brand loyalty among smokers

Smokers take pride in their brand of choice. You may experience a kind of allegiance, a feeling of loyalty or pride, in your brand. You may even put down people who prefer other brands, who smoke filtered versus nonfiltered cigarettes, slim versus regular cigarettes, and so on. In other words, you may feel proud to be a Marlboro man (or woman). You may think that Kools are cool. Or perhaps you feel that you're a cut above the crowd because you're a Cohiba fan. You may define yourself and the group you run with on the basis of what you smoke.

Advertising further drives home loyalty to particular brands. The old Joe Camel ad was extremely popular, but what was it about, really? The ad depicted a ludicrous cartoon character, cigarette drooping from mouth, as a walking, talking phallic symbol.

Legal effects

The legal effects of tobacco deserve a book of their own. Hundreds of lawsuits have been brought against tobacco companies. These suits allege that tobacco users' illnesses, resulting disabilities, and deaths were the direct result of tobacco use, and that the companies sold and promoted their products while feigning ignorance of tobacco's ill effects. The cumulative damages as described by the plaintiffs run into the hundreds of billions of dollars.

It took many years for legal efforts against tobacco to get off the ground. Earlier efforts to hold the tobacco companies responsible for smokers' illness and death failed, due in part to the limited financial and legal resources on the part of plaintiffs. The culture and legal environment has changed a great deal in the past two decades, though. In 1994, Mississippi was the first of 22 states to launch lawsuits against tobacco companies to recoup millions of Medicaid dollars spent on treating sick smokers. The legal notion of *contributing negligence* — that smokers were at least partially responsible for the consequences on their health — has given way to precedents of partial and even strict liability on the part of the tobacco companies.

In 1998, the tobacco companies reached the Master Settlement Agreement with 46 of the U.S. states. Part of the rationale for this agreement was to combine the efforts of thousands of potential litigees into massive class-action lawsuits on the state level. According to the terms of this agreement, the tobacco manufacturers who signed agreed to place funds each year into an escrow account for annual dispensation to the 46 states. The money is intended to support education and prevention efforts in each state, although complaints and allegations have been raised that the money has not been targeted appropriately in some states.

The U.S. government pushed back against tobacco use in the 1960s by creating the Surgeon General's Advisory Committee on Smoking and Health. The year 1964 saw the publication of *Smoking and Health,* which came out and declared that cigarette smoking caused lung cancer in men. Carcinogens in tobacco smoke, like cadmium, arsenic, and DDT, were named. Although the statistical relationship between lung cancer and smoking was not quite as robust for women as it was for men, the risk was still very much present for women. The little warning box that appears on every cigarette ad, billboard, and package was mandated by federal law in 1965, through the Federal Cigarette Labeling and Advertising Act. Cigarette advertising on the radio, on television, and in movies was banned in 1971. By 1990, smoking on interstate buses and on U.S. flights of six hours or less was illegal.

Political effects

The political fallout of tobacco production, manufacturing, sales, and use is global. The tobacco industry itself is global in reach, providing jobs and a way of life for hundreds of thousands of people. As I hope you gather from this book, tobacco's impact on the physical and therefore financial health of nations is enormous. The tobacco industry is gargantuan and, like other corporate behemoths, gobbles up market share and consumers wherever and whenever it can.

As a result of legal and tax disincentives in the United States, along with Big Tobacco's compliance with health warnings and "prevention" efforts, marketing efforts are increasingly targeted internationally. If you're interested in a politician's stand on the issue, his or her voting record on various tobacco-related issues is a matter of public record and is available in a variety of formats. Although it's rare for politicians to endorse the manufacture and sale of tobacco directly (except perhaps in districts where tobacco agriculture is the major source of income), you can "read their lips" by checking out their voting records. Although we give lip service to harm reduction and to keeping tobacco away from minors in the United States, the push is on overseas to sell as many cigarettes as possible.

Cultural effects

Tobacco has many cultural effects, perhaps the most prominent being its everpresence on the silver screen. The tobacco industry knows that the movies are a terrific medium in which to advertise cigarettes. It is well known that the industry has paid actors and film studios to use cigarettes on screen in an effort to promote the image of smoking as cool.

The number of examples of brand-name cigarettes being smoked by leading actors or otherwise being used in movie scenes are legion. In *Superman II,* for example, Lois Lane smokes Marlboros. At one point in the movie, Superman and the villains hurl a truck bearing the Marlboro name back and forth. Philip Morris paid to have its product featured prominently.

Other companies involved in the aggressive promotion of cigarettes in the movies have included R. J. Reynolds and Brown and Williamson Tobacco. Despite the industry's promise to self-regulate, some infractions have been proven.

Chapter 3

Knowing Why You Get Addicted

. . . .

In This Chapter

▶ Listing the benefits and downsides of smoking

▶ Counting up the poisons contained in tobacco smoke

▶ Understanding addiction, dependence, and other key concepts

▶ Defining tolerance, abuse, and other important terms

▶ Looking at how the brain's neurotransmitters work

▶ Exploring why people get addicted to nicotine and other substances

. . . .

*I*n recent decades, clinical scientists have accumulated increasing knowledge about the whys and wherefores of addiction. You and every other potential quitter can benefit from the great leaps forward that have been made in understanding this problem. Not too long ago; addiction was considered a result of weakness, of deficient morals. More recently, scientists have been able to elaborate the brain chemistry behind addiction, and today we regard many forms of addiction as alterations in brain chemicals, or *neurotransmitters*.

Understanding the science behind addiction empowers you in your attempt to quit smoking because it helps you understand exactly what you're facing when you quit. Your contribution to quitting and staying quit is critical. This chapter interacts with you and helps you participate fully in the process of achieving smoke-free health.

Looking at the Benefits and Risks of Smoking

Quitting smoking is one of the best and most important things you can do for yourself. You will find that the best way to do it is to do it comprehensively. You must arm and fortify yourself not only with the facts, but also with self-knowledge and with commitment on an intellectual, emotional, and perhaps even spiritual level.

A little history of substance abuse

There's a history to substance use. The use of alcohol and other drugs waxes and wanes in popularity, depending on a number of factors, including

✔ Availability

✔ Popularization by celebrities and other role models

✔ Price

✔ Moral climate

✔ Legality

In the 1960s, recreational drug use was a significant part of the prevailing youth culture. Using marijuana and psychedelics, usually accompanied by cigarettes, became the norm for many. The 1990s saw a return to the cultural sensibility of the 1920s, when illicit drug use was largely frowned upon and seen as an unfortunate habit of poor city dwellers, musicians, others "on the fringe" ... and affluent suburban kids and their parents.

By contrast, many drugs that are considered dangerous today were widely available over the counter in the late 19th century. The original Coca-Cola, for example, contained cocaine, as did a number of other nostrums and remedies available in drugstores to the general public (without a doctor's prescription) wherever powders and specifics were sold.

Why do you want to quit? Maybe you think you need to, although you would prefer to smoke forever. Take an in depth look at the personal costs and benefits of smoking. Take a pen to paper and draw a line down the center of the page. Label one column Benefits of Smoking and the other Risks of Smoking, as in Table 3-1. Then, in each column, fill in what you think are the benefits and risks of this habit.

Table 3-1	Charting the Benefits and Risks of Smoking
Benefits of Smoking	*Risks of Smoking*

Devote as much time as you need during an undistracted part of your day to completing this chart. Search your own memories and experiences as well as the experiences of others over the years to come up with items for each list. The items that jump to mind first are likely to be those that are most immediate and contemporary for you — the perks and downsides of smoking now.

You can always add to your list later. In fact, I'm sure you'll add to it later as you enjoy more smoke-free time and come to appreciate all the benefits of cutting cigarettes out of your life. You can assign points to each of the items on your list, using the following scale: 1 means that the risk/benefit has little impact on your life, while 10 means that the item has enormous impact. Add up the columns and see what you come up with. Do the risks outweigh the benefits?

I quit smoking 12 years ago, when our first son was born. I had been a confirmed pack-a-day man for years up to then, but what firmly and finally made me decide was my unwillingness to expose our newborn to the smell and chemicals of burnt tobacco. At the time, I went through a lot of list-making myself. The following lists include some of the risks and benefits that I came up with.

Risks:

- ✔ Developing chronic lung disease such as bronchitis, emphysema, or lung cancer.

- ✔ Developing diseases of other body systems, such as bladder, throat, or mouth cancer.

- ✔ Relying on cigarettes every time I need a goodie or a distraction or need to feel alert.

- ✔ Needing a pack no matter where I am — in the middle of nowhere, skiing, or flying an F-19, I'd still have to find a pack.

- ✔ Having to sneak out of work or social engagements or whatever I'm doing to smoke.

- ✔ Enduring disapproving looks from nonsmokers in public.

- ✔ Being considered an addict by myself and others.

- ✔ Spending ever-increasing amounts of money that I could have spent on healthier, more constructive pastimes.

- ✔ Waking up with a smoker's cough.

- ✔ Having to kiss someone with the rancid taste of cigarette smoke in my mouth.

✔ Desensitizing my taste buds so that subtle flavors and fragrances escaped my notice.

✔ Forever emptying and cleaning out ashtrays.

✔ Lining the pockets of tobacco companies.

✔ Setting a poor example for my family.

Benefits:

✔ Looking cool (although a 40-year-old physician doesn't necessarily need to emulate James Dean or Humphrey Bogart, do you think?).

✔ Keeping my fingers and mouth busy at most times.

✔ Enjoying conversational breaks.

✔ "Earning" a reward for completing work or exercising — or anything!

✔ Being able to follow a meal or lovemaking session with another pleasurable activity.

✔ Suppressing my appetite when I don't have the time or money to eat or interest in eating.

✔ Energizing myself when I need an extra boost.

✔ Conforming to peer pressure and being one of the gang when others are happily lighting up.

When you look at the "benefits," you can begin to appreciate how compelling smoking can be. The idea, though, is to be even more impressed by the cumulative risks and potential adverse consequences of continuing to smoke.

Naming Your Poison

When you smoke, you get a lot more than you paid for. And you get a lot more than you expected. Along with nicotine, cigarette smoke and other forms of combusted tobacco contain hundreds of highly poisonous substances, many of them illness-causing when present in sufficient amounts, and some of them carcinogenic.

Among the main culprits are

✔ **Tar,** which itself contains hundreds of hazardous and carcinogenic compounds.

✔ **Carbon monoxide,** which is released from burning tobacco leaves and actually squeezes the oxygen out of your red blood cells, significantly reducing the amount of life-giving oxygen that gets to your heart, muscles, and brain. Moderate amounts of carbon monoxide cause dizziness and nausea (again due to lack of oxygen), and large amounts can cause death. Many suicide victims have quit this life with the help of carbon monoxide from automobile exhaust.

✔ **Hydrogen cyanide,** which is one of the most poisonous compounds in cigarette smoke. Modest amounts of this killer cause weakness, headache, nausea, vomiting, breathing difficulty, and skin irritation.

✔ **Formaldehyde** and **benzene,** which are present in significant amounts in cigarette smoke and are considered to be probable cancer-causing agents.

Cigarette smoking is known to be the number-one cause of preventable death in the United States. Choosing not to put these toxic substances into your body is a very wise move. Nicotine fuels the addiction to smoking, but the hydrocarbons, tars, and free radicals that tobacco smoke contains are highly toxic and contribute to the diseases and deaths that result from smoking.

Understanding What Addiction Is

People have been trying to understand addiction for thousands of years. Every epoch has brought its own cultural, historical, and social biases and orientation toward this understanding. For example, ancient peoples (up to and including medieval Europeans) often attributed socially unacceptable behavior such as addiction to demonic possession. Not too long ago, society often chastised and derided people who had addictions no matter what the type — booze, tobacco, drugs, or other substances.

The tobacco-alcohol link

According to the National Clearinghouse for Alcohol and Drug Information (NCADI), daily cigarette smoking is associated with the use of illicit drugs among youth. Individuals under the age of 18 who were daily smokers or heavy drinkers were more likely to use recreational drugs than daily smokers or heavy drinkers who were older. Furthermore, those youths who used both cigarettes and alcohol in the month preceding the survey were more than twice as likely to have used street drugs than youths who used only alcohol or cigarettes alone. See Chapter 17 for information about talking to teens about the dangers of smoking — and helping them quit if they've already succumbed to temptation.

Fortunately, the addiction treatment field has made a lot of progress in recent years. Individuals who use substances regularly despite the destructive effects and problems these substances cause are considered to be *chemically dependent,* or to be abusing chemicals. If you're dependent on a substance, you build *tolerance* (where it takes more and more of the drug to cause the same effect) and experience *withdrawal* (uncomfortable symptoms when you stop using the drug).

Many researchers and clinicians in the field believe that tobacco dependence and abuse are true medical disorders and, as such, deserve medical interventions, such as the use of the nicotine patch and/or the anticraving drug Zyban. As medicine has entered the playing field, addiction has become less of a stigma — and those with addictions are more willing to ask for help.

Defining addiction, dependence, and abuse

It seems like everyone's an addict these days. Cigarettes, alcohol, pills, sex, shopping, food, exercise — the list of habit-formers is endless.

Addiction and addictive behaviors are as old as humankind. The Bible records numerous instances of drunkenness and its consequences. The vote is not yet in on whether contemporary society experiences more of these problems than previous ones did. One possible result of the increasing focus on public health issues is a greater awareness of addiction problems.

So what is addiction? *Addiction* is any behavior that's repeated over and over despite significant negative consequences. Another term for addiction is *dependence* (as in *chemical dependence*).

Could addiction include breathing smog-filled air, driving on freeways, or drinking polluted water? Not really. Most of us who do these things don't have much of a say in the matter. *Addiction* refers to behavior that on some level is elective. People choose to drink, smoke, or go to the racetrack and gamble — or at least they consciously make the choice the first few times they do it, before they become addicted.

Lesser forms of addiction have been termed *abuse.* Of course, a fine line separates abuse and actual dependence. With alcohol, for example, many heavy drinkers imbibe heavily but episodically; they don't qualify for the label *dependent* because they can get by for days or even weeks at a time without drinking. On the other hand, even a single use of a dangerous drug like PCP or cocaine can result in a catastrophic series of physical or mental changes, even if the user is not addicted to the drug.

The real cost of cigarettes

Cigarettes are responsible for costs to society in the billions of dollars. According to the Centers for Disease Control, from 1995 to 1999 in the United States:

✔ Smoking caused about 440,000 premature deaths annually.

✔ Smoking cost the nation about $157 billion in annual health-related economic losses.

✔ There was an annual average of 264,087 deaths among men and 178,311 deaths among women due to smoking. Smoking-related deaths were usually attributable to lung cancer, heart disease, and chronic pulmonary obstructive disease (COPD).

✔ As a result of maternal smoking during pregnancy, almost 600 baby boys and more than 400 baby girls died each year.

The CDC also estimates that in each year covered by the survey, about 1,000 people died from fires caused by smoking, and another 37,000 died from heart disease or lung cancer caused by exposure to secondhand smoke. How's that for expensive?

Nonetheless, the abuse concept is meant to capture the idea that the use of a substance — even the very infrequent, recreational use of cigarettes — can be abusive if it causes harm to the user.

Abuse, dependence, addiction . . . experts have devoted unthinkable amounts of time trying to clarify these concepts. The consensus still isn't in. Most of those who work in the addiction field prefer to describe their clients as "chemically dependent individuals" rather than as addicts. The term *addict* has taken on many negative connotations — it has a definite stigma attached to it — and obscures the fact that chemical use may be a disease and not a moral shortcoming.

As important as it is to have a common language when discussing these matters, it's also important to recognize these definitions are *not* written in stone.

Defining other key terms

The hallmarks of dependence are *tolerance* and *withdrawal.* Any drug or substance that involves tolerance and withdrawal is considered to be addictive.

Tolerance

Tolerance exists when it takes more and more of something (cigarettes, booze, shopping, or whatever) to get the same effect, the same high. Tolerance can be either of the following:

> ✔ **Metabolic,** as when your liver becomes more efficient at breaking down repeated and/or ever higher doses of alcohol and other substances
>
> ✔ **Cellular,** where the brain cells just don't get the same buzz that they used to

The physiological basis of cellular tolerance remains a mystery. A more complete understanding would likely lead to terrific advances in the treatment and prevention of addictive disorders. Metabolic tolerance, on the other hand, is fairly well understood. Liver enzymes break down, or *metabolize*, nutrients, drugs, and other foreign substances. As the body is exposed to repeated doses of a drug, certain liver enzymes are induced — that is, they become more efficient at metabolizing the drug. This explains, for example, how a seasoned drinker can fly a B-52 or write a novel long after you or I would have passed out under the table.

Withdrawal

When your brain and body have become accustomed to repeated doses of nicotine, or alcohol, or any other drug that causes major changes in mood and brain function, they react when the drug is taken away. Quite often, the *withdrawal* experience is the very opposite of the drug use experience. With nicotine, for example, withdrawal features restlessness, distractibility, and fatigue — all opposites of the way you feel when you've just smoked a cigarette.

Famous addicts

According to at least one biographer, a typical drinking day for writer Ernest Hemingway began with vodka and tequila, followed by Bloody Marys at noon, succeeded in turn by scotch and mixed drinks and untold amounts of wine to usher in the evening. The Hemingway story is not that great a stretch when it comes to some smokers' habits.

Other famous owners of hollow legs (and other appetites) include

✔ John Belushi

✔ Ty Cobb

✔ Robert Downey, Jr.

✔ William Faulkner

✔ W. C. Fields

✔ F. Scott Fitzgerald

✔ Janis Joplin

✔ Jim Morrison

✔ Edgar Allan Poe

✔ Babe Ruth

✔ John Steinbeck

Why people smoke — and why it's hard to quit

Nicotine has been shown to be a powerful reinforcer in animals, which in laboratory cages will press levers to get it. Nicotine has also been shown to be a powerful reinforcer in humans, who will go to great lengths (even walk a mile!) to cop a smoke. Cigarettes reduce anxiety, increase alertness, and become associated in smokers' minds with powerful rewards — reinforcers — like decreased anxiety, increased alertness, post-meal gratification, and post-coital bliss.

The average pack-a-day smoker takes some 70,000 puffs over the course of a year. It takes a major commitment to quit anything you do that often! Like coffee drinkers, smokers who quit may find themselves bedeviled by definite withdrawal symptoms, including fatigue, irritability, anxiety, and decreased alertness. Of those who quit, two-thirds have begun smoking again after one year. Those who switch to lower-nicotine brands usually find themselves simply smoking more cigarettes per day to make up for the fact that they're getting less nicotine from each butt.

Conditioning

When a reward — a pleasurable experience — is connected with a given behavior, the nervous system somehow adapts to that behavior and tends to want it to be repeated. If these behaviors are particularly pleasurable, the brain is reluctant to give them up. Laboratory mice who are rewarded with food pellets for pressing a bar will continue to press the bar in order to keep getting the pellets. Likewise, a number of positive reinforcements become connected to smoking, such as appetite suppression, feeling cool, and feeling more alert. This linkage of a contingency that eventually results in a specific behavior is known as *conditioning*.

Neuroadaptation

Neuroadaptation describes more than tolerance and withdrawal. It is the basis of the gradual diminishing and eventual disappearance of a person's awareness of incoming sensory stimuli. Imagine what life would be like if you couldn't tune out the sensation of clothing on your skin or the constant rain of ambient noise on your eardrums!

In *The Doors of Perception*, writer Aldous Huxley bemoaned our usual inability to appreciate things as they first looked or felt to us, before tolerance or neuroadaptation set in. His solution was psychedelic drugs like mescaline, peyote, and LSD, which can make things seem new and exciting again. Unfortunately for smokers, the nervous system does not adapt to repeated doses of nicotine. Instead, your brain and body experience nicotine withdrawal when you haven't smoked for several hours, and you find yourself reaching for another cigarette.

Drugs like nicotine that are highly rewarding to the brain because of their relaxing, distracting, energizing, and appetite-suppressing properties actually condition users to want more. In laboratory studies, animals that become conditioned to press a lever to get more drug will preferentially press for nicotine, sometimes to the exclusion of food or rest. Talk about bad choices!

Knowing How Neurotransmitters Function — and How Substances Like Nicotine Mess Things Up

Getting a better handle on how neurotransmitters normally work, and how drugs like nicotine affect these processes, may help you understand addiction in general and your own addiction(s), if you have any, in particular.

Hundreds of millions of brain cells, called *neurons,* communicate with one another by means of highly organized relays and loops. *Neurotransmitters* such as dopamine, norepinephrine, and serotonin are the chemical messengers that enable brain cells to communicate. Neurotransmitters are released into the *synaptic space* between neurons and either excite or inhibit the *receptors* of the next brain cell in line. Think of it as a physiological bucket brigade taking place on a microscopic level. Or think of it as a neurophysiological relay race.

Crossing the synaptic space between brain cells, neurotransmitters stimulate (or inhibit) the next neuron in the circuit, which in turn releases or shuts off further neurotransmitters, which then stimulates or inhibits the next neuron in the circuit, and so on. These neurotransmitters are ultimately taken back up into their brain cells of origin and are then either recycled for further use or metabolized (broken down). When brain chemicals are taken back up into the nerve cell, the brain chemical's (neurotransmitter's) trigger action on the system is terminated.

Some psychoactive drugs, such as nicotine, act directly on the receptors, while others block the re-uptake mechanism, resulting in increased neurotransmitter presence in the synaptic space and increased and continued stimulation of the neuron receptors.

Drugs also appear to have dramatic effects on the brain's reward systems, such as the endorphin/enkephalin system. Euphoriants such as heroin may temporarily shut down the brain's ability to manufacture its own pleasure molecules (endorphins and enkephalins). In the absence of a continued supply of heroin, the user's brain feels horrible. Alcohol, opiates, and other drugs either stimulate or compete for specific receptor sites, which may explain why drug users (including smokers) experience great pleasure and experience persistent and severe withdrawal symptoms when they stop using the drug.

Withdrawal can be relatively mild — the garden variety Sunday morning hangover is nothing but a form of mild to moderate alcohol withdrawal — or devastatingly painful, sometimes to the point of seizures or even death. Withdrawal also differs from one drug to another. The severity, discomfort, or risk to health depends not only on the substance used but also on the frequency of use, the level of tolerance, the amount ingested, and the elapsed time since the last use.

The brain is like a symphony. To sound right, all the different instruments must play together.

Analyzing Drugs (Including Nicotine) and Why People Use Them

According to *Webster's Collegiate Dictionary*, a *drug* is "any substance used as a medicine or as an ingredient in a medicine." A *medicine* is defined as "any drug or other substance used in treating disease, healing or relieving pain." Nicotine doesn't treat disease, promote healing, or relieve pain, but it is still a drug.

Broadening the definition of "drug"

The *Webster's* definition of the term *drug* as a substance used as a medicine is overly narrow. People drug themselves not only with substances, but also with

- ✔ Shopping
- ✔ Gambling
- ✔ Sex
- ✔ Sports
- ✔ Television
- ✔ Money
- ✔ Work

- ✔ Religion
- ✔ Computers
- ✔ Pornography
- ✔ Power
- ✔ Hatred
- ✔ Travel
- ✔ Materialism
- ✔ Cars
- ✔ Relationships

Classifying drugs

This is a *functional* classification of psychoactive drugs:

- **Alcohol,** including but by no means limited to beer, wine, port, schnapps, kir, aquavit, champagne, vermouth, scotch, rye, whiskey, absinthe, rum, ouzo, tequila, mezcal, sherry, brandy, cognac, amontillado, vodka, gin, and sloe gin (hic!).

- **Sedatives/Hypnotics** (sleeping pills), including all classes of benzodiazepines, other types of sleep medications, and barbiturates.

- **Stimulants,** such as cocaine, amphetamine, dexedrine, pemoline, caffeine, khat, ephedrine, methylphenidate, and biphetamine. Stimulants are used to get high, reduce weight, and increase alertness.

- **Opiates,** including, but not limited to, opium, heroin, "laudanum," paregoric, methadone, dilaudid, percocet, percodan, demerol, oxycontin. Opiates are the most potent painkillers around. Some of them find legitimate medical use in the treatment of severe or intractable pain.

- **Hallucinogens,** an ever-expanding (some would say mind-expanding) group to which new members are added all the time. LSD, mescaline, peyote, cannabis, THC, hashish, angel dust, PCP, ketamine, psilocybin, and even morning glory seeds and nutmeg ('the Sailor's High") have been used to induce visions, alter reality, and change states of consciousness.

- **Various prescription pills,** such as Fiorinal, Darvon, Elavil, Doriden, Soma, Cogentin, and Artane. These pills are prescribed for various medical purposes *and* can be found on the street, where they often fetch sky-high prices.

- Last but not least, the deadliest drug of all: **nicotine.** Nicotine is both a stimulant and a sedative. Smoking or chewing tobacco is directly related to thousand upon thousands of deaths each year from cancers of the mouth, throat, and lungs; emphysema; chronic bronchitis; and heart disease. Cigarette smoking aggravates hypertension and peptic ulcer disease. Absent these horrible diseases, cigarette smoking runs you down and depletes your energy and self-esteem.

The further you get from the natural source of a substance — the more concentrated the active ingredient becomes — the greater the likelihood of trouble. This blanket statement applies to all classes of intoxicants. Severe paranoia or delusions or other kinds of psychiatric problems are more likely to occur with pure THC (thetrahydrocannibol, the active ingredient of marijuana and hashish) than with smoked marijuana. Similarly, it's easier to get wasted on hard liquor like vodka or scotch than on beer or wine.

Nicotine, on the other hand, is completely harmless. That is, unless you take into account the hundreds of thousands of deaths each year from cancer, hardening of the arteries, and chronic lung disease that we know are directly related to use of tobacco products. Not only that, but tobacco use accounts for approximately 400,000 deaths each year. Far fewer are directly attributable to alcohol. Annual deaths directly related to the use of illicit drugs, on the other hand, have been estimated at some 20,000 to 30,000.

Tobacco wasn't always this harmful. Pre-Columbian Indians who chewed or smoked tobacco in pipes certainly did not have the widespread and severe lung problems that beset modern cigarette smokers. Less potent forms of drugs taken by less effective routes of delivery (for example, chewing tobacco leaves instead of inhaling tobacco smoke, or drinking beer instead of distilled spirits) are less likely to cause serious harm.

The comparison of tobacco with illicit drug use is again instructive. Although there may be 3 million American users of illicit drugs, cigarette smokers are estimated at 50 million (that's one-third of those over age 12) and heavy drinkers at 10 million. Based on these numbers, it's easy to work out the comparative degree of damage for yourself.

What do drugs do?

Different drugs have different effects on the brain and the body. While some drugs, such as alcohol and LSD, have only one *psychoactive* (acting on the mind) compound, others, such as marijuana and tobacco, have many active compounds. Not only that, but many drugs affect more than one type of neuronal receptor, which means that you can expect multiple physical and mental effects. Some drugs exert different effects depending how much of the drug is taken. For example, nicotine in small amounts acts as a sedative, whereas two or three consecutive smokes later the smoker definitely feels *wired*.

One way to understand drug effects is to classify them. There's no single right way to classify drugs. You can, for example, classify them by legal status, as the U.S. Drug Enforcement Agency does: Cocaine, marijuana, heroin, and LSD are all considered Schedule I — that is, they're considered to have no legitimate medical use (although the compassionate use of marijuana for treating chemotherapy-induced nausea has been a raging political controversy on the state level for years). Drugs can also be categorized by structure (type of molecule) and by function (effect on the body).

Why do people use drugs?

People use drugs such as nicotine for a variety of reasons. They use drugs

- ✓ **Because it feels good . . . though not always!** In one study, a third of the subjects who used alcohol or street drugs reported that they actually felt worse after using the substance. With drug use, *changing* the way you feel may be as important as *improving* the way you feel.

- ✓ **To feel that they belong.** Peer pressure can be the gateway to alcohol and drug use, particularly among teenagers. Strategies aimed at the young seek to prevent the crystallization of identities around deviant behavior such as drug use. In other words, drugs are not cool.

✔ **To feel different.** Shy people, for example, may use drink or drugs to remove inhibitions and to make themselves feel and act more outgoing. The weak may feel strong under the influence; dispirited outcasts may become loquacious and assertive after having a few.

✔ **Because cigarettes, alcohol, and other drugs act as social lubricants.** Certain individuals with social phobia — fear of interacting with others in public — use drugs to loosen up in public. This strategy may work to a certain extent, but having to rely on a smoke or a drink every time you want to shine socially can be a real obstacle.

✔ **To enhance their performance at various tasks, from schoolwork to athletics to job performance.** Athletes bolster their speed and strength with steroids. Soldiers have used amphetamines to stay awake and forestall hunger during prolonged combat. Dancers and musicians have relied on speed, cocaine, and numerous other drugs to boost their stamina and creative flow. But countless others do fine (if not better) without chemicals.

✔ **Because their parents or other role models did.** Evidence suggests that alcoholism runs in families. Close relatives of alcoholics have a three to four times greater risk of alcoholism. Studies have also demonstrated a higher likelihood of alcoholism in identical twin children of alcoholics and among children of alcoholics who were raised in nonalcoholic homes. This doesn't mean that children or relatives of alcoholics are fated to become alcoholics themselves, though. Environment and other factors, including personality and intelligence, strongly influence the individual's susceptibility to addiction.

Drug use can begin as experimentation — "Let's try something new!" In other cases, the wish to self-medicate — to take something to dull painful emotions such as depression, loneliness, and fear — kicks off the cycle of addiction. Consistent relationships between certain psychiatric disorders or personality traits and specific drugs of abuse have not been proven. Nonetheless, there have been many reports of opiate use to self-medicate rage and *psychosis* (loss of contact with reality).

Drug use in the service of self-medication can set up a vicious cycle: People find that they need to smoke a joint (or cigarette) in order to accomplish a creative task may find their energy and inspiration levels reduced by the marijuana (or tobacco). In other words, Beethoven's *Fifth Symphony* and Michelangelo's *Pieta* were probably not created under the influence. See Chapter 14 for more on self-medicating.

Some artists, of course, swear by marijuana, booze, or other drugs. The smoking, drinking piano player or painter (think Jackson Pollack) is a cultural stereotype. But usually, a morning-after look at their midnight efforts finds an illegible, fuzzy-brained, or downright laughable parody of inspiration. Many successful artists, performers, and businesspeople enhance their output with solid self-care in the form of good nutrition, exercise, and adequate rest.

Looking at the Various Theories of Addiction

People have been grappling with the question "Why do people use drugs like nicotine?" since history began. A related question — "How is it that some people can use drugs sparingly or episodically while others become truly addicted?" — is just as challenging to answer. Leading theories of addiction include the following:

- ✔ **Behavioral models** explain substance use and other addictive behaviors on the basis of *conditioning* and *reinforcement*. Experiments with laboratory animals show that drug highs, especially nicotine highs, are extremely reinforcing — a rat will work to the point of starvation, exhaustion, and even death to press a lever that causes the drug to be released into its brain. Rats (and people) become *conditioned* — that is, they associate previously "neutral" environmental cues (such as music, sex, or a given restaurant or neighborhood) with the drug effect and start craving the drug the moment they're exposed to these deeply embedded reminders of the drug. Drugs act as their cue or reinforcement, while environmental factors associated with drug use (such as peer approval and positive self-regard) also act as reinforcers.

- ✔ **Social learning theory** highlights the effect of social influences, such as peer pressure and cultural and family values (or the absence of them) on the acquiring of addictive behavior. Alcoholics Anonymous and similar self-help groups for recovering addicts emphasize the importance of avoiding "people, places, and things." Exposure to drug cues may not only provoke conditioned responses but may instill values and behaviors that need to be unlearned at later points in time. For example, you *can* enjoy a meal without a cigarette for dessert.

- ✔ **Biological explanations** cite *neuroadaptation* as the key process in addiction. The brain somehow adapts to repeated exposure to nicotine and then experiences states of deprivation, or withdrawal, when the nicotine is withheld. Specific changes in brain cell receptors and brain blood flow accompany states of intoxication and withdrawal.

✔ **Self-medication hypotheses** posit a relationship between painful mood states such as anxiety and depression and the use of tobacco and other drugs. According to this theory, people drink or use drugs in order to change or improve the way they feel. This process is circular, since withdrawal from nicotine and other substances often ends up aggravating the baseline mood problem.

Granted, nicotine is one of the most addictive substances around. But none of these models adequately explains how or why Person X becomes a regular smoker and Person Y does not. Addiction may result from the impact of numerous factors — availability of smokes, peer pressure, desire to take or smoke something in order to feel different — on what has been called an addictive personality.

Research has demonstrated that addictive behavior can be inherited. Studies of twins and children of alcoholic parents raised by nonalcoholic parents show that there is some genetic transmission of alcoholics. On the other hand, other studies show that individual factors such as intelligence and specific character traits such as resourcefulness can override or make up for a strong genetic predisposition to tobacco or alcohol use.

In the 1960s, thousands of American soldiers used cheap and potent heroin while stationed in Vietnam. Yet only a tiny fraction remained addicted upon their return to the U.S. Addiction (including to tobacco) results from the interplay of *mindset* (personality, expectations) and *setting* (environment). In the familiar, safer, and more supportive setting of home, these same soldiers no longer needed to self-medicate with drugs.

This is often the case for adolescent "experimental" tobacco and drug use as well. During the teen and early adulthood years, defying authority and trying new and possibly dangerous experiences — taking risks — are the norm. Later in life, such behaviors come to be considered inappropriate or deviant and are discarded.

Speaking of self-medication: If people do self-medicate anger, depression, and anxiety with substances such as nicotine, then you would expect mentally ill people to be self-medicating *big-time* . . . and they do! Cigarette use among those with psychiatric disorders, especially among the chronically mentally ill, is a problem of epidemic proportions. Research has shown that nicotine actually helps reduce the blood levels of certain psychotropic medications, reducing their effectiveness. Some people with depression, severe anxiety, and other psychiatric disorders smoke in order to counteract the mind-altering medications they take.

Gateway drugs

What about this idea that using one drug (the "gateway" drug) makes using another more likely?

Careful study of individual drug use reveals that many people do progress from cigarettes, alcohol, or marijuana to hard drugs like cocaine and heroin. Gateway drugs are associated with later use of more dangerous drugs (although it's hard to come up with any drugs — seriously! — that are more dangerous than tobacco). Concern about this tendency fuels some of the arguments against the legalization of marijuana and provides part of the rationale for higher and higher cigarette taxes. It's a well-known economic fact that as the price of a drug rises, the number of users diminishes.

Chapter 4

Figuring Out Why You Smoke

Why would anyone *choose* to smoke? Beyond a certain point, of course, you really stop choosing. Nicotine is one of the most fiercely addicting substances on earth. This fact has been borne out in numerous studies of both laboratory animals and humans. Quitting smoking is tough. Learning more about nicotine addiction and about addiction in general should give you greater respect for yourself and your courage in overcoming this dependence.

Addiction to tobacco — to nicotine — has both physical and psychological components. Laboratory experiments have demonstrated that among drugs of abuse, nicotine is way up there on the habit-forming scale. Like many other behaviors, addiction has many factors. Whether you get hooked on cigarettes has a lot to do with who you are, how you handle things, your family background, and the environment in which you place yourself.

They say that knowledge is power. Knowing more about why you smoke arms you for the leap into smoke-free freedom.

Smoking Out the Smokers: Who Smokes?

Cigarette users are found in all age ranges, among both sexes, and across all social groups. Forty million people in the United States smoke today.

If you've had at least 16 years of school, you're less likely to smoke than adults who have less education. Population surveys also indicate that people with lower annual incomes (especially those below the poverty level) smoke more frequently than those who are more affluent. Among the states, Nevada has the highest rate of smokers, and Utah has the lowest.

The ethnic groups with the highest percentage of smokers are Native Americans and natives of Alaska. You probably won't be surprised to learn that as smoking has declined among Caucasians and other white (non-Hispanic) people in recent years, the tobacco companies have increasingly focused their marketing and advertising efforts on people of other races — mainly Hispanics and African Americans. The number-one cause of cancer mortality among Hispanics is lung cancer. Percentage-wise, more African-American males smoke than white males.

Women are up there on the list of smokers, too; at least 22 million women in the United States smoke. As a group, they're heavily targeted by tobacco advertising. Female high school seniors are smoking more than ever, and in general women are starting to smoke earlier in their lives. According to the American Cancer Society, lung cancer takes the lives of at least 60,000 women each year, with the annual mortality rate among women having increased fourfold since 1960.

Young people aren't immune to the lure of cigarettes, either. Dr. David Kessler of the U.S. Food and Drug Administration stated in 1996 that half of all nicotine users begin using nicotine *by age 13*. The National Youth Tobacco Survey reported in 1999 that about one in eight middle schoolers admitted to having used some kind of tobacco product. Surveys indicate that one-third of high school students acknowledge having used a tobacco product in the past 30 days. Approximately 25 percent of high school students claim to be active smokers.

Almost 50 million people in the United States have quit smoking. You can, too!

Recognizing Why You Started

Why did you start smoking? The next time you're with one or more fellow smokers, you might consider raising this question. Imagine the variety of responses you will get.

You may have started smoking because

- ✔ Your partner or spouse or close friends did.
- ✔ You couldn't imagine getting sick because of tobacco use.

✔ Cigarettes were less expensive than food.

✔ You didn't believe the party line about the harmfulness of tobacco.

✔ You wanted to be defiant.

✔ You wanted to make a statement.

✔ The future didn't seem like it would ever arrive.

✔ Cigarettes were a natural fit with drinking and partying.

Undoubtedly, you can add your own unique reasons to this list. You may have thought that smoking was cool. There is a time in our lives when we feel invulnerable, as if nothing can harm us. You may have taken a philosophical stance that smoking was okay. Whatever your reason for picking up smoking, that reason is definitely not the reason you have continued to smoke. Smoking is addictive, and the personal choice to smoke or not to smoke probably left the building long ago.

Understanding Why You Smoke Now

Excuse the play on words, but many people, including nonsmokers, make light of tobacco addiction. It's as though an unspoken scale of addiction severity existed, with tobacco coming in somewhere on the less severe end of things. "Bad" addictions include illegal drugs like crack and heroin.

Actually, nicotine is one of the most addictive substances known to exist. The reason you smoke in spite of your reluctance to do so is precisely because nicotine is so addictive.

Cut yourself a mental break. Don't give up on quitting just because it seems so difficult. Many others have been down this road, and you can succeed at quitting, too.

Smoking is usually not hidden or covert. The habit is highly visible. But compared to other addictions, addiction to tobacco is more challenging to your life and more demanding of your time. Believe it or not, many users of opiates, heroin, and methadone continue for years and even decades without becoming ill. "Maintenance" drinkers regularly consume alcohol over a lifetime, sometimes with less drastic consequences than may follow from continued smoking. Certain countries such as England license the prescription of heavy-duty painkillers such as heroin, and people take steady amounts for decades without developing medical problems. Granted, you may be able to think of friends or acquaintances who smoke without health consequences, but healthy long-term smokers are the exception. Think about the long-term smokers you know. A smoker's cough is not a sign of robust health!

Don't minimize the seriousness of smoking. Just because millions of people do it and it's legal and therefore socially sanctioned does not reduce the gravity of the potential harm that smoking can cause.

Tobacco is not competing with any other drugs or substances for first prize among addictions. Still, if such a prize existed, tobacco might win the blue ribbon. What other addiction — including alcoholism and dependence on drugs — involves hour-by-hour use? Most other drugs stick around in the body long enough to require refills only every few hours (the single notable exception being crack cocaine, which is used as often as possible until the supply is gone).

Why do you smoke now? Probably for numerous reasons — the biggest of which is that you are addicted and can't stop. Here are some other possible reasons:

✔ You use tobacco as a remedy for anxiety.

✔ To you, smoking is an escape from this world and a window into another world; smoking shuts down your mind, if only for a moment.

✔ Addiction may be your attempt to slow down the clock and think less about the passage of time.

Of course, addiction isn't the only reason people smoke. At some point — right now would be a good time — take stock of your life and your values. What does picking up a cigarette tell you about your choices? It tells you that, at best, you are expending energy by forcing yourself not to worry about the future. At worst, you may have decided that life is such a struggle that you literally don't care what happens tomorrow or next year.

Smoking, like any addiction, is not only about putting off thoughts about the risks of cigarettes. Like all addictions, it is about the murder of *now*. Granted, I am making this point quite dramatically. When you think about it, though, the act of smoking is a statement about the intolerability of the moment and about your (lack of) commitment to your life.

Smoking to be cool (cigarettes aren't!)

When Jack Webb, Sharon Stone, Rod Serling, Grace Kelly, James Dean, or Marlon Brando lit up, that was cool. Hollywood and the media bombard us with images and fantasies that seem cool. Luke Skywalker having a life-or-death light saber duel with Darth Vader is cool, too, but chances are you'll never do that, and even if you could, you probably wouldn't want to.

Having a monkey on your back is definitely *not* cool. Neither is ending up permanently attached to a 5-liter-per-minute oxygen hose or being unable to walk half a block without losing your breath.

In the 1960s, in the era of sex, drugs, and rock and roll, the counterculture celebrated the rebellious, deviant lifestyle. The glamour figures of the time were Jimi Hendrix, Jim Morrison, and Janice Joplin. Where are they now?

If you take a careful look at the pop stars who are making it big today, it's very apparent that the real success stories are those who spend a great deal of their time offstage taking great care of themselves. These people have personal trainers, work out every day, and spend plenty of time and money figuring out how to eat right and preserve their talent, energy, and looks for as long as humanly possible.

If you smoke because you think that it's cool, try to come up with an alternate image of cool. Can you imagine enjoying the full and unrestricted use of your lungs and the rest of your body? High energy, stamina, and good health are very cool. Smoking as a sign of coolness came and went. That was then and this is now.

Smoking to control weight

Yes, tobacco takes the edge off your appetite for food. Yes, millions of smokers use cigarettes and other tobacco products to replace food. Nicotine even gives you an edge, a feeling of being wired, that you don't get from food. For these reasons, many smokers lean on the excuse that they need to keep smoking to control their weight.

If weight gain is a concern for you, I'm happy to tell you that most people who quit smoking don't gain more than 10 pounds. The rest is up to you, meaning that you need to think of weight gain — if you experience it at all — as strictly temporary and as something that you can remedy. It's a matter of priorities.

Gaining several pounds for a relatively short period won't kill you. Continuing to smoke might.

Good nutrition is important. Are there ways to help yourself feel more fit, trim, and healthy? Your physical engine runs much more smoothly and efficiently on a mix of protein and fruit and vegetable carbohydrates than it does on fat-loaded fast foods. Eating right gives you more energy, which is something you may have relied on cigarettes for. If you're overweight, you can find excellent resources in books and on the Internet. Highly trained professionals such as nutritionists and dieticians can review your food intake and exercise schedule and help you devise an optimal plan.

Having said that, I'm now going to do a 180-degree flip and recant much of this wonderful and wise advice.

The history of Hollywood and smoking

In a raw self-disclosure in *The New York Times,* Hollywood writer Joe Eszterhas acknowledged personal responsibility for smoking deaths. As the screenwriter for 14 extremely successful films, many of which portray smoking as glamorous, sexy, and desirable, he feels guilty for promoting the use of tobacco.

Recently, Eszterhas learned of his own throat cancer. He admits that as a "militant smoker," smoking was part of a defiant, rebellious image that he enjoyed portraying. In *Basic Instinct,* the vampy Sharon Stone deliberately blows smoke in the face of Michael Douglas, who's trying to quit. In the movie's best-known scene — in which Stone's character tries to get her interrogator, Douglas's character, to take a peek between her uncrossed legs — she's holding a cigarette.

Eszterhas has since sacrificed his larynx to cancer and has difficulty making himself understood. He has quit smoking (he hopes) for good and instead has turned to prayer and exercise. He describes the people he has seen on cancer wards, struggling for their next breath. He no longer believes that smoking is a right. He believes that tobacco should be policed in the same way as heroin. The ex-smoker likens a cigarette in the hands of an onscreen actor to a smoking gun aimed at teenagers. Screenwriters contribute to the problem, he says, because they know that some actors are more likely to take a part if the character smokes. (Some actors are so addicted that they can't put cigarettes down long enough to shoot a scene.)

Legal authorities working both for and against the film industry have unearthed documents relating to agreements regarding cigarette placement in a number of movies, including *The Jazz Singer* and *Arthur.* These agreements include lists of celebrities who agreed to appear in those motion pictures. Other examples that are hard to forget are James Dean in *Rebel Without a Cause* and John Travolta in *Pulp Fiction.* Interestingly, a 1994 study done at the University of California of films from 1960 to 1990 found that during this period, the number of characters who lit up increased by a factor of three. Some of these revelations were published in *Tobacco Control,* a British medical journal devoted to antismoking themes. Product placement agreements — tobacco in movies — is the hot issue at stake. According to the journal's report, R. J. Reynolds, working through a publicist, arranged to provide free tobacco in the 1980s to actors and directors such as John Cassavetes, Liv Ullmann, and Shelley Winters.

One group, Smoke Free Movies, has been running a full-court press to wipe out smoking in the movies. The group's strategies include full-page ads in major newspapers, objecting to the frequency of cigarette-wielding actors. The group cites a study claiming to have found that nonsmoking teens exposed to smoking in the movies are much more likely to begin smoking than teens who don't witness these visual depredations. The group has made highly vocal accusations that Philip Morris paid to have Marlboros prominently displayed in the film *In the Bedroom.* Smoke Free Movies proposes a number of specific strategies, such as a ban on mentioning cigarette brand names in movies to limit the visibility of cigarettes in the cinema.

The tobacco industry was confronted more than a decade ago by Congress about its aggressive product placement in movies, and the tobacco companies agreed to a self-imposed and self-monitored halt to the practice. Nonetheless, chances are that the next time you go to the movies — unless you're watching *Harry Potter* or a Disney flick — one or more of the adult characters will light up.

If comfort food is what it will take to get you to quit smoking, go for it. This recommendation is somewhat controversial, I suppose. I'm not endorsing a leap into the hog trough, nor am I suggesting that you cram your pantry full of cookies, chips, and cake. I'm acknowledging that during the first few days of quitting, or maybe longer, you may find yourself wanting an oral substitute. Obviously, you can make healthy and not-so-healthy choices. Just about anything you put in your mouth is better than a cigarette.

Plenty of liquids are highly recommended. Some people feel that the more (healthy) liquids you drink during your initial days of quitting, the better. Water, carbonated water, juice, and even diet soda are fine.

You can be as elegant and refined as you like with your substitute oral gratifications. Some newbie quitters find that it helps to carry around a bag of celery or carrot sticks to munch on throughout the day. Gum chewing (sugarless, unless you're looking to give your dentist more business) is an old standby as an over-the-counter replacement for smokes. If you enjoy cooking, this is your chance to invest the time and energy it takes to cook up the most varied and tasty dishes you've ever made. If you're somewhat less ambitious, quit-smoking week is a great time to treat yourself to some dinners out. The more delicious the food, the less likely you are to obsess about smokes.

Smoking to control stress

For many people, smoking is a remedy for anxiety and stress. Although nicotine in low doses is a stimulant that temporarily boosts your alertness and ability to concentrate, higher doses act as a sedative, relaxing you and "dumbing down" your neuromuscular system. Smoking does relieve stress, but it *adds* to stress in many ways.

What's the point of reducing stress with cigarettes when each cigarette heightens your risk for disease, makes you feel guilty, and causes you aesthetic and financial discomfort? Aesthetic discomfort? You may call this sensation "guilt." Whatever you call the feeling of having succumbed to the craving for a smoke, the feeling is usually unpleasant.

Has anyone ever told you, "I smoke because I have too much stress," or, "I drink because of my wife"? This is the language of rationalization, of blaming outside forces or other people for the things you do to yourself. You smoke because you have strong cravings for nicotine, and you package those cravings in a variety of elaborate or not-so-elaborate justifications. These justifications often cause you mental anguish when you consider them at a distance.

Pursuing personality

Behavioral researchers have been trying for many years to refine their understanding of personality. The effort began thousands of years ago with the "humoral" theory: Character and behavior were said to be based on the deficit or excess of various *humors* (hormones) in the body. For example, a melancholic person was thought to have too much black bile flowing in his veins. A phlegmatic person had too much . . . phlegm! You get the picture.

Many other typological systems for human nature have come and gone since those days. Psychiatric observers in 19th-century Europe erected arcane and complex systems for describing people's traits. Other observers, particularly medical psychiatrists and neurologists working in insane asylums, noted that the seriously mentally ill seemed to belong to one of two main categories. Some patients, despite severely disabling symptoms, eventually improved, even to the point of being able to return home. They were manic depressives. The other group, who never really enjoyed remission, had premature dementia. The latter group is now termed *schizophrenic*.

What does any of this have to do with the addictive personality? Plenty. The evolving classification system — and it is still evolving — became somewhat more sophisticated. Doctors realized that mental states such as insanity and depression could be temporary, whereas mental traits such as perfectionism, suspiciousness, or excessive expressiveness were fixed, long-term qualities. Diagnosticians came to utilize what is now known as a multiaxial or multidimensional diagnostic scheme. A person could be diagnosed with both a state disorder, such as depression or manic depression, *and* a more enduring typological problem, such as a hysterical, compulsive, or paranoid personality. This scheme refined the ability to label people, for better or worse.

Personality disorders — the long-term stuff that character is made of, the traits that make your behavior in various situations somewhat predictable — can also be described in this classification scheme.

When I first quit smoking, I actually found that I felt too *relaxed*. It turned out that the cigarettes had been pumping me up, and I found the more serene feelings brought about by the lack of nicotine in my system uncomfortable. But eventually, I found ways to appreciate and even enjoy the relaxed feelings and the downtime, just like you can find ways to relieve stress without turning to cancer sticks. The physiological action of nicotine is dual. Certain amounts of nicotine cause activation and stimulation. Other amounts are sedating. Understanding this duality helps you understand why quitting smoking is sometimes accompanied by tiredness *and* wiredness. Whatever sensations you experience when you quit smoking, remember that they are transient and are worth the price of freedom from smoking slavery.

Quitting is the time to exercise, take walks, play golf, and spend time with other people. If certain activities are particularly relaxing or rewarding for you, by all means pursue them. On the other hand, if certain activities are particularly stressful and usually make you reach for a smoke, avoid them as much as possible, especially during your first week of quitting.

Understanding the Addictive Personality

In recent years, the media has paid a great deal of attention to the so-called addictive personality. Mr. or Ms. Addictive Personality has been typecast as a person for whom getting hooked is much easier than it is for most people. The addictive personality is viewed as predisposed to developing addictions of many types: drinking, drug use, gambling, sex, binge eating or anorexia, shopping, you name it. A related notion is that those with addictive personalities, having for the moment mastered or overcome one dependence or habit, easily slide into another.

Additive personality is not recognized as a personality disorder in contemporary psychiatry. You don't have to reflect too long or too deeply to appreciate that some people gravitate more readily than others to addiction. Why, for example, did only 1 percent of heroin-addicted GIs returning home from Vietnam remain on opiates? Why is it that, with addicting substances like tobacco and alcohol being freely available, only certain people get hooked?

Scientists are still working out the fine points of the addictive personality, but we do know that predisposition to addiction can be inherited. If one or both of your parents are or were smokers, you are more likely to be one yourself. And if you are a thrill seeker who enjoys trying new things, your need for stimulation can raise the odds that you will self-medicate with tobacco or other substances. Self-medication is the process of giving yourself one or more drugs including nicotine in order to change the way you feel. On the other hand, it's possible that *resistance* to tobacco and perhaps other kinds of addiction can be passed along genetically as well.

The amount and degree of stress in your life is also a factor in determining how much of an addictive personality you have. Fortunately, your stress level is somewhat under your control. You can work toward changing your internal and external environments if they are significant sources of stress for you.

The connections between stress and addictive personality are complex and intimate. People with addictive personalities — those who regularly and habitually reach for a smoke or other source of comfort that is external and potentially damaging — increase their stress levels by their substance use. If you have an addictive personality, your perception of stress may be different from that of other people. You may be more sensitive to stress. Some people react to stress with a message to themselves, "Gotta relax." You may say, "Gotta relax, must have a smoke."

Pressing the lever: Animal models

Many experiments have demonstrated that nicotine is one of the most reinforcing drugs in the world. Lab animals will go to great extremes to continue getting nicotine delivered to them, even forgoing sleep and food in their effort to get a hit.

Some organizations are opposed to the use of animals in lab experiments. Objections to the use of mice, dogs, and other animals in tests of smoke and tobacco tars include the concern that laboratory conditions don't come near natural conditions involving people. Conclusions drawn from animal research apply to humans only loosely or very indirectly. Some of the experiments are in fact cruel and involve exposing test animals to smoke via tubes inserted into their lungs. Other experiments involve shaving mammals and applying tars from tobacco directly onto the exposed skin. Even with these intrusive types of experiments, conclusions are controversial and can be construed as being for or against the safety of tobacco products in people.

Tobacco companies fund many of these research studies, so legitimate concern exists about the validity of the findings and the potential or actual conflict of interest in industry-sponsored safety research.

So-called animal models of drug dependence have been in use for some time. These studies use various laboratory animals, even insects and bacteria, to test the addiction potential, toxicity, and mutagenicity of different drugs. (*Mutagenicity* is the tendency for something to cause mutations.) A typical model used in labs to study the dependence liability of a drug is to have the animal self-administer the substance. (*Dependence liability* is the potential of a drug to cause addiction.) The animal presses a bar or lever, and nicotine or other drugs are administered through an intravenous line or by a tiny catheter inserted directly into the animal's brain.

As a result of these types of experiments, researchers have found that nicotine has a sky-high abuse or addiction potential. Lab animals will keep pressing bars in order to continue self-administering nicotine. (This is similar to what happens when lab animals — or people, for that matter — are given free access to cocaine.) With both cocaine and nicotine, self-administration continues until the drug supply is gone. This work amply demonstrates that nicotine is extremely *reinforcing* — that you will walk a mile, and then some, to get a smoke.

There are no blood tests or so-called biological markers for addiction or even for the tendency toward addiction. Nonetheless, asking yourself a series of common-sense questions can help you refine your awareness of how automatically you reach for a smoke.

- ✔ Do you smoke?
- ✔ Do you reach for a cigarette or an alcoholic drink or food whenever you feel nervous or anxious?
- ✔ Have you ever had a problem with other substances, such as marijuana, cocaine, or pills?

✔ Have you ever been treated for substance abuse or dependence?

✔ Do you easily develop self-destructive habits, such as binge eating or spending more than you can afford to, that are hard to shake?

If you answered yes to any of these questions, you have a proclivity toward addiction. Now, don't go running scared. "Addiction" is a label. If it frightens you to think of yourself in this way, substitute the word *dependence* or the phrase *bad habit*.

More knowledge about yourself is more power. If you know that you have the addictive Achilles heel, you're on the road to doing something about it. You know that certain triggers make you crave smoking, and you will have increasing control over your exposure and response to these triggers.

Seeing Your Brain on Nicotine

Part of understanding why you smoke is understanding the brain circuitry involved. When you understand how the brain works in normal health, without any drugs or smoke, you are better positioned to recognize the effects that tampering with the system (that is, by adding tobacco) has.

The complexity of the adult human brain is staggering — it's so finely tuned that its workings and architecture are almost beyond description. Nonetheless, decades of research have succeeded in identifying some of the major information pipelines in the brain. The adult brain weighs only several pounds — but, oh, what a several pounds it is!

Your brain contains 2 to 3 billion *neurons,* or nerve cells, each of which is connected to one or more other neurons, making for billions upon billions of *synapses* (connections) in the organ. The possibilities of information flow are nearly endless.

Neurons communicate with each other electrically and chemically. Once an *action potential* (a wave of electricity) sweeps down the trunk of a nerve cell, it depolarizes the cell membrane, causing a flow of ions like potassium and sodium through special channels in the cell membrane. Next, chemical packets of neurotransmitters are released from the nerve terminal across the *synaptic space* (the gap between nerve cells), where they trigger receptors on the surface of the next neuron in the sequence. You can think of the arrangement as an elaborate, effective bucket brigade on a microscopic scale. See Figure 4-1 for an illustration of the arrangement.

A great deal has been said and will continue to be said about these neurotransmitters. Although the main neurotransmitters — acetylcholine, serotonin, norepinephrine, and dopamine — seem to be featured in every issue of *Newsweek* or *Time,* a number of other chemical transmitters have additional functions and may work to antagonize or boost the effect of the better-known ones.

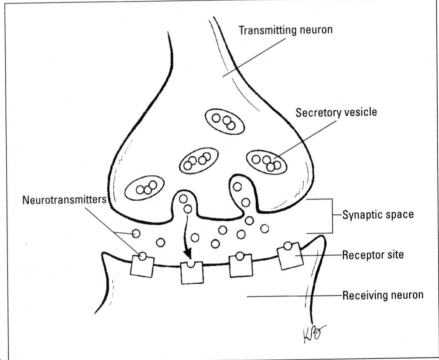

Figure 4-1:
How
neurons
communi-
cate.

Nicotine hits neuroreceptors. It is known to have major effects on acetylcholine (nicotinic) receptors, and there is strong evidence that nicotine affects dopamine receptors as well. Dopamine receptors, in turn, may be involved in the brain's feel-good system, the endorphins. Nicotine and other addictive substances may be so habit-forming at least in part because they trigger the brain's own reward system, and when the brain feels good, it wants to keep on feeling good.

There's more to smoke than just nicotine. Tobacco smoke contains hundreds of chemicals in addition to nicotine.

Recent research using brain imaging suggests that tobacco smoke may contain psychoactive chemicals in addition to nicotine. It also shows that some of these "fellow traveler" chemicals can affect the way you feel and behave. A number of the other chemicals that are along for the ride in cigarette smoke have potent effects on the brain and behavior.

Smoking 'til You Choke

As you get closer to understanding why you smoke, you want to equip yourself with as many reasons as possible never to smoke again. Try the reasons in this section on for size.

Do you remember your first puff of tobacco? It probably wasn't very pleasant. Have you had the experience of picking up a cigar or cigarette after quitting for a lengthy period? At those times, you probably asked yourself, "Why am I doing this? This is crazy!" The choking fits, the coughing, the harshness of the taste, the exposure of the delicate mucus membranes in your mouth, throat, and lungs to this toxic invader — what's the point?

Doctors see people with chronic lung disease fairly often. These people may be wheelchair bound, oxygen bound, or bedridden. Many other smokers drag themselves from place to place, tragically put upon by the slightest exertion. Walking around the block, let alone up a flight of stairs, can be an intolerable strain for people whose lungs no longer cooperate. *Emphysema,* a form of chronic lung disease that can result from smoking, makes it increasingly difficult to get rid of inhaled air. Having emphysema is like walking around with an inflexible barrel of a chest that no longer moves flexibly to allow you to exhale freely.

Pulmonologists — chest doctors — have a variety of ways of evaluating your pulmonary function. In addition to listening to your lungs with a stethoscope, they can assess the capacity, content, and functional parameters of your lungs with the use of X-rays, CAT scans, MRIs, and pulmonary function tests. Some of these tests involve the inhalation of various gases to measure how much you can inhale and exhale and how effective your lungs are at allowing gases to diffuse from the capillary system to the tissues.

I hope that you don't get to the point where smoking is grossly damaging your health. See Chapter 5 for details about the effects that smoking has on your body.

If you're concerned about a cough, pain, or any other aspect of breathing, consult a physician.

Chapter 5

Evaluating the Health Risks of Smoking

*E*very breath of clean air you take is filled with healthful, life-giving oxygen, nitrogen, and other gases. Every puff of tobacco you take is packed with poisonous chemicals and gases, including tars, carbon monoxide, and carcinogenic hydrocarbons.

You probably already know that smoking is bad for you — that fact is hard to avoid. But if you still smoke even though you know it's harmful, it may help you to understand the damage that smoking does to your body. Knowing the specifics just might be what it takes to get you to decide to quit, *now*. In this chapter, I explain the health risks of smoking and give you the information you need to be able to assess your own health risk.

Breathing: A Mini-Primer

Understanding how breathing works helps you see where potential roadblocks and problems can arise. (Smoking causes most of these problems, as you will see.)

Breathing is a miraculous process that goes on all the time, even while you're asleep. Most adults breathe between 12 and 20 times a minute; the rates are generally faster for children. The fact that the respiratory system works so well on its own that most times you aren't even aware of its presence is a testament to its incredible complexity and efficiency.

The job of the respiratory tree (it's called a *tree* because the trachea, bronchi, and bronchioles look like the spreading branches of a tree held upside-down, as shown in Figure 5-1) is to move fresh, clean, oxygen-rich air into your lungs and to expel used air that's depleted of oxygen and loaded with carbon dioxide. The body combines that oxygen with water and nutrients from your diet to create energy and to form new cells. This process, which occurs in hundreds of millions of cells in every organ throughout the body, gives off carbon dioxide as an end product.

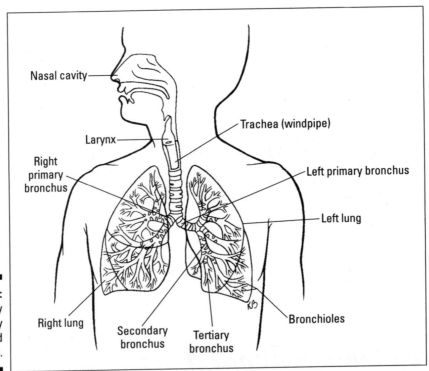

Figure 5-1:
A healthy
respiratory
system and
all its parts.

Nasal cavity

Larynx

Trachea (windpipe)

Right
primary
bronchus

Left primary bronchus

Left lung

Right lung

Secondary
bronchus

Tertiary
bronchus

Bronchioles

Interestingly, plant respiration works in the opposite way. Plants take in carbon dioxide and emit oxygen. This helps explain why saving the forests is such a critical issue for the survival of the planet. Plants and trees replenish the oxygen that we need to breathe!

The lungs (you get two of them, one on either side of your *thoracic cavity,* or the area between your neck and abdomen) also eliminate waste matter and other substances that are harmful to the body. Alcohol, for example, is at least partially excreted through the lungs; that's why you can often tell if someone has been drinking — they have the odor of alcohol on their breath. Carbon monoxide, a prominent toxin in tobacco smoke, is also eliminated through the lungs.

The lungs are a collapsible, almost infinitely divided series of tubes, tubules, and tiny air pockets. The larger *bronchi* branch off into finer *bronchioles,* which end in the gas-filled cul-de-sacs known as *alveoli* (see Figure 5-2). The inner linings of the lungs are moist and have an extremely rich network of capillaries running right beneath the surface. These *alveolar capillaries* are where the oxygen-carbon dioxide exchange takes place.

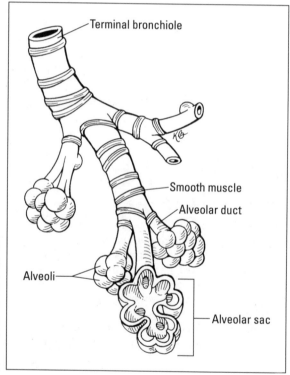

Terminal bronchiole

Smooth muscle

Alveolar duct

Alveoli

Alveolar sac

Figure 5-2:
The bron-
chioles end
in tiny air
pockets
called
alveoli.

The other important structural feature of your lungs to be aware of is their inherent elasticity. Because of special protein fibers distributed throughout the respiratory tract, the lungs are very flexible and can withstand a lifetime of inhaling (expanding) and exhaling (contracting). Few manmade machines can work so dependably and for so long without breaking down.

Breathing also involves the *diaphragm* (the muscle that separates your chest from your abdominal cavity) and the rib muscles. When these muscles expand, air rushes in from the upper respiratory tract (the nose, mouth, and pharynx) and fills the lungs. When you exhale, the same muscles relax, the volume of your chest cavity decreases, and air flows back out.

Air passes through several anatomical structures on the way to and from the lungs. These body parts are worth knowing about because tobacco smoke can adversely affect them. Air passes through your nose and mouth into the *trachea,* or windpipe, which sits in front of your esophagus and is the swallowing tube that leads from mouth to stomach. Air moves through your vocal cords (located in your larynx) until it reaches the bronchi.

Oxygen spreads across the *alveolar membrane* into the pulmonary capillary. Likewise, carbon dioxide and other gases such as carbon monoxide diffuse out of the capillary and back into the alveoli, into the bronchioles, and then into the air.

As soon as the oxygen enters the bloodstream (via the pulmonary capillary), it binds with hemoglobin in the red blood cells, which carry the oxygen through circulation to every part of the body, where it is eventually released and used for cellular work.

Looking at Smoking's Effects on the Respiratory System

The respiratory system is where smoking does the majority of its damage. For example, smokers are at a much higher risk than nonsmokers of developing cancer and other diseases of the head and neck. I hope that the following list of just some of the respiratory-system damage that smoking can cause will lead you to decide to quit smoking once and for all.

- ✔ **Lung cancer:** Millions of people die from lung cancer. See the section "Cigarettes and cancer: A match made in heaven," later in this chapter, for much more on this devastating disease.

  Chronic lung changes following years of smoking include *cavitation* (the collapse of alveoli into large, ineffective cul-de-sacs that reduce adequate ventilation), mucus oversecretion, tumor development, and *emphysema.* Emphysema results from alveolar destruction and from reduced elasticity of the bronchioles, which in turn diminishes the ability to exhale. People with emphysema can inhale but can't exhale adequately. Figure 5-3 shows the various harmful effects that smoking can have on the lungs.

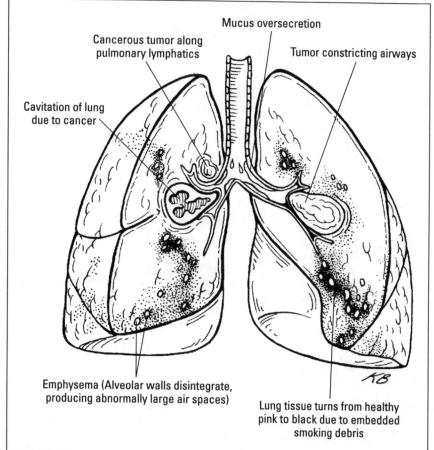

Mucus oversecretion

Cancerous tumor along
pulmonary lymphatics

Tumor constricting airways

Cavitation of lung
due to cancer

Figure 5-3:
Smoking
wreaks a
great deal
of havoc
on the
lungs,
causing
cancer,
emphysema,
and other
problems.

Emphysema (Alveolar walls disintegrate,
producing abnormally large air spaces)

Lung tissue turns from healthy
pink to black due to embedded
smoking debris

- ✔ **Gingivitis:** *Gingivitis,* an inflammation of the gums, is fairly common among smokers. It is due, as are most of the respiratory ailments that smokers fall victim to, to constant irritation from tar and other toxins in tobacco smoke.

- ✔ **Laryngeal cancer:** Chances are that the person you noticed with a mechanical voice box (an artificial larynx) had his or her larynx removed due to cancer. Laryngeal cancer is right up there on the cigarette hit parade.

- ✔ **Chronic obstructive pulmonary disease (COPD):** Also known as chronic bronchitis and emphysema, COPD is very difficult to treat and is irreversible. The most effective way to halt the progression of COPD is to quit smoking. *Bronchitis* is an inflammation of the delicate mucous membrane lining of the bronchi that results in irritation, pain, coughing, and production of excess mucus. *Emphysema* is another heartbreaker, involving the progressive loss of elasticity of lung tissue. A person with emphysema can inhale but has greater and greater trouble exhaling. As a result, the alveoli and lung tissue essentially expand, blow up and blow out, creating larger and ever less functional ventilation space. People with emphysema literally struggle to breathe, and some even get to the point where oxygen tanks are necessary. You may have seen some of these unfortunates, forever accompanied by a green canister of oxygen that relieves the suffering but doesn't eliminate it.

✔ **Asthma:** *Asthma* is a condition that often arises in childhood and involves the constriction, or tightening, of the bronchi and bronchioles, effectively reducing the amount of air that can be taken in. Smoking aggravates underlying asthma and can provoke episodes of asthmatic breathing in those who have the illness. Asthma can be life-threatening. If you've ever seen an asthmatic person struggling for air, you know what I mean. Fortunately, medical care is usually effective and provides fast relief.

✔ **Carbon monoxide poisoning:** Carbon monoxide is a colorless, odorless gas that's found in automobile exhaust fumes and cigarettes, among other things. You don't want to breathe in carbon monoxide because it competes with oxygen. The amazing molecule hemoglobin is the oxygen carrier in red blood cells, moving oxygen from your lungs to the rest of your body. When you smoke or are exposed to carbon monoxide in some other way (such as in an unventilated car), the carbon monoxide binds much more readily to the hemoglobin molecules, and your blood level of oxygen can drop dramatically. If you've ever smoked too many cigarettes in too short a time, you may have experienced acute oxygen deprivation as a result of carbon monoxide overload. Carbon monoxide poisoning can be fatal.

Figure 5-4 shows you how red blood cells react positively to oxygen and negatively to carbon monoxide.

Celebrity smoking casualties

The following is a short list of some of the more notable victims of cigarettes and lung cancer. If you have a morbid streak, check out www.tobaccovictims.org, which names dozens of celebrities who have fallen victim to the hype, addictiveness, and lethality of tobacco.

✔ Humphrey Bogart

✔ Betty Davis

✔ Walt Disney

✔ Sigmund Freud

✔ Clark Gable

✔ Ulysses S. Grant

✔ Dean Martin

✔ Pat Nixon

✔ Roy Orbison

✔ Vincent Price

✔ Lee Remick

✔ Babe Ruth

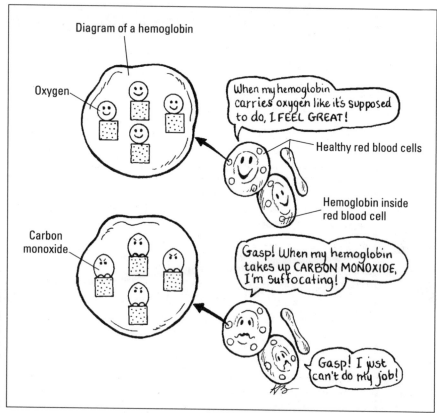

Figure 5-4:
Carbon
monoxide
robs your
blood cells
of oxygen.

Damage to the lungs and bronchi caused by smoking accumulates over time. If you get sick from smoking, the illness results from longstanding and repeated injury to the delicate respiratory tract lining. The good news is that once you stop smoking, your lungs and bronchi instantly go to work to heal themselves. The best time to quit smoking is before any irreversible damage (such as emphysema) is done.

Smoking Out the Health Risks of Tobacco

At this point in your quest to quit smoking, you surely have gotten the idea that tobacco in any form is bad for your health, as well as for your wallet and your overall well-being. Although many people are aware of the obvious negative consequences — a persistent cough, stained fingertips, and smokers' breath, and lung disease — many remain unaware of the far-reaching effects that tobacco products have on the rest of the body. This section describes some of those effects. Read on . . . and quit!

Smoke gets in your eyes (and mouth and heart and lungs . . .)

The physical and medical consequences of smoking are numerous, and the extent and seriousness of smoking-related illness are shocking. More than 450,000 Americans die each year as a result of smoking. Between 3,000 and 5,000 more die as a result of exposure to smoke in the environment (known as secondhand smoke).

Smokers get sick and die at younger ages than nonsmokers, too. According to the World Health Organization, half of regular smokers who began smoking during adolescence will die as a result of their tobacco use. Experts estimate that up to 30 percent of cancer deaths in the United States could be prevented if cigarettes were banned.

Cancer is one of the worst effects that smoking has on the body. Organs that have direct contact with tobacco smoke — the throat, lungs, and esophagus — are the most likely to develop cancer. Here are some of the other effects you are likely to experience if you continue your habit (if you aren't experiencing them already!):

- Your fingers and fingernails become discolored with tarry, mustard-hued stains that can't be scrubbed off.

- Your breath takes on the odor either of the cigarette or cigar you're smoking or of old, lingering tobacco.

- Over time, your skin takes on the appearance of advanced age, with exaggerated wrinkles, crevices, and worry lines.

- Your gums and teeth suffer, with periodontal disease, including *gingivitis* (painful, swollen, bleeding gums), a prominent part of the not-so-pretty smoking picture. Teeth become stained in unwelcome shades from mustard yellow to dark brown. Stained teeth are a social liability.

- Chronic tobacco users may develop *tobacco amblyopia,* a condition that involves difficulty with symmetric aligned eye movements.

- Smoking can cause or worsen peptic ulcers and can make them recur.

- Cigarettes are implicated in the development of *osteoporosis,* a thinning or weakening of the bones often associated with the elderly.

- Female smokers over the age of 35 who take oral contraceptives ("the pill") are at greater risk for heart attack, stroke, and blood clots.

- In the United States, half of all strokes are attributable to cigarette smoking.

✔ Peripheral vascular disease, which causes pain, a loss of sensation, and poor circulation in the legs, is a serious condition that can lead to infection and even necessitate amputation. Smoking is the primary risk factor for the development of some types of peripheral vascular disease.

✔ If you are overweight or have high blood pressure or diabetes, smoking will aggravate these conditions and could lead to more severe symptoms and/or greater need for treatment.

✔ At least one in eight cases of high blood pressure is due to smoking.

✔ Babies of mothers who smoke are at greater risk for SIDS (Sudden Infant Death Syndrome) and of being born at a low weight.

✔ Children of mothers who smoke stand a greater chance of having asthma, ear infections, and upper respiratory infections.

Smoking is also one of the major risk factors for developing cardiovascular disease, including heart disease, stroke, abdominal aortic aneurysm, and impaired circulation to the extremities — and cardiovascular disease is the number-one cause of death in the Western world. The more you smoke, the greater your risk of getting some form of it.

Smoking is a major culprit in heart attacks (myocardial infarction). Studies demonstrate that your risk of dying from a heart attack is directly related to how deeply you inhale, how long you've smoked, and the number of cigarettes you smoke per day. Smokers are almost twice as likely to have a heart attack as nonsmokers are.

Insurance companies *cost share,* which means that they spread the wealth — or in this case, the costs of bad habits that lead to poor health — among all those who pay for insurance, including nonsmokers.

Cigarettes and cancer: A match made in heaven

Cigarette smoke contains dozens of *carcinogens* (cancer-causing chemical compounds), such as nitrosamines, aldehydes, and aromatic hydrocarbons. Urine samples from smokers applied to microbes in laboratories have caused genetic mutations in these organisms. Carcinogens interact with the genetic material (DNA) in cells, causing mutations in the genetic code, which then give rise to aberrant and sometimes cancerous cells.

Despite the tobacco companies' decades-long advertising crusade, there's no doubt that smoking causes lung cancer, which is the number-one cause of cancer mortality. Experts note that 90 percent of lung cancer is related to smoking.

A smoker's odds of developing lung cancer are 12 to 22 times higher than a nonsmoker's. The more you smoke (including the number of cigarettes, the depth of the inhale, and the number of years of smoking), the greater your chance of developing lung cancer. The statistical rate of lung cancer has an element of predictability to it. Studies show that as the number of smokers in the population increased, the rate of lung cancer rose dramatically. The good news is that public health education efforts, including government-mandated warnings, school-based prevention efforts, and books like this one, do help. Studies have demonstrated the positive impact of certain preventive programs.

Lung cancer isn't the only cancer caused by smoking. Cancer of the larynx is usually caused by smoking, and a lifetime of heavy alcohol use further increases the risk of acquiring this illness. Smoking is also a principal cause of oral (mouth) cancer, esophageal cancer (four out of five cases are caused by smoking), kidney cancer, and bladder cancer. Up to a third of pancreatic cancer deaths are caused by cigarette smoking, and smokers have a significantly increased chance of developing stomach cancer, cancer of the cervix (in women), and leukemia.

If you're living with and suffering from a fear of cancer because you continue to smoke, you're being realistic! I'm presenting you with the most accurate and up-to-date information, much of which is truly sobering. The upside is that you can translate your newfound awareness into immediate action. The moment you stop smoking, your body begins to clean and repair itself. You can facilitate the healing process by getting plenty of exercise, adequate rest, and good nutrition, and by practicing what used to be called "mental hygiene." Right thinking leads to healthier living.

If you're concerned about a physical problem or symptom, such as a nagging cough, persistent fever, or malaise, by all means consult your doctor. If you don't have a doctor, get one! If you're ill, the best and fastest way to overcome the problem is to have it diagnosed and treated.

What nicotine does to your body

Within seconds of the first puff (or chew or sniff) of tobacco, your heart rate, blood pressure, and breathing rate increase. Your body immediately releases adrenaline, which puts it in a state of readiness for fight or flight. The stimulant action of nicotine is similar to what has been called the stress reaction. All body systems are put on high alert — a kind of physiological DefCon 4. You remain in physiological high gear, with increased heart rate and blood pressure, as long as you smoke and for some hours after, until the nicotine has left your system.

As you can imagine, a continued stress response is harmful to the body. As a result of the continued release of adrenaline, cortisol, and other stress hormones, the body's immune and other systems become overtaxed. You need to be able to wind down from this condition of tension, vigilance, and extreme alertness.

With greater amounts and a longer duration of use, nicotine exerts a sedating effect — so much so that large enough amounts can be toxic, causing nausea, vomiting, and shaking. High doses of nicotine may even prove fatal. Insecticides are made from compounds that are identical in action to nicotine. There are known cases of accidental ingestion of tobacco products by infants and children that have led to severe poisoning.

Nicotine has other immediate effects. You probably remember the very first time or two you tried to smoke, because you probably coughed, retched, or became quite nauseated. Nausea is a direct effect of nicotine.

One to 12 hours after the last cigarette, confirmed smokers begin to experience nicotine withdrawal symptoms. These symptoms include

- Irritability
- Fatigue
- Mood swings
- Insomnia or hypersomnia (too much sleep)
- Trouble concentrating
- Headache
- Increased appetite
- Anxiety
- Depression
- Shifting energy levels

Interestingly, many of these symptoms are similar to symptoms that arise with depression and other types of mood disorders, which may help explain why Zyban helps some newly abstinent smokers through the process of quitting. See Chapter 9 for more on Zyban and other therapies that lessen nicotine withdrawal symptoms.

Evaluating Your Own Health Risk

"Smoking can't be that bad" is a typical response to a review of the far-ranging and horrific health consequences of tobacco use. But dismissing antismoking messages as typical authoritarianism — the older generation once again telling the younger generation what to do — is a mistake. The motivation behind the antismoking campaign is pure and simply saving lives.

Your health risk is based on your responses to the following questions:

- ✔ Do you smoke?
- ✔ Do you inhale?
- ✔ Do you think about cutting down?
- ✔ Does it irritate you when other people ask you to consider quitting?
- ✔ Do you smoke first thing in the morning?
- ✔ Are there times when you will literally walk a mile — or drive 10 miles — to replenish your cigarette supply?

If you answered yes to *any* of these questions, you need to quit! I was going to say that you need to seriously consider quitting, but what is that? Chances are you've been thinking about quitting for some time already — otherwise, you wouldn't be reading this book.

By looking at your smoking patterns, you can get a more specific idea of your particular health risk from smoking. Your risk of developing any of the myriad illnesses and health problems that smoking can cause increases with

- ✔ The amount of time you've smoked
- ✔ The number of cigarettes you smoke each day
- ✔ How deeply you inhale each puff

If you have any medical problems now, such as hypertension, obesity, asthma, diabetes, or peptic ulcer, smoking is likely to aggravate these problems. Your doctor can help you evaluate your personal situation and what you can do to improve your health.

The inspiring news is that the longer you stay quit, the more repair and healing your body undergoes. After five to ten years off of cigarettes, your health risk for a number of these disorders approaches that of nonsmokers.

Quitting While You're Ahead

If you started smoking only recently, or if you've been smoking for a relatively short time, you're ahead of the game. It will be easier for your body to recover to where it was before you started smoking, and the recovery may take less time. If you're a take-it-or-leave-it type of smoker, someone who smokes only on weekends or at social events, you're in an especially enviable position: You're not truly hooked (yet). If you really can take it or leave it — if you believe that you aren't addicted — see how you feel going without a smoke the next time you would ordinarily have one.

There is evidence that some pulmonary function (your lungs' ability to expand, inhale, and exhale properly) returns over time when you quit smoking. All your body systems, including the circulatory system, the immune system (white blood cells), and the lymphatic system (part of your body's defense network), go into mop-up mode and remove or cordon off as much of the tobacco toxins and damaged cells as possible.

According to statistics, if you're 65 and female, quitting smoking now will add about four years to your life. In the same study, reported in *The American Journal of Public Health,* those who quit by age 35 live an average of 7 to 8.5 years longer than those who kept on smoking. Quitting also means that you'll have fewer upper respiratory infections over the course of your life. Tell me that having fewer colds and flus is not a major selling point for quitting! Likewise, women who quit before pregnancy or within the first three months of pregnancy lower their risk of miscarriage and of having a low-birth-weight baby to the risk levels of nonsmoking women.

If you've quit recently, terrific. Take advantage of your newfound freedom from tobacco and slam the door in the face of cravings and temptations to "have just one." You need to be especially wary — and modest — if you're newly quit and you feel like you have the habit licked and can pick up the occasional cigarette.

Like someone once said about alcohol, "One is too many, and a thousand are not enough."

Chapter 6

Adding Up the Damage

. . . .

. . . .

The actual cost of a pack of cigarettes goes far beyond what you pay out of pocket — although that cost alone can be significant, as this chapter shows you. You also have to take into account the cumulative cost to your health, your well-being, and society's health, financial and otherwise. Thousands of people who get seriously ill as a result of smoking have to rely on federal funds to pay for their healthcare. And where does some of the funding for some of that healthcare come from? Your tax dollars! The damage isn't just in your own land, either; tobacco places a burden of ill health and financial strain on countries all over the world. This chapter gives you the opportunity to evaluate these costs and think about whether you really want to continue accruing them.

As you launch your effort to quit smoking, you also need to know how to deal effectively with some of the feelings that arise as you quit and then stay quit. Remember that quitting smoking is both a personal and a social decision. When you quit, you benefit yourself *and* the rest of society.

Evaluating the Actual Cost of Smoking

There are dozens of ways to figure out the dollars-and-cents cost of your cigarettes. Obviously, the total expense depends on how many cigarettes you smoke each day and how much you pay for each pack. Several facts help simplify your calculation:

- ✔ People tend to either stabilize or increase the amount they smoke over time. You seldom decrease the number of cigarettes that you smoke each day.

- ✔ The price of tobacco products, particularly cigarettes, continues to increase. Some people have switched to generic brands in order to reduce their tobacco costs. Others buy their smokes "off the back of a truck" — they buy cigarettes that are smuggled, do not carry tax stamps, or are otherwise contraband.

The following sections help you take an honest look at how much you spend on cigarettes each year — and how much you'd save by saying no to smoking.

Adding up what a pack a day costs in a year

The cost of cigarettes may seem like small change when you buy a pack today, but it adds up as you accumulate each day's $4 or $5 that goes toward packs of smokes. If you smoke a pack (20 cigarettes) a day at a cost of $4.50 a pack, you will have spent $135 after one month. After a year (time flies when you're having fun!), you'll have spent a grand total of $1,620. Table 6-1 shows you how much you can pay out in a variety of smoking scenarios.

Table 6-1	How Much You Spend on Smokes	
Butts per Day	*Cost per Month*	*Cost per Year*
10	$67.50	$810.00
20	$135.00	$1,620.00
30	$202.50	$2,430.00
40	$270.00	$3,240.00
60	$337.50	$4,860.00

Money saved and invested grows with the aid of a miraculous fertilizer known as *compound interest.* Table 6-2 shows you how much you'd save by quitting and investing the amount you would have spent on cigarettes at a mere 5 percent interest.

Table 6-2	Quitting: How Much You'd Save at 5% Annual Interest	
Smokes per Day	**After One Year**	**After Two Years**
10	$850.50	$1,743.53
20	$1,701.00	$3,487.05
30	$2,551.50	$5,230.50
40	$3,402.00	$6,974.00
60	$5,103.00	$10,461.15
90	$7,654.50	$15,691.23

Bear in mind that these figures are on the conservative side; I'm using only a 5 percent annual interest rate, and these estimates are based on one bank deposit per year rather than on true compound (daily) interest, which would yield a considerably higher return. For example, after five years, the $810 saved from quitting a pack a day for just one year would have turned into $1,033.70. At a slightly higher interest rate — say, 8 percent — the savings from one year of not smoking would amount to $1,190.16. If you remained smoke-free, you would continue to accumulate savings, and before you knew it you would own Boardwalk and Park Place, too!

See Chapter 22 if you need help coming up with ideas for ways to spend the money you'll save by quitting.

Adding up what each pack costs society at large

The Congressional Office of Technology Assessment estimates that each pack of cigarettes costs society somewhere between $2 and $3 after healthcare and other related costs are factored in. This cost is *in addition to* how much you lay out each time you buy a pack.

You may feel that smoking involves no cost to society, believing that each person is responsible for his or her own behavior. This civil liberties issue is not unique to smoking; it also includes potentially risky behavior like riding a bicycle or a motorcycle without a helmet. You can argue the situation both ways, probably endlessly, but you'd still be smoking!

Realizing the triple savings of quitting

Quitting smoking involves triple savings: to your wallet, to your health, and to your self-esteem. I think I've already made it clear in this chapter where the financial savings come in, and Chapter 5 goes into great detail about smoking's negative health effects. The self-esteem savings may be less obvious, so let me explain.

One of the many amazing things that happens when you quit smoking is that you begin to believe in and plan for the future. Part of the baggage of smoking addiction is a live-for-the-moment attitude by which you basically tell yourself, "Who cares what tomorrow brings?" The seeds you plant today — whether they're zinnias, cucumbers, or positive feelings about yourself — will come back to you in time. The same holds true for money. If you've been able to save and invest money over the years, you don't need to be reminded how the stuff tends to grow.

Probing Public Health Issues

The numbers involved in Big Tobacco are *big*. For example, in 1992, Philip Morris was one of the top earners among all corporations. This company is one of the largest in the world. The company's balance sheet shows revenues of $80 billion in the year 2002.

Unlike the United States, a number of countries haven't made great strides toward tobacco control, particularly in impoverished parts of the world. The belief that little can be done to quell the use of tobacco leads to inaction. On top of that, various lobbies and interest groups convince regulators and lawmakers that stricter regulation will lead to increased criminal activity (smuggling) and adverse economic consequences, such as falls in national revenue and job loss. Understandably, unemployment — or fear of unemployment — is a major motivator to maintain the status quo.

The tobacco companies spread the idea that jobs and economic security would be lost if tobacco were more heavily regulated. However, in most countries tobacco production and manufacturing are not the largest industries. An international reduction in tobacco use would undoubtedly occur on a gradual basis, hopefully giving tobacco-focused economies a chance to shift to different industries and adapt to the change. Tobacco cultivation is a large industry in China, India, and parts of Africa.

The argument that increased tobacco control means economic ruin for countries, most vocally articulated by the tobacco companies, oversimplifies the situation. Some would argue that if tobacco consumption drops, people will have more money to spend on other things. Reduced spending on tobacco products doesn't necessarily mean reduced spending in general. Alternative economic studies suggest that the number of jobs could actually increase as a result of more discretionary income being available for purchases other than tobacco.

Debates in the United States

The concern about increased controls on and reduced demand for tobacco in the United States is particularly strong in the southern states, where tobacco farming is a big industry. Some experts believe that reduced demand for tobacco and tobacco products would lead to more money being available for other commodities or services. Others argue that if fewer people smoked, tax revenues would fall. This may be true in the short run. Nonetheless, if the mission of government is to promote public health, a potential fall in tax revenue from the sale of tobacco products may be a small price to pay. Also, a reduction in the amount of smoking-related illness means lower healthcare costs for which the government must foot the bill.

Recent history demonstrates a rising awareness of the public health risks related to smoking. In 1989, California passed Proposition 99, which levied a tax on cigarettes to support a robust antismoking crusade in the state. Efforts included airing of video segments showing heads of tobacco companies swearing that their products were not habit forming. Another ad showed a patient with a *laryngectomy* (a hole made in her trachea to allow her to breathe) who was smoking through the surgically created opening. Despite these efforts, the rate of smoking among California's young people increased in 1994.

International issues

One reason the industry is called Big Tobacco is that tobacco is one of the most frequently traded and sold commodities in the world. Internationally, consumers spend some $400 billion each year on the leaf. To make grim matters even darker, up to one-fourth of all cigarettes produced on Earth pass through smugglers' hands, according to the World Health Organization. Which gives you the added "satisfaction" of knowing that a significant part of tobacco revenues is being siphoned off to criminal groups.

Concerns about tobacco smuggling and illegal trafficking extend around the globe. According to some legal authorities, cigarette smuggling may be a strategy that some cigarette companies employ to penetrate markets abroad.

By doing so, the tobacco company gains market share and weakens the local producers. Big Tobacco may negotiate with foreign governments to lower tobacco tariffs as a means of dealing with the contraband trade. R. J. Reynolds was indicted at one point for its Northern Brands' alleged practice of smuggling cigarettes into Canada. The problem is said to be particularly prominent in Iran, while anti-tobacco attorneys in Europe state that monies derived from cigarette smuggling may be used to bankroll terrorist groups.

NAFTA and other international trade and tariff agreements receive a great deal of media attention. What isn't so widely trumpeted is that many of these trade agreements include provisions that facilitate the shipping, trade, and import and export of tobacco and tobacco products. Consumer demand is heightened as a result of looser trade regulations, and tobacco advertising flourishes at the same time that reductions in tariffs result in lower cigarette prices.

Talk about cost containment: Experts from Phillip Morris in Czechoslovakia are publicizing a study that demonstrates how tobacco consumption helps the country's economy — national medical expenses are reduced with each tobacco-related (premature) death.

Massaging the Media: Advertising and Cigarettes

Understanding cigarette advertising, which has a long and complicated history, is a way of understanding people. Cigarette advertising appeals to some of the deepest human impulses and strivings. Influencing consumers' choices is a fine art that decades of practice have honed to a high degree of sophistication. The tobacco companies have spent as much as $6 billion a year on advertising alone.

As glamorous and catchy as some cigarette ads may be, always think *cost*. The advertisements cost stratospheric amounts of money, which translates into a direct out-of-pocket expense for you, the smoker. Plus, cigarette ads are meant to appeal to your vanity, to your desire to look and feel young and sexy. The only real way to get there is to quit smoking and take good care of yourself.

Old ads for Chesterfield cigarettes were simple, direct, and powerful. "Chesterfield cigarettes? *They satisfy.*" Can't you just taste the gratification promised in every puff? Old Gold attempted to allay smokers' concerns about tobacco-related health problems by promising "Not a cough in a carload." Mentholated cigarettes were supposed to be smoother and to go down easier. While the Joe Camel ad campaign was clearly targeted at younger people, a number of cigarette brands were aimed directly at women. Virginia Slims were manufactured for women, and their sleeker, longer look was meant to appeal pretty much exclusively to women. The practice of targeting specific, albeit huge, groups of smokers and potential smokers continues to this day.

Another favorite ploy of cigarette advertisers is strategic product placement. Phillip Morris, for example, provided the chain-smoking Lois Lane (played by Margot Kidder) with Marlboros in the movie *Superman.* The sequel featured trucks and billboards touting the Marlboro logo. If you think about it, product placement is a *super*-effective form of advertising. Millions of people watch these films; market penetration is likely to be much higher than it is with magazine advertising.

As part of the continuing effort to raise the public's awareness of tobacco-related hazards, educators, policymakers, and social scientists have been promoting various strategies to limit access to tobacco products and tobacco product advertising. Such efforts include community education, stiffer taxes, increasingly prevalent bans on smoking in public places such as restaurants, and stricter limits on where advertising can and can't appear. Fortunately, medical and scientific efforts to reduce smoking have kept pace with the political and preventive programs. Studies demonstrate conclusively that nicotine replacement therapies such as the patch and nicotine chewing gum really help smokers quit.

The impact on kids

Cigarette advertising has a tangible influence on children and other potential consumers. Tobacco companies sponsor major sporting events such as the Marlboro Grand Prix and the Virginia Slims tennis championships. At one point, as many children recognized the Mickey Mouse logo as were familiar with the old Joe Camel figure! The California Tobacco Tax Initiative prepared a very instructive table called "The REAL Cost of Marlboro Gear and Camel Cash Goods." The cigarette companies offered all kinds of merchandise, from boots to T-shirts to a mountain bike, in exchange for coupons awarded for buying their cigarette brands. The real cost of these goods went far beyond the cash or redemptive value, measured in lost school days, workdays, and life that cigarette smoking brings.

If you started smoking when you were very young (during your childhood or your teen years), you have an increased probability of becoming a serious — heavy — smoker. It also increases your chances of getting and succumbing to a smoking-related illness at some point. Sad to say, but tens of thousands of children all over the world start smoking *each day.* The better and more encouraging news is that prevention and education efforts have had a gradual but growing impact on some younger smokers and on those who are thinking of quitting.

Part of the issue may be that younger people bring a different mindset to their lifestyle. The teen years are typically a time of establishing independence and exhibiting defiant attitudes and behaviors. The purpose of teen rebellion is to show the world that teens have their own identities and can make their own choices, for good or for ill. Many teenagers simply don't buy into the notion of mortality (their own, that is). Younger people may feel that they're living under a lucky star and that no consequences will arise from fast living, reckless driving, drinking, and smoking. If any changes in lifestyle need to be made, they can be made later: "Later, dude, much later . . . ."

Some experts blame Hollywood for getting young people to regard smoking as hip. Winona Ryder, Julia Roberts, and Johnny Depp, among others, have helped promote the idea that smoking is cool by smoking on camera.

The tobacco industry and advertising

If you want a really interesting experience in mass marketing and winning friends and influencing people, take a visual stroll through the cigarette ads of the 1940s and '50s. These graphic masterpieces depict a variety of people in a variety of situations. Each ad shares the message that cigarettes bring relaxation, energy, adventure, excitement, and career and romantic success! The drawings and photos depict stunning blondes and smiling or sultry brunettes, dapper guys in fancy cars, each model cheerier and toothier than the last.

Many of these glamorous and glamorizing ads can be viewed on the Web at sites like www. chickenhead.com. The extravagant claims run the gamut, with some ads insisting that their smokes will relieve the "burned-out" over-smoked throat, will leave the smoker's mouth feeling clear and clean, and will allow you to smoke all you want with impunity. More recently, the ads promise high living and even suggest that those who smoke are somehow aristocratic.

Consider the psychological appeal, the pitch for elegance and high living that the cigarette advertisers make. In plain language, the ads refer to English royalty: Marlboro, Winston, Parliament, Viceroy. Salem and Newport, I suppose, are meant to evoke other choices and snobby settings. Many more recent ads show great-looking people having great fun: water-skiing, romancing, and enjoying young, healthy, sexy lives. Looking back on it now, the cigarette sales pitch was (and still is, actually) shameless. The tobacco industry had no difficulty promoting their product with the utmost zest, zeal, and entrepreneurial abandon.

Aside from the visual impact of these gorgeous people spending their time smoking while they did other wonderful things, there were the myriad, sometimes bizarre claims made for the healthful effects of tobacco. Cigarettes add pep to your life; cigarettes are the perfect solution to those low-energy moments in the day; the delicious blend of Turkish and other tobaccos help clear scratchy and sore throats. Right!

The impact on families

At the end of the day, who can really quantify the cost of smoking and other kinds of tobacco use on families? Attorneys attempt to do it all the time, of course, but financial compensation for prolonged illness and death always falls short of the mark. There's no way to replace a person, a valued family member, a parent.

In addition to the physical toll of tobacco is the ethical or moral expense of being a really poor role model. Children and teenagers who observe adults smoking seek to imitate the behavior or condemn it (or both). Everyone loses. You might even say that the family who smokes together chokes together. In light of what we now know about secondhand smoke, it's accurate to say that anyone around a source of tobacco smoke suffers.

As a smoker, you need to know that exposure to tobacco smoke really can harm your kids, including in the following ways:

- ✔ Children whose parents smoke have an increased chance of developing serious respiratory infections such as pneumonia.
- ✔ Kids exposed to secondhand smoke are more likely to get coughs and wheeze.
- ✔ Middle ear infections and asthma are prominent consequences of exposing children to smoke.

If you're still smoking, don't smoke near children. Make your home a smoke-free environment. Putting obstacles in your way to smoking gives you incentive to quit. You might even consider finding out about the smoking policy and smoking areas at your workplace and encouraging management to spell them out. The harder it is to smoke, the less likely it is that you will. As public awareness of the dangers of smoking heightens, public barriers are erected that make it more difficult for everyone to access tobacco.

In 2002, a Family Court judge in western Australia decided to prohibit a mother from smoking in the presence of her 10-year-old son. The secondhand smoke issue is one of the major concerns you need to have about smoking around others, especially children. What was once casually dismissed as the overwrought cries of antismoking "fanatics" turns out to be scientifically proven fact. Secondhand smoke injures and kills.

Put this in your pipe . . .

"I see you are inhaling tobacco, puffing, smoking, spitting. (I do not object to your spitting.)"

— G. K. Chesterton, *Faber Book of Parodies* (Faber and Faber, 1984)

Scanning the Statistics

Tobacco has been in use for at least several hundred years, although the cigarette did not start getting mass-produced until the 19th century. As you probably know, cigarette consumption since then has taken off like wildfire. Current estimates are that over 1 billion people in the world smoke. (In other words, approximately one in three adults on the planet smokes.) The vast majority of these smokers reside in countries on the low end to the middle of the socioeconomic spectrum. Of this majority, about 80 percent live in low- and middle-income countries. The total number of smokers worldwide is expected to keep increasing.

Although all forms of tobacco can cause disease given frequent enough use and/or susceptibility on the part of user, some forms of tobacco are more toxic than others. While chewing tobacco and smoking pipes were fairly popular in the past, by far most tobacco is now used in the form of cigarettes, either manufactured or hand-rolled. Bidis, another form of rolled tobacco, are widely used in India and in parts of southeast Asia. Bidis are increasingly popular among students in the United States.

Smoking around the world

Cigarette use in nations with low or midrange incomes has been increasing for more than 30 years. At the same time, a general reduction of smoking among men in high-income countries has occurred. The other side of the statistical coin is that, as a group, women and teenagers are smoking more than they used to.

The World Health Organization has been studying smoking trends and statistical patterns across the globe and has found the following to be true:

- ✔ A good deal of variation exists from one part of the world to another. Many more women smoke in Eastern Europe than in East Asia and the Pacific Region. Eastern Europe itself has a particularly high rate of smoking, with up to 59 percent of adult males smoking.

- ✔ As with other substances of abuse, such as alcohol and cocaine, the global frequency of tobacco use varies by social class, historical era, and culture. Historically, smoking had been a pastime of the rich. This trend has changed dramatically in recent decades. It appears that economically advantaged men in wealthier countries have been smoking less. The more years of education you've had, the less likely you are to be a smoker.

✔ Most smokers begin early in life, before they are 25 years old. According to World Health Organization studies, the vast majority of smokers in affluent countries begin in their teens. A decline in the age of starting smoking has been observed worldwide.

✔ As a wannabe quitter, you're in excellent company. People all over the world are trying to quit and stay quit. There appears to be a correlation between a country's standard of living, level of education, and income and the number of people who have quit smoking. The more and better informed people are, the more likely they are to quit smoking.

The World Health Organization met in Geneva in February 2003 to finalize the wording of a treaty to control tobacco and its almost immeasurable effects on global health. The treaty is intended to reduce cigarette advertising, forbid false and misleading information from being passed along to consumers, encourage higher taxes, and promote the tobacco industry's responsibility and liability for its goods. Proponents of international smoking reduction would like to see a global ban on cigarette advertising and sponsorships of sporting events by tobacco companies. Britain recently enacted a nationwide ban on all tobacco advertising. Ireland will ban smoking in all workplaces, including bars and pubs, starting in 2004. A far-reaching ban on public smoking has already been enacted in Thailand, with observers reporting that, for the most part, the law seems to be upheld.

The U.S. smoking scene

Following 20 years of declining smoking rates in the United States, the percentage of people who smoke has reached a steady plateau of about 25 percent. In other words, smoking rates have stopped declining. Numerous statistical studies have shown that an inverse correlation exists between the price of tobacco and the number of people who smoke. In the 1970s, when cigarette prices in England fell, the number of smokers increased. In the 20 years that smoking in the U.S. decreased, cigarette prices steadily rose.

Recent estimates of smoking's annual cost to the United States in healthcare and lost workdays are at least $100 billion a year. Yes, you read that right: $100 *billion*. And tobacco's impact goes far beyond lost work*days*. If you are a regular or heavy smoker, you spend significant amounts of time finding ways to get out of the office to light up. Your focus and energy are diluted by the near-constant necessity to calculate, to strategize, to sneak in those out-of-office smokes. Some people's attitudes about their work are quite casual, and they may feel that they're simply punching in and punching out to earn a wage. But you may not be one of those people. To the extent that you are focused on your work and that what you do really matters to you — and you believe in your heart that your work makes a difference to others — you must regret the time and energy that go into the pursuit of smokes.

Despite all the clamor from the Surgeon General, health authorities, antismoking activists, and those who have suffered physical illness as a result of smoking, almost one in four adults in the United States still smokes. Up to half of smokers try to quit during any given year.

There's plenty of good news in the United States regarding quitting smoking, too. Recent years of legislation represent a virtual monsoon outlawing smoking in public places like restaurants, transportation centers, and municipal offices. Educational efforts aimed at young people and other groups who are demographically poised to begin smoking have been effective. The hope is that the United States will pour more public funds (including those garnered from tobacco company lawsuits) into preventive and educational efforts. Already, there are volumes of news clippings related to events on the local and national level to stop smoking.

Smoking Even if You Don't Want To: Secondhand Smoke

Secondhand smoke, also known as *passive smoking,* is smoke from other smokers that bystanders may inadvertently inhale. The smoke may originate from a burning cigarette, cigar, or pipe or may be exhaled by a smoker.

The stir about secondhand smoke

What's all the fuss about secondhand smoke? The Environmental Protection Agency (EPA) published a report in 1993 clearly stating that environmental tobacco smoke can cause major medical problems in people of all ages. Since then, many experts have analyzed the report, and the findings hold. Just like firsthand smoke, secondhand smoke contains thousands of chemicals, dozens of which are known agents of disease. Some of these chemical compounds have been shown to cause cancer in laboratory animals. As you learn more about secondhand, or environmental (another term for it), tobacco smoke, you'll encounter statistics that at first may seem exaggerated. The actual figures may shock you.

The EPA unequivocally states that secondhand smoke causes lung cancer. It also estimates that about 3,000 people *die* each year from lung cancer caused by passive smoking. And just like firsthand smoke, smoke that's passively inhaled can do much more than cause cancer and death. Breathing problems, worsening of asthma, and chronic lung disease are all caused by exposure to tobacco smoke and probably occur far more frequently than tobacco-induced cancer does. If you've ever seen someone with moderate or severe chronic lung disease, you know how awful this kind of respiratory disease is. People with this disease can't fully exhale; they constantly feel like they can't breathe properly. Not only that, but inadvertent or accidental inhalation of tobacco smoke causes dizziness and headaches and wears down the body's ability to fight off germs and infections. The more often you're exposed to secondhand smoke, the higher your risk.

Some people dismiss the impact of secondhand smoke. I wish it were that easy. Secondhand smoke

- ✔ Is especially harmful to children, whose lungs are still developing.

- ✔ Is especially harmful to people with asthma and other respiratory diseases, making their conditions worse.

- ✔ Causes thousands of deaths each year from lung and heart disease. The mechanisms are multiple. Components of cigarette smoke are directly toxic to the lungs and heart. These vital organs have to work harder to compensate for the added burden imposed by smoking.

- ✔ Causes inflammation of the airways, leading to coughing, mucus production, wheezing, and possible chronic breathing problems.

Despite the nearly ubiquitous presence of tobacco smoke, you can protect yourself and your family by doing the following:

- ✔ Ask visitors to your home to smoke outside.

- ✔ If you smoke, avoid lighting up at home.

- ✔ Never smoke in the presence of children.

- ✔ Practice harm reduction: If people must smoke indoors, have them smoke in a well-ventilated area, such as near an open window or door.

- ✔ Nag. If you nag people enough, they may change their behavior. Sometimes bugging people about their smoking, such as by asking them repeatedly if they've spoken to their doctor about it, eventually hits home. (As a smoker, you've probably gotten many comments on your smoking, which you may have perceived both as caring and as a nuisance.)

- ✔ Avoid lighting up in a car, which can easily turn into a humidor. Plus, the odor can linger for the life of the vehicle.

An unacceptably high number of toxic compounds from tobacco smoke linger in the air long after the cigarette or pipe is finished.

There are ways to say no to secondhand smoke:

- ✔ Say yes the next time someone asks, "Do you mind if I smoke?"
- ✔ Ask to be seated in the nonsmoking sections of restaurants and other public places.
- ✔ Remember that you have a right to work in a smoke-free environment. If you're inhaling other people's smoke at work, talk to management about improving the arrangement.

Getting smoke out of public places

I was recently in a restaurant in a state where smoking in public places is still allowed (still suffered, you might say). Smoking is an integral part of the bar scene but fortunately is becoming less and less of a social ingredient at restaurants.

The EPA has made efforts to protect nonsmokers from environmental smoke. The agency suggests that companies put policies in place that effectively designate nonsmoking and smoking areas. The idea is that you have a right to work in a place where you are not exposed to toxic substances such as tobacco smoke. Many companies have taken up this challenge and have created smoke-free environments for their staff.

Simply separating smokers and nonsmokers within the same area, such as a one-room cafeteria, may reduce the nonsmokers' exposure, but nonsmokers are still exposed to recirculated smoke or smoke drifting into nonsmoking areas. The ideal is to work out a physical, architectural solution. People at work and at school have a right to go about their business without inhaling toxic compounds.

The smoke-free environment issue has been especially acute in hospitals, strangely enough. People who are admitted to hospitals for treatment of medical or psychiatric conditions are reluctant to give up their smoking habit and occasionally insist on their right to smoke even in a setting where health and wellness are top priorities.

Not that long ago, you could light up on an airplane or in a train. People didn't give it a second thought. In more recent centuries (that's a joke!), the hazards posed by the presence of flames and smoke in airplanes have been taken more seriously. Nowadays, the reaction to a passenger lighting up on board would most likely be one of unconcealed horror. Not to mention the issue of recirculated air; people in enclosed spaces are the unwitting and usually unwilling victims of smokers.

Which direction do you think the smoking-in-public-places issue will go? Do you think smoking restrictions are likely to be relaxed, or that concerns about public health will win out and the wave of health-promoting ordinances will become tidal, with smoking increasingly marginalized and banned?

A terrific direction to go with your belief is to your local, state, and national government. Take your concerns to the top. Harnessing your energy in the direction of healing, in the service of being heard, is an unbeatable way to champion your personal cause of quitting smoking.

Appreciating the Ripple Effects

Moving from the global level to the personal level is natural. The personal level of quitting smoking flows effortlessly from your awareness of macro events. Likewise, your personal mission to quit smoking has many ripples in the larger world. Linking up the personal consequences of the smoking habit with the social cost is another way to motivate yourself to quit.

The morning after

The morning after — the classic alcohol hangover — has been forever embedded in popular awareness as a result of films like *The Lost Weekend; Bright Lights, Big City;* and *28 Days.* Maybe you've been unlucky enough to have had one of these Hollywood-size hangovers. Obviously, I'm not talking about drinking here, but about a different kind of hangover: a *moral* hangover.

A rebound of conscience can sweep over you like a tidal wave the morning after you've slipped. Many smokers experience waves of heart-wrenching guilt because they smoke, period. The message to yourself might be something like, "How can I do this to myself?" The compunction, contrition, and self-abasement can be particularly intense if you've decided to quit and, so to speak, fall off the wagon. If you've been through this kind of experience, then you know how painful it is. If people depend on you emotionally, you may double or triple the heartbreak and hand-wringing.

Of course, the morning after (smoking, that is) has physical components, too. Every smoker has had the experience of waking to the unpleasant feeling of a parched and polluted mouth. Taking it a step further by visualizing the accumulation of tobacco toxins down your bronchi and lungs only amplifies the anxiety and despair. When it's your turn to clean out the ashtrays, you can't help but notice the dark patches and rings of tar on the tamped-out cigarette filters. What you see is what *you* get.

The only way to rid yourself of realistic worries about ongoing harm to yourself from smoking is to quit.

Recognizing the guilt

How about sending a relative, perhaps one of your children, to the store or a cigarette machine to buy you a pack of smokes? (Of course, these days it's much more difficult for underage people to purchase a pack.) How many scenarios can you visualize or recall where you've cringed while "arranging" a smoke?

Curious parallels exist between smoking and other addictions. If you're familiar with 12 Step programs such as Alcoholics Anonymous, you can't fail to see the similarities that all addictions share. Smoking can make you feel like your life is out of control. It can become a monstrous burden, a quiet but steady consumer of your time and energy. As with alcoholism, tobacco dependence causes you to rearrange your time, energy, and priorities. You may sacrifice time spent with family, work, or self-care in the pursuit of a cigarette. Any and all of these sacrifices results in guilt and shame of massive proportions. When you feel enough guilt and shame, you reach for a smoke. Eliminate these feelings and you have less of a reason to smoke.

Guilt and *shame* are pretty strong words. This kind of language is usually reserved for egregious acts that harm people and cause permanent and irreversible damage. That's what smoking does. Although a nicotine addict may simply be trying to maintain a steady nicotine level in order to feel "normal," each puff ratchets up the chance that serious, permanent damage to health will result.

If you don't feel much guilt and shame about smoking, *try to.* A good strategy for finding and maintaining this healthier perspective is the following: Next time you see someone lighting up, visualize the smoke particles bombarding the lining of that person's throat and lungs and interacting with the bronchial cells. Visualize the respiratory cells being attacked by sheets of dense tar. Think of the chronic mobilization of defender white blood cells that rush to the scene of the crime in an attempt to contain and engulf the toxins. While all that goes on, the person takes another puff! Remember, too, the first time you smoked. Remember how harsh and poisonous the incoming smoke felt. Undoubtedly you coughed, possibly you retched, and very possibly you wondered how anyone could ever smoke on a repeated, not to mention hourly, basis.

You're probably wondering why I would encourage you to feel guilt and shame. Next time you think about lighting up, turn up the gain on the guilt switch.

The accumulation of regret, repentance — whatever you want to call it — will eventually outweigh the "benefits" of smoking. Another reason to pursue these difficult feelings is that, like it or not, they act as moral policemen. The opposite of feeling guilty and shameful is feeling proud of yourself and liking yourself more. Once you get past feeling bad about your cigarette addiction and actually do something about it, pride in yourself starts to kick in. Being able to give yourself a pat on the back for your courage, persistence, and, yes, heroism is a great feeling.

Not everyone is able to quit. Those who do succeed have faced themselves in a direct and deep way and are taking active steps to feel, live, and perform better. It's called personal growth.

I've quit a thousand times

Those who quit may make six or seven attempts before they make it stick. I think it was Mark Twain who said, "I have no trouble quitting: I've done it a thousand times." If you're like most smokers, you can relate to his experience. For most smokers, quitting isn't something that happens overnight. Quitting is not a casual thing. It takes determination, a detailed plan, and a strategy for every eventuality. Every time you try to quit is a respite for your lungs and for your health in general. Feel good about the days and weeks of nonsmoking that you have accumulated.

Even if you've never tried to quit before, remember that you didn't enter this world as a smoker. Even if you started smoking at a tender age, you had years of carefree breathing. When you were playing in the sandbox, you weren't bedeviled with the thought of finding a smoke. Quitting smoking will refresh not only your body but also your spirit. No one enjoys feeling like a failure. No one enjoys repeated experiences of failure. Once you have smoking licked, you'll be able to move far beyond the arena of smoking/not smoking and quitting/not quitting.

Rejecting rationalizations and looking inside yourself

Do any of these rationalizations sound familiar?

- Everyone in my family has lived a long time. My great uncle Waldo smoked until the last day of his life. He died at the age of 90.
- It will harm me more if I start eating and gain weight. I prefer to continue smoking.
- I have so few pleasures in life.
- Now is not a good time to quit. I'll do it seriously and with more commitment at a later time.

If you came to see me as a patient and presented these rationalizations, the first thing I would do is find out what *you* want. I would want to know your smoking history: how much you smoke, how often, and what kind of cigarettes. I would further flesh out your smoking history by asking you when you are least likely and most likely to smoke. What triggers make you reach automatically for a cigarette? What is the longest period of abstinence from tobacco that you have had? What was going on at the time that made you resolve to quit smoking? What allowed you to stay quit for as long as you did?

Once you told me that you want to stop smoking, I would try to find out *why*. Why do you want to stop at this particular point in time? What kind of pressure are you getting from other people to quit? Is smoking making problems for you? Has smoking caused problems for you in the past? What is the actual cumulative cost of smoking to you, not only in dollars and cents, but also in health, illness, and self-esteem?

I would also like to learn more about *you*. How do you see yourself? What resources and strengths do you have that you can draw upon to succeed at quitting? How do you see yourself in five days, five weeks, and five months from now? Do you know someone who has quit? Do you know someone who has gotten sick as a result of smoking? How did you feel about that? I also need to find out about your lifestyle — how you treat yourself from day to day. Do you encourage yourself to succeed at projects that you undertake, or do you see yourself as a loser? Have you ever had to think about yourself in this way before?

My assessment gets even more detailed. If you're going to beat this, I need to know how you spend your time. What kind of work do you do? Is it easy or difficult to smoke at work? Do you ever find that smoking interferes with working, that it distracts you from what you are doing? How about the people you work with — as a group, are they smokers, or do they look askance at people who sneak outside to light up? How do you spend the rest of your time, your evenings and weekends? Who are the important people in your life? How does smoking impact each one of these people? Do you have children, or are you close to kids of your friends or family? What hobbies and interests do you have? How are they related to smoking? (For example, let's say you enjoy watching birds or camping. How do these activities mix with smoking? Now that I mention it, what activities *do* fit with smoking? Drinking in a bar, perhaps, or being a detective in a 1930s pulp fiction thriller . . . .)

So you say you want to quit. Are you ready to quit now? What plans have you made to insure that this will work, that quitting will last? Is everything else in your life exactly the same, except that you have decided to quit? Are there components of your life that could be rearranged, or revised, or chilled out, to give you some wiggle room while you're adjusting to the change?

When do you want to quit? (Some people do just quit, keeping all the other activities in their life exactly the same as before.) Perhaps you could make it work by setting aside a week to quit. Taking a vacation from work, from routine, from ordinary life, is sometimes effective in making a quit plan succeed. What is your plan? Do you want to just quit, or do you prefer to taper? What are the pros and cons of each approach?

Have you thought about using one of the many nicotine replacement therapies, such as the patch, nicotine gum, or spray, to help you with your goal? What kind of support will you have? Will you be extra active, because being around people helps to take your mind off smoking? Have you thought about where you will be spending your time during the first week that you stop smoking? Who will be around? Are they smokers or nonsmokers? Have you spoken to your friends and family about your intention? What have they said in response? What measures are they willing to take to support your effort? What measures would you like them to take?

What environmental changes will facilitate your quit effort? Do you need to get rid of the lingering odor of tobacco from your home and car? Do you need to do a house-wide sweep to remove all ashtrays, matches, cigar boxes and other mementos, appliances, and smoking memorabilia? You will need to do a concurrent inner spring cleaning, too. When you go through your storehouse of memories, I have no doubt that you will have packed away among all the other belongings trunks full of fond and nostalgic tobacco moments. Most smokers have these moments. Smoking becomes intimately connected over time with so many of the meaningful and personal things you do that at first try it is hard even to get enough psychological distance to appreciate the broad and multilayered impact smoking has had on your life.

Once you decide to side with reality and recognize these smoke memories and dreams for what they are — nostalgic and one-sided views of a nasty, health-devouring habit — the fog will begin to lift. Instead of thinking about cigarettes as romantic and exciting, remember all the times you couldn't believe that you were lighting up. Remember the first few times you smoked (and probably choked, too). Think about the times you were feeling under the weather with a cold or a headache and you lit up anyway. Did those cigarettes go down smooth? Think of all the negative press that smoking has earned, all the criticism and negative commentary you've received and heard over the years. Do you imagine that people are making these issues up, that the antismoking crusaders are merely fanatics rallying around a meaningless and worthless cause?

Look inside. During your first week of quitting, you will rely on as many supports as you can muster, and it's extremely helpful to have *internal,* psychological supports as well as external ones.

Speaking of smoking bans

In 2003, New York's Nassau County placed a total ban on smoking in bars and restaurants. This measure is as welcome as it is difficult to enforce. One health department official stated that the initial enforcement efforts would consist of responding to complaints from consumers. A similar ban on smoking in New York City's bars, clubs, and restaurants is in effect. Stiff penalties, including fines of up to $2,000 and loss of operating permits, are part of the new law.

In a related event (and geographic area), Westchester County, New York, was recently commended by the regional Lung Association for its effective use of funds awarded to the state from the class-action lawsuit (the Master Settlement Fund) against tobacco companies. The Mississippi state legislature appears to be moving rapidly toward prohibition of smoking in public buildings including restaurants, stores, arenas, and office buildings. Many other municipalities are moving in identical directions. Find out where *your* region is moving as far as discouraging and banning smoking goes.

Part II
Packing It In:
Taking the Leap

The 5th Wave   By Rich Tennant

"No, I said Phillip is using <u>a</u> patch to help
him quit smoking, not <u>the</u> patch."

In this part . . .

This part enables you to have an extended conversation with yourself. Take a detailed look at your use of tobacco and decide whether the tobacco lifestyle is something you're willing to continue living with (and for). Once you've decided to quit, you want to outfit yourself with the most up-to-date and effective tools available. Quitting smoking is not just about saying no, and it doesn't have to be a matter of grim determination and white knuckles. It involves the informed, active, and ongoing use of quitting tools. Medical treatments such as nicotine replacement therapy and the anticraving drug Zyban can diminish nicotine withdrawal symptoms to tolerable levels. This part gives you an in-depth look at the ammunition currently available in the war to reclaim your body and your health.

Chapter 7

Breaking a Bad Habit

Smoking is more than just a bad habit. It's a lifestyle that comprises dozens of decisions that you make on an hourly basis. These decisions affect you today and play a major role in your future health and well-being. Quitting smoking is a decision to cut loose not only the act of smoking but also the many behaviors that go along with smoking.

You can make dozens, if not hundreds, of lifestyle accommodations to ensure your continued supply and use of tobacco. These accommodations are all-inclusive, ranging from what you wear to where you spend your time. It's quite possible that many of your decisions are actually based on smoking; this is one of the hallmarks of the habit. When you realize that your lifestyle choices are dictated by smoking, you may want to consider a different way. Taking back control of your life by quitting smoking means that you'll have more time, more energy, and more options.

Not deciding to quit is also a decision. As you think back over the course of your life, you can't help but conclude that the future does arrive — you can't just think that you'll get to quitting at some unidentified "later." Today is the unfolding of yesterday's events and decisions. What you think about and decide now helps determine the reality that will eventually be yours.

Looking in the Mirror: Analyzing Your Smoking Patterns

Your behavior is regulated by a fantastic array of chemical and physiological reactions. The study of these biological processes demonstrates that there are patterns in addiction, in illness, and in health. Many living creatures have peak activity during daylight hours. Feeding and mating times tend to follow a phasic or predictable pattern over the course of days and seasons. Your smoking behavior is also understandable from a behavioral point of view.

Appetites can be physical, emotional, and/or spiritual. If you have a continual gnawing in your gut for food or for nicotine, it's possible that this yearning is reflected in parallel changes in your brain chemicals. I'm not saying that you need medication (although nicotine replacement therapies can be helpful in your quit attempt — see Chapter 9). I'm saying that the mind and body are continuous and consistent. Think of your brain chemicals achieving the right levels as the tobacco chemicals exit your body.

There are clearly recognizable patterns of smoking. You may be a weekend warrior, or you may be a regular smoker. Many smokers smoke once or twice an hour. You may not even think of yourself as following a formula when it comes to smoking. Nonetheless, to an observer, your lighting up is probably as predictable as the tides. Realizing that you are a slave to your smoking routine may be a great incentive to quit.

An interesting and sobering exercise is to create a log sheet with the hours of the day on it and jot down the times you smoke — each and every time. Table 7-1 is a sample log that you can use; just put an X in each box that corresponds to a smoke. How many cigarettes did you smoke on Monday? Tuesday? The following Monday? You're likely to be amazed at the consistency of the numbers.

Table 7-1			Smoking Log Sheet				
	Mon	*Tues*	*Wed*	*Thurs*	*Fri*	*Sat*	*Sun*
7:00 a.m.							
8:00 a.m.							
9:00 a.m.							
10:00 a.m.							
11:00 a.m.							
Noon							
1:00 p.m.							
2:00 p.m.							
3:00 p.m.							
4:00 p.m.							

	Mon	*Tues*	*Wed*	*Thurs*	*Fri*	*Sat*	*Sun*
5:00 p.m.							
6:00 p.m.							
7:00 p.m.							
8:00 p.m.							
9:00 p.m.							
10:00 p.m.							

The more time and energy you spend on assessing your habit, the more emotional and cognitive distance you gain on it. You reach a point where continuing the habit becomes unacceptable to you on one or more levels.

Take a look at the following statements and think about how many of them apply to you. To what extent is your smoking behavior "textbook"? To what extent does being this predictable motivate you to quit?

✔ I smoke every day.

✔ I think about smoking shortly after waking.

✔ I must have a cigarette after coffee or a meal.

✔ I have driven just to buy a pack of cigarettes.

✔ I have asked strangers for cigarettes.

✔ People close to me have suggested that I quit.

✔ I get angry when people suggest that I cut down.

✔ I have a smoker's cough.

✔ I would rather smoke than do almost anything else.

✔ I'm concerned about how much money I spend on cigarettes.

✔ I've tried to quit before.

✔ I dislike the lack of control I have over my tobacco use.

If you checked any one of these items, you have a smoking problem. You are addicted to tobacco. If you remain uncertain about whether you're addicted, try to stop for one week. If you don't miss the smokes — if the week goes by and you don't pick one up — you may not be addicted. By all means, don't break your stride at this point. If you've been able to stop for a day or a week, keep going!

Realizing that there is no such thing as a seasoned smoker

Smoking is not a casual thing. If you've already tried to quit, you know this. If smoking were a casual thing, you would have been able to stop already.

Your body never really adjusts to smoking. It can take a lot of abuse, but it has its limits. After a finite amount of time and exposure to tobacco, it literally breaks down. The good news is that your body often gives off warning signals before breaking down completely. For example, you may develop a smoker's cough before you get into serious respiratory trouble.

Recall any time you have been able to lay down the gauntlet and quit smoking for a while. Perhaps you relapsed long enough after quitting to feel the difference. Remember how harsh that first cigarette tasted?

There's no such thing as a seasoned smoker. Throw that idea away. Tobacco traumatizes the delicate lining of the mouth, throat, lungs, and gastrointestinal tract no matter how long you've smoked or how many cigarettes you regularly smoke in a day.

Smoking may have been your solution for stress for a long time. One of the first steps toward overcoming the self-defeating smoking lifestyle is to recognize it as a lifestyle. Do you smoke

- ✔ Even though you often don't want to?
- ✔ Despite frequent resolutions to quit?
- ✔ In spite of advice to quit?
- ✔ Instead of eating or getting exercise?
- ✔ Instead of relaxing or thinking?
- ✔ One cigarette right after another?
- ✔ And hate yourself right afterward?
- ✔ And force yourself to not think about it?
- ✔ And rationalize it away?

Do you agree that smoking is a lifestyle? For most people, smoking is not a take-it-or-leave-it decision.

Using tobacco usually involves all kinds of personal concessions and accommodations, such as making sure that you have the accessories (matches, lighter, ashtray), wearing clothes that have a pocket for a pack, and finding out ahead of time whether the place you're going allows smoking. The trend has been for smoking to be banned in public places so that the smoking lifestyle is becoming increasingly inconvenient. Who needs the excess baggage?

Perhaps these words and sentiments seem foreign to you. Maybe you believe that smoking really isn't a big deal. Follow the trail of a puff of smoke.

You light a cigarette and inhale. The superheated tobacco leaf burns, and hundreds of chemical compounds travel through the rolled leaf, concentrating in strength as you inhale. The white cloud, now so dense that it leaves brown markings on the filter each time you puff, hits your tongue, your cheeks, and the back of your throat before descending down your windpipe and hitting your upper bronchial tree. There, the cells of your mucosal lining do their best time after time to repel the nasty particles, but the cells can do only so much. Even with mucus secretion, coughing, and repeated exhalation of smoke, significant amounts remain behind. This smoke coats the lining of the lungs and is eventually taken in by the cells. The substances are irritating in the extreme and actually cause the cells to scar; some of the cells transform into abnormal and even cancerous cells. Fortunately, in most cases your body recognizes these changed cells as foreign and gobbles them up.

Sometimes the outcome is not so positive, and the transformed cells linger and flourish. Then you really have a problem.

Do you really want to continue doing this to yourself? Do you really want to continue to have such an estranged relationship with your body?

Recognizing common smoking patterns

A number of fairly recognizable smoking patterns exist. I know a number of people who light up two or three times an hour. Perhaps you know people like this — folks who actually go through two or three packs a day. You may be one of them. The more you smoke, the more challenging your detox will be.

Catching up

Although regular smokers tend to level off at a fairly steady intake of tobacco from day to day, your system can be thrown out of whack if you go without tobacco for a while. You may actually go through a rebound period during which you overshoot the mark and try to catch up on your "deficient" or flagging nicotine level. The next time you go without a smoke for longer than you'd planned, observe whether you smoke more or inhale more deeply when you first "catch up."

A typical pattern of use involves smoking a pack of cigarettes a day. Many other people smoke socially — in the evenings, at gatherings, and on the weekends. Recent converts to the habit find that that their frequency of use picks up over time. Seasoned smokers usually hit a plateau — you hit a steady level of use.

Whatever your smoking pattern, it is excessive, unnecessary, and unhealthy. Preachy enough for you? (I guess you could say that I'm trying to make "light" of the issue.)

Evaluating What Went Wrong Before

This may be the first time you've tried to quit, or it may be the 14th. Don't be discouraged; millions of people all over the world have succeeded at quitting smoking. Most of those who have quit had tried several times before making it last.

Don't let what you're reading and hearing about other people who relapsed, or who failed their first time around, get you down. Statistics are made up of individuals. Many people have succeeded at quitting on their first try — maybe you will, too!

Just because you tried to quit smoking in the past doesn't mean that you can't succeed now. Most people who quit successfully try to quit up to a half-dozen times before making it stick. Look at your experience from the opposite point of view: If you've quit in the past, whether it was for two days or two months, you've already demonstrated that you can do it. You got through that period without tobacco. When you're supplied with a quit plan (see Chapter 11) and all the other resources that are currently available, your chances of staying quit are that much better.

Identifying common triggers — and the specific ones that get you

What made you relapse to smoking before? If you can recall the specific triggers that made you pick up again, you can be extra wary of them. Common relapse triggers include

> ✔ **Believing that you've got the habit licked.** You may have felt that you could have "just one." Shortly after, you may have convinced yourself that having just one more would cause little harm. By the third cigarette, you were as addicted as before.

✔ **Catastrophizing.** You slipped and had one or more cigarettes despite your best intentions. You felt so guilty, like you'd let yourself down so much, that you threw up your hands in despair and essentially gave up. "I may as well enjoy myself" is the theme song that accompanies this self-pitying wail.

✔ **Stressing.** An event occurs in your world and you panic. You cower emotionally and retreat to an earlier position: "I've got to have a cigarette." Actually, you don't have to have a cigarette. Having a cigarette actually amplifies your stress. Not only do you still need to deal with whatever is taking place in your life, but you now have additional stressful stimuli such as a rapid heartbeat, coughing, and a bitter, smoky taste in your mouth — not to mention the supremely unpleasant feeling of self-betrayal.

Remember the phrase *grace under pressure*. Someone somewhere used that phrase to describe a hero. As someone trying to quit smoking, you are a hero. The philosopher Nietzsche's aphorism, "Whatever doesn't kill me outright makes me stronger," might apply, too. Or you may feel that Nietzsche is overstating it a bit. Besides, quitting smoking can't come even remotely close to killing you. Cigarettes can kill you, however.

✔ **Relaxing.** Being on vacation or kicking back on a weekend day is the perfect excuse to have a cool drink and light up. *Wrong.* Take a closer look at what relaxing is all about. Letting down your hair and unwinding has to do with smelling the roses, feeling the cool breeze, and every other form of slowing down and feeling good. Cigarettes are not about slowing down. Cigarettes are stimulants that kick up your pulse rate and blood pressure and unwind the spool of your life — rob you of your time — that much more quickly.

✔ **Watching other people smoke.** You may think, "If they can smoke without consequences, why can't I?" This self-pitying routine comes up fairly regularly when you first stop smoking. You feel sorry for yourself because you have to give up something you like. Remember that you've been through this before. You had to give up crawling, for example, in order to walk. You had to give up babbling in order to talk. Giving up smoking is letting go of an oral fixation that you really don't need. The path toward health and heroism involves taking care of your whole body and your whole mind. You do so by attending carefully to yourself: You find a workout that makes you feel good; you find new ways to think, look at things, and behave that are consistent with the person you want to be.

✔ **Accepting substandard health.** You may already have a cough or congestion in your lungs first thing in the morning. Following this line of logic, you may try to convince yourself that the damage is already done, so why not at least enjoy the smokes?

✔ **Being tired of feeling tired.** It's true that cigarettes give you a lift. Bit feeling run down is a normal part of life. Your energy flows in waves.

Everyone has energy peaks and valleys throughout the day. Quitting smoking will add enormously to your available energy after the first few weeks.

Zyban, the anticraving medication, helps control the fatigue that can accompany nicotine withdrawal. Exercise, good sleep habits, and a positive enthusiastic outlook also contribute to a high-energy life.

✔ **Trying to control your weight.** You are eating too much and are super-concerned about gaining weight. (See Chapter 15 for details on the links between smoking and food.) Look around you: Countless numbers of people who don't smoke manage to remain slim. Oral gratifications such as cigarettes and food are not the only pleasures in life. As you find others, you will find increasing rewards in your appearance and improved feelings of well-being.

✔ **Keeping up appearances.** You like the way you look when you smoke. Smoking, you tell yourself, is cool. Fast-forward the picture a few years and imagine if that will always be the case. You've seen how chronic smokers look and cough; you've seen the telltale wrinkles that betray their addiction.

Think back to a time when quitting didn't work. Where were you? What were you doing at the time you broke down and smoked? Who were you with? People, places, and activities can be triggers, too. Do any of the following excuses sound familiar?

✔ I became too nervous.

✔ I got very irritable.

✔ I couldn't sleep.

✔ I slept too much.

✔ I couldn't focus my thoughts.

✔ I was at loose ends at work.

✔ I was on vacation.

✔ I cut myself a break and had a smoke.

Don't fall for these tricks the next time around.

Evidence suggests that adding on quit tools such as counseling, following up with a doctor, using a nicotine replacement therapy, and/or using Zyban to reduce cravings for cigarettes increases your chances of staying quit. See Chapter 9 for more information about nicotine replacement therapies.

Lose your fear, lose your warts: The power of hypnosis and positive thinking

The journal *Developmental and Behavioral Pediatrics* reported that in 1994, R. B. Noll claimed that he was able to cure warts completely in six of seven patients for whom all prior attempts at treatment had failed — previously, the warts had disappeared only to return later. This news was spectacular. Noll's patients received between two and nine sessions of hypnosis as well as training in visualization exercises that were intended to boost their immune systems so that the warts would not reappear.

Studies that compared hypnosis with no treatment found significantly greater wart loss among the hypnotized subjects. Even more interesting, wart-bearers treated with a *placebo* (a sugar pill, a make-believe treatment) did better than those who received no treatment.

This tells me that hypnosis — the power of suggestion — actually affects the body's immune function. The power of the mind is no joke. Libraries are full of books about the power of "positive thinking": think your way to health, to a perfect life partner, to millions. Some people actually do it. Pointed in the right direction, the mind can create worlds of untold beauty. Untended, the mind can turn in on itself and wreak havoc.

Without going to extremes, it may be possible to take the same awesome energy that destroys warts — or sculpts a masterpiece — and use it to lose anxiety. Or tobacco! Right now, you can surrender and cower in fear of your life without tobacco. Or, through focusing your actions, educating yourself, and meditating and/or harnessing the power of positive thinking, you can lose those unsightly warts — and bad friends like tobacco.

Staying positive about past failures

If you tried to quit before and didn't succeed, your previous quit attempts probably failed for numerous reasons. However, try to avoid thinking of your previous efforts as failures. While you were quitting, you were fighting the good fight. The idea is that you may have lost the battle, but you still can win the war.

Perhaps you were overwhelmed by the thought of the odds. You've heard of how many quit attempts people make. You know Mark Twain's jibe about "I have no trouble quitting — I've done it a thousand times"? Statistics and demographics are wide open to interpretation. You can look at a given set of data in any number of ways. Yes, many would-be quitters go back to active smoking. But *millions of people* have stopped. You can be one of them.

Were you fully prepared to quit? You need a quit plan, a calendar that accounts for every moment of every day of your first quit week (see Chapter 8). A critical part of a quit plan is a firm decision to make quitting your number one priority. Quitting supersedes everything else going on in your life at the time. If you aren't smoking but you feel lousy, tired, wired, irritable, or whatever, you're still succeeding. You must be willing to trade two or three days of feeling less than perfect for a lifetime of breathing freely.

Things of high value — like health and dignity — come from hard work. Quitting smoking is hard work. But it feels great!

Overcoming Your Fear of Failure

You probably know people who have sacrificed their lives, who have not lived out their dreams because of their fear of failing. Fear of failure is a kind of spiritual cancer. You want to grow, to achieve, to be something, but your fear and inhibition stand in the way.

Habit gets in the way, too. The customary way of doing things is a roadblock. Old habits die hard, as they say. Likewise, new habits are brought into the world with great difficulty.

Do you have a fear of failure? Ask yourself if you're a perfectionist. Are you reluctant to go ahead with a project unless you know every detail ahead of time and are assured a perfect result? Have you made quit-smoking attempts before that were short lived? Did you convince yourself that you would never succeed?

An alternate way to look at quitting tobacco is that every tobacco/smoke-free moment is a success. Every smoke-free moment is another moment that your lungs and the rest of your body can go into healing mode. Each moment that you avoid smoking is a moment of success.

Instead of picking up a smoke, pick up the phone to call a buddy or pick up the keys to get out of the house.

A practicing occultist I know prescribes the exercise of self-denial as the bedrock of self-empowerment. Fortunately, for your purposes, self-denial need only apply to smoking! Nonetheless, it's a big NO to tell yourself. When you do tell yourself no, it's a major achievement. The occultist would say that it's a "magical" achievement. You're substituting what you want for instinct or blind habit. You have countless moments like these. Every time you choose to reach for something you care about, each time you choose to think or feel "outside the box," you are striving beyond inertia and habit toward the new. You already know what it's like to give in to the old habit of smoking. When you act different, you are different.

At the end of the day, you want to feel that you fought the good fight. You want to feel that you did everything you could to feel well, to live well, to be a good steward of your body and your mind. Why? The question is not rhetorical. All of nature is about maximal living. Birds and dogs and plants reach for the light and the food and the good feelings. Why should it be any different for you?

Fear can be a killer. Don't let fear get in your way. Analyze your fear. Put your fear of quitting into words. Are you scared of

- ✔ Trying something new?
- ✔ Not fitting in with a smoking crowd?
- ✔ Having to explain yourself to others?
- ✔ Withdrawal feelings?
- ✔ Not knowing what to do with your hands?
- ✔ Not knowing what to do with your time?
- ✔ Feeling uncomfortable when among others?
- ✔ Low energy?
- ✔ Fear?

President Franklin Delano Roosevelt once said, "The only thing we have to fear is fear itself." When you quit smoking, a great deal of the struggle is with the anticipation of quitting. You may find yourself wondering, "How can I get through this experience without a cigarette?" or "I always have a cigarette after dinner." You can undoubtedly think of many other knee-jerk thoughts like these.

What is your very worst fear related to quitting smoking? Is it really so terrible? You may be scared of how you will feel once you quit. The anticipation can be worse than the experience itself.

The worst (or best) thing that can happen if you fail at quitting is that you can try again!

Think about other positive decisions you've made in your life. Perhaps you decided where to go to school or where to live. You may have faced the decision of whether to marry, or the even more challenging decision of whom to marry. Your life is a collection of decisions, some small, some not so small. When you rise in the morning, you decide which socks to put on. You may even decide how you're going to feel that particular day.

When you choose a quit day, you choose health and lose fear. Health and fear are incompatible.

Chapter 8

Taking Your First Steps

- -

In This Chapter

▶ Breaking your bond with tobacco

▶ Going cold turkey

▶ Saying no gradually or by varying your smoking routine

▶ Replacing the "reward" of cigarettes with a better, healthier reward

▶ Ending your love/hate relationship with tobacco

- -

*T*raditional methods of quitting smoking include quitting cold turkey, gradually reducing the amount you smoke, and replacing the "reward" of cigarettes with other, healthier rewards. In this chapter, you will "just do it." I talk you through the alternatives so that you can consider which option is best for you. But don't think about it too long. As they say, *carpe diem:* Seize the day. There are many ways to get it right. The most important thing is to quit smoking and quit smoking soon. Planning is important, but so is action. It's quitting time.

Quitting Time

The consensus is that it's best to plan your quit as carefully and in as much detail as possible. You want to avoid an impulsive quit attempt because you don't want to give in to impulses and because you don't want a quitting impulse to be followed by a smoking impulse.

Surrendering to the impulse to smoke is physically and spiritually toxic. No can do!

Mark your calendar. The day you choose to quit is a special day. On that day, you turn back the hands of time. You take back control of your life and begin to breathe freely. Your body and cells begin to rid themselves of the accumulated toxins of tobacco and renew themselves with vitality, energy, and oxygen.

One key to quitting success is to look forward to quitting day. Quitting smoking is an excellent thing to do. It's one of the greatest gifts you can give yourself.

With a view toward detailed planning, go beyond picking your quit day. Work out the specifics of how you will spend that day. Will it be a workday? Whom will you spend the day with? What ingredients of the day will make it work for you? Having a plan and knowing what to expect will make it much easier to you to deal with this often difficult (but great!) day.

Leafing the Nostalgia Behind

As a smoker in the process of quitting, you will experience all kinds of nostalgia (as well as regret) for the habit you're giving up. A key to success is not to romanticize your involvement with tobacco. Thinking back upon my own long years of experience with the leaf, I come up with the following memories. Can you relate?

Cigarettes were something to turn to in a pinch. When I was lost for a thought or action, or when I was hungry or tired (or lonely or angry), I would reach for a smoke. Just like you, I belonged to the fellowship of the smoke ring. I was a member of the near-universal order of the "gotta light?" society. Smoking was often easier than eating. I would reward myself for working out by smoking.

On the other hand, I had more tobacco traumas — true nicotine nightmares — than I can recall. Once, in Greenwich Village, I smoked two cigarettes in a row, became overwhelmed with dizziness, and passed out right on the sidewalk. Nice! I can't remember how many other times I lit up despite the harsh sensations of the acrid smoke making its way down my respiratory tract.

Humans are one of the few, if not the only, species that go out of their way to harm themselves. When was the last time you saw a leopard or an orangutan drive to a convenience store in the middle of the night for a pack of Luckies? I smoked when I was sick. I smoked first thing in the morning. Looking back on it now, I wonder how I could have been so cruel to my body — fresh from a night's sleep and BAM! — I socked it to my heart and lungs with a half-dozen good, deep inhales. Morning-afters, I would see littered ashtrays, ash heaps, and little graveyards of tamped-out butts, half-smoked cigarettes, and lipstick-smeared filters.

Have you ever gotten so desperate for a smoke that you went after one of those discards and actually lit it up? Remember how those taste? Half-smoked cigarettes have all the accumulated tar and nicotine concentrated in them so that even one hit is enough to make you dizzy and nauseated. And then there are the first cigarettes after variable periods of quitting. Those cigarettes taste particularly foul. They are repeat experiences of "How can I do this to myself?"

Another exceedingly unpleasant experience as a smoker is finding out that someone has lung cancer. It's either someone you know or a celebrity. If someone you know has lung cancer, that's especially bad. If it's a celebrity, that's bad news, too, because you think about the person's brilliant career shot down in mid-arc because of this stupid and unnecessary habit.

You don't have to be a doctor to witness the ravages of lung disease.

As you read, think, and discuss your smoking experiences with others, you will come upon many moments of regret, anger, frustration — even grief. If you know people who have become seriously ill as a result of smoking, these kinds of feelings about smoking are certainly there to be experienced.

Letting Go

Letting go can be one of the biggest and scariest steps you take in your life. You become accustomed to doing things in a certain way. You become accustomed to smoking a certain number of cigarettes at particular times of day. You quickly get used to the taste, rhythm, and feel of lighting up. There is a kind of dance, a ritual, to the act of striking a match and lighting up a cigarette. The cigarette (or pipe or other tobacco product) becomes a regular part of your life. When you think of going about your life from morning until night, you think of having a smoke. Cigarettes are the constant accompaniment to both work or school and time at home.

Change is hard. Scientists who study change have noted that even positive change — such as getting a promotion, moving to a nicer place, or getting married — can be stressful. There's something reassuring about a habit, no matter how destructive it can be in the long run. Some people develop consistent patterns of self-destructive behavior. The explanation for this behavior may lay deep in their past . . . or there may be no available explanation. At any rate, you and I and most people we know tend to hold on to old and even stale, outmoded patterns of behavior.

It's more important to drop a bad habit than to understand why you do it!

Unfortunately, the saying "once bitten, twice shy" doesn't always apply. Look at unhealthy, unhappy relationships. Why do people stay in relationships that make them so unhappy? Why do people continue to do things over and over again that aren't good for them? Why is the sky blue? (My questions aren't really intended to be rhetorical.)

Long-term patterns of self-defeating, harmful behavior are widespread and definitely aren't limited to smoking. People harm themselves with all kinds of things that feel good at the time. Break it down. Think through having a smoke from start to finish. You may be amazed at the sheer number of rationalizations and other mental strategies you pull together to get past the fact that you're doing something that's bad for you.

When you quit smoking, you're letting go of a dependency. You're letting go of an old and familiar way of doing and handling things. Instead of running away in your mind, feeling overwhelmed, or coming to the conclusion that you can't and won't handle quitting, look at the individual components of your attachment — the physical, emotional, and mental.

- **Physical:** The physical component is the least of your concerns, because you can temporarily replace the nicotine in tobacco with a nicotine replacement therapy that minimizes any withdrawal symptoms you may have. (See Chapter 9 for more on replacement therapies such as the nicotine patch and nicotine gum.)

- **Emotional:** The emotional component has been described as psychological craving. Feelings of loss, deprivation, and nostalgia (among others) come up when you cut cigarettes loose. These feelings of bereavement are to be expected. For many people, smoking is a constant companion, a "friend" who is always available, who can always be relied on to make them feel a certain way. Who wouldn't feel saddened by the loss of this "friend"?

- **Mental:** The mental component is stickier and more complex. You're attached to the idea that you need and want a smoke, particularly at certain times. This is called desire. Desire is by no means unique to smoking. You experience desire all day long. You constantly make choices about things that you prefer over other things. Some desires are mild and fleeting, such as the choice of which show to watch on television. On the other hand, you may be shopping and decide that you *have* to have something you just saw, whatever the price.

The wish for a smoke is at the extreme end of the spectrum of desire, especially if you haven't had a smoke in a while. You get to the point where it's hard not to think about smoking. The urge presses you, prods you, until you finally give in.

Or maybe you don't give in. The first step is not to give in to the desire for a smoke. See how great it feels to overcome what feels like an instinct, a reflex. Sigmund Freud once said that the aim of psychoanalysis is to replace what he called the *id* — uncontrolled, unexamined drives — with what he called the *ego*. To him, the ego was the mature, logical navigator of the mind. I'm not a great fan of Freud; in fact, I think most of what he had to say was nonsense. Nonetheless, it's always better to be in control of your drives and appetites than to have your appetites (such as for cigarettes) control you. It's better to be the captain of your choices.

Don't be a slave to nicotine. It's better to do something because you've made a decision to do it. Smoking, overeating, or whatever is something that feels like it does *you*. The more control you have over your life, the better you'll feel, and the more things will go your way. Having control over your life doesn't mean that you become a stiff, humorless prig. Having control means that you have much more input over what you do, how you feel, where you go, why you do things, and when you do them (or not) . . . including smoking.

Sure, saying that quitting is liberating is easy for me — I quit years ago. But I'm not trying to hand you a line. When you don't have to think about buying cigarettes, hiding the telltale odor, making excuses, or apologizing to yourself, you free up an enormous amount of time, money, and energy that you can spend on so many other life-promoting activities.

The time and energy you save don't have to be spent on life-promoting activities, by the way. You can use your extra time to kick back and do whatever you like. Sleep more! Think less! Indulge yourself in a way that's not going to put you in the hospital.

Enough of the sermons. Quitting smoking is a serious pursuit. It's every bit as challenging and important to your survival as giving up any other unhealthy attachment. If you've been in a toxic relationship that you've managed to break free of, then you know what I mean.

Save yourself because the future is real. If you live for today, what will you do tomorrow?

Putting Smoking to Rest

Because quitting smoking is a major life step, a major step forward, you may want to mark this milestone with a ceremony. Rituals are very useful at life's milestones — they provide emotional markers of endings and beginnings. Following are some suggestions that may appeal to your sense of ritual:

> ✔ Take your pack of cigarettes and bury it in the ground. If you're so inclined, say a prayer to promote your plan. You can also eulogize your friend who is now among the departed.

✔ Count how many cigarette ads, posters, and accessories with logos you see today. Think about this propaganda war. Who wants to be among the brainwashed?

✔ Light a match and watch it burn down. Contemplate the energy of the flame and how it can be used for good or ill. Fire can heat a home or a delicious soup . . . or light a cigarette full of poisons.

✔ Pick a workout. Experiment. Try walking or running a few blocks or pay a quick visit to the local gym to see what it looks like. Today is the day to begin a new life, and there's no better way to mark it than to engage in a health-promoting activity like exercise.

If you want to memorialize your smoking days, don't think of tobacco as a pink cloud. Just recall a few of the really uncomfortable times you've had as a smoker. Remember the first time you smoked. Remember the way it felt when you smoked while you had a cold. Remember how it felt when you smoked too much and felt like barfing. This is the world you're saying good-bye to. Good riddance!

The ritual idea is challenging because it's nice to have a sense of closure, to feel like you're really shutting the door on this lifestyle. On the other hand, you want to avoid lingering among these memories, because too many memories of smoking can trigger intense cravings. Be creative and active. The goal is to be too busy to be distracted by longing.

A breath of fresh air

You may get to a point where you feel like you're drowning in clichés — "a breath of fresh air," for example. If you take a closer look, though, the breath-of-fresh-air concept *is* completely new and fresh. There's nothing trivial about it.

The wise men of the east had a name for breath — they called it *prana*. This term means more than just "breath." It also means vital energy, life. The idea is that when you breathe, especially when you breathe intentionally, as in meditation or yoga, you fill yourself with the spirit of life and energy. The root of the word *spirit* — *inspire* — can also be traced back to the idea of breathing. A breath is an inspiration.

Controlled breathing can be a source of fuel for your mind, your heart, and your life. I'm not trying to hit you with more clichés. You can go to very deep places with focused breathing and thinking, as Chapter 10 explains.

Now consider the opposite. What is the opposite of inspiration, of controlled breathing, of taking in waves of energy, *prana*, renewal? You got it! Tobacco. Would you rather be a walking advertisement for one of the mega-tobacco companies, or would you rather be the master of a realm of oceanic power and calm? The choice is yours.

Doing Without: The Cold-Turkey Method

When you think about the phrase *cold turkey*, you may come up with a slain waterfowl lying on a dinner table surrounded by cherry tomatoes and cranberries, or the phrase may call to mind visions of some poor street addict, huddled and shivering in a corner of a miserable room, his eyes bulging as he prays for a grain of his drug. You've probably seen pictures, movies, or TV shows about addicts, junkies, unfortunate souls who have had to live through gut-wrenching deprivation of their substance of dependence. Usually, these extreme scenarios are related to heroin or other opiate-based drugs, but withdrawal rears its ugly head seen with tobacco as well.

Stopping your use of tobacco won't kill you. It will save your life. But for a while, it may feel like it's going to kill you! But I guarantee you that it won't. You can stop — millions of people already have and millions more will.

To lessen the discomfort caused by withdrawal symptoms, try the following techniques:

- Meditating
- Exercising
- Finding help from support groups
- Learning as much as you can about health so that you can fully appreciate the good you're doing for yourself
- Using a nicotine replacement therapy (see Chapter 9)

Is cold turkey — quitting smoking suddenly and completely — the right approach for you? Most approaches endorse total cessation. If you take a more gradual approach, such as having the first smoke of the day a little bit later each day, you run the risk of relapsing into old, familiar habits. The best and perhaps only way to find out whether cold turkey will work for you is to give it a try. I know many people who quit this way, without counseling or nicotine replacement therapy. They just quit. If you find that you just can't say no, that's okay, too; so many quitting tools and resources are available to you now. There's no harm in trying — but don't give up! If the cold turkey method doesn't work for you, one of the many others will.

Cutting Back Gradually

Many people quit smoking by using the gradual method, also known as the *taper method*. Wherever you're starting from — a pack of cigarettes a day, 13 pipefuls a day, two cigars a day, a tin of chew a day — is your baseline from which to cut back. No magic formula determines by what amount it's best to reduce your daily tobacco intake (although many experts argue that quitting altogether is the best approach). Cutting down a bit at a time is sensible. If you smoke a pack a day, try smoking 18 cigarettes a day for the next week, then 16 a day for the next week, and so on.

Kids' cigar bar: What do you think?

With his woolen cap pulled down tightly, his parachute pants just below and exposing his navel and raccoon rings orbiting both eyes, he looked like a junior Kurt Cobain. He sashayed to the front of the line, cutting several of us off, and demanded a triple-shot espresso and a Macanudo (a Cuban cigar).

The counter person grimaced but kept his peace, as if to say, "We get this all the time."

"Sorry, dude," the server finally said, "but I'm gonna have to card you."

"No way," his youthful customer rejoined. "I'm 11 years old. You *have* to serve me!" He sneered. "Besides," the young hooligan added, "My dad's a lawyer!"

I had to wonder how a medical ethicist would handle this situation. My imagination ran wild.

"Dear Ethicist," I wrote in my mind, "my daughter, a stridently vocal 7-year-old whose hedge fund and commodities portfolio has outdone mine for three years running, insists on having coffee with her meals. She shows no interest in diluents such as milk or even whipped cream. Last year, after a fine meal in the city honoring her great-grandfather's 95th birthday, she startled us all by insisting upon Turkish coffee for dessert. The waiter said that they had none. My daughter sighed and asked for arabica, drip ground. As if that weren't enough, she then whipped out a pack of Gitanes (filterless French cigarettes) and lit up. What should I do?"

The ethicist would probably answer like this:

"What, as a great writer once asked, is to be done? These days, you have to go out of your way to avoid a good cup of joe. Quality java joints are multiplying faster than rabbits. And so are cigar bars. (I understand that next year's Yellow Pages will be issuing a separate book just to house these listings.)

"I fear that as a society we are experiencing only the tip of the iceberg of this problem — a problem whose size and scope are so vast as to threaten to sink, *Titanic*-like, our entire ship of state.

"We have become a nation of nicotine nuts, coffee aficionados, cigar cravers, caffeine addicts, java heads. To make matters worse, our children now emulate our worst practices. Hospitals — hospitals, mind you! — routinely feature coffee franchises such as Starbucks and Green Mountain Coffee — in their food courts. Automatic brew machines interrupt corridors in practically every municipal agency across the land. The next logical step will be cigar bars in daycare centers. The toll on our health will be beyond accounting. Already, we are becoming a society of goggle-eyed, tar-spewing, mocha-breathed souls.

"The remedy? That, my friend, is between you and your conscience. You can pull over to the very next Dunkin Donuts, drop in at the nearest package store, and buy some crayons, some video games, and some smokin' children's cheroot. No one over 18 allowed!"

This downward progression may be too slow for you. I'm not your police officer; I'm your advisor! Your body and mind know best. I can tell you that you will get resistance from the "feeling" part of your brain — it will tell you, "Smoke more! Smoke more!" But the *cognitive,* or rational, side of your brain can and should win out. Hang in there. Stick with it and you'll add years to your life. Plus, there's no measure for the gains in quality of life that you'll experience as a result of quitting.

It doesn't really matter how you quit. When it comes to quitting smoking, the end justifies the means.

Varying Your Nicotine Routine

The advocates of alternatives to all-or-nothing approaches to quitting often suggest varying your nicotine routine as a preliminary step toward quitting altogether. Others insist that you need to stop smoking, period. Still others have found that a gradual reduction worked for them. The state of the art is that we don't yet know why some approaches work for certain people and don't work for others.

The idea behind varying your nicotine routine is to get you out of the habit of smoking at the same times, in the same way, and in the same amount every day. If you have your first smoke of the day the moment you step out of bed, then wait a while before lighting up. If you always smoke after meals, delay the after-dinner cigarette by half an hour or longer and see how that feels.

Mix up your smoking routine. The more you get outside the box of routine, the more likely you are to start to examine the practice of smoking itself. A great example is when you wait longer and longer each day to have your first cigarette of the day. Eventually, many smokers wonder why they're lighting up at all.

Varying your nicotine routine enables you to transform yourself from a creature of habit to . . . whatever you want to be!

Giving It Up — and Getting Something Else Instead

Something you hear quite often in the addiction treatment and recovery world — because it's true! — is that in order to give up a dependence, you need to take on a substitute. You (and I and the next guy) need something to replace whatever significant things you surrender in life. Seriously. If you lose an important person, you may find another. Or you may replace that person with a lasting sadness or grief. Similarly, habits don't leave easily. If you are to lose tobacco, gain health. Or happiness. Or spirituality. Or a sunny disposition. Or a predilection for eating celery stalks, or collecting antiques, or whatever. The point is, you are a creature of habits.

So work out two or three specific substitutes — treats — that can immediately take the place of tobacco. For example, you may decide that for every day you don't smoke, you will take $10 to buy new clothes or a personal training session at the health club.

There are thousands of substitute gratifications for tobacco.

You need a focus for your energy and drive. *For your passion.* Granted, it sounds a bit funny: passion — for tobacco? Smoking is a passionate attachment for many people. Try giving it up sometime and finding a more worthy object of your desire. See Chapter 22 if you'd like specific suggestions on how to treat yourself with all your unspent money.

Dealing with the Changes You'll Be Going Through

As you move from what has been termed the *pre-contemplator stage* to actually quitting, you go through changes in a variety of areas: physical, emotional, financial, social, and spiritual. Some of the changes are painful and involve struggle and a good deal of commitment on your part; most of the changes are positive and excellent! You have a lot to look forward to as you move from planning to quitting.

Ten terrible tobacco remedies

- Chaining yourself to an immovable object

- Getting an anti-tobacco vaccination (actually not that farfetched)

- Sprinkling foul-smelling toxins in your cigarettes

- Going to medical school

- Watching someone have a bronchoscopy

- Observing lung surgery

- Joining a cult that forbids smoking

- Tearing up a $20 bill every time you light up

- Donating the money you would have spent on cigarettes this month to your least favorite charity

- Inhaling a cigar instead of a cigarette

Separation from tobacco

In an episode of the television show *Curb Your Enthusiasm,* Larry David reacts to the portrait of a recently deceased friend by getting really captivated by the shirt the dead man is wearing. While everyone else is running around beating their breasts and tearing their hair out in grief, Larry has only one thing in mind: "How can I get my hands on that shirt? Where can I get that shirt?"

Too bad it's not that easy for the rest of us. Separation and loss are tough nuts to crack. Ask any newborn *anything* separated from its mother. Ask anyone who has recently split up with a partner or spouse. Ask anyone who's trying to stop smoking!

Scientific studies have demonstrated beyond the shadow of a doubt that newborn mammals separated prematurely from their mothers not only fail to thrive but actually die. Further along the evolutionary axis — among people — things are not that much different. Infants who do not get enough attention and coddling can wind up as highly impaired adults with defects resembling brain damage.

Those who are contemplating or are actually going through separation or divorce feel brain damaged, too. "My whole world was rocked," a 49-year-old veterinarian told me. "I just couldn't get past this for months. I guess I had gotten so used to coming home, to seeing the kids, to the routine of things, no matter how unhappy everyone was. It just plain hurts."

Another man, a diplomat at a Latin American mission, agreed that the hardest part for him was not being able to see his kids at night. "When you get used to seeing them every night, tucking them in, touching and kissing those sweet little heads — and then you can't do it anymore — it breaks you up. It broke me. I'm a broken man."

Neither man has yet recovered from his loss.

Separation and *divorce* are terms that are relevant to your relationship with tobacco. Separation from a long-standing relationship of any kind kicks off a number of deep physiological alarms that put the body and brain into DefCon4 alert. It's a stress reaction that fires away 24 hours a day.

The solution? Think outside the box. Loneliness, though not necessarily a universal condition, is widespread. As strange as it may sound, you really are *not* alone. Another solution is good health. A great solution is dignity. Being able to face yourself in the morning with pride, knowing that you treated yourself as least as well as you would a child or a dog (would you light up a cigar for a tot?) can make you feel super.

The *physical* changes take place immediately and over the mid- and long-term as well. The acute or immediate changes following the cessation of tobacco use can include depression, anxiety, restlessness, jitteriness, increased appetite, and diminished energy. Some people describe feeling wired, or simultaneously wired and tired. These are the average, expectable withdrawal symptoms that many people who stop smoking experience.

Emotional changes can include increased alertness (or increased tiredness), moodiness, irritability, and even depression and anxiety. One reason you smoke is to regulate your moods, to control how you feel. When you stop smoking, your brain's emotional circuits go on rebound activity, and you may feel the opposite of the way you feel when you light up. These emotional changes are mostly temporary. Within a matter of weeks, you will feel better, more alert, more vital, and better able to handle whatever stresses life may throw you. Chapter 14 contains a great deal of information about the emotional changes that accompany smoking and quitting smoking.

The *financial* changes that accompany quitting smoking are all for the good. You'll save at least $4 to $5 a day if you smoke a pack a day. If you enjoy those fine Cuban-type cigars (at $20 a pop) and cut them loose, you'll save even more money. You'll have the satisfaction of having more money to spend and of knowing that your decision to quit smoking put that extra money in your pocket.

Inner Strategies for Success

A recent report in the *Archives of General Psychiatry* shows that exposure to smoking cues specific brain regions that are involved in the craving sensation. Your job as a quitter is to start activating other areas of your brain by rewarding yourself with these kinds of thoughts:

- ✔ Quitting smoking takes a lot of courage and strength. You're a hero! Half of all smokers attempt to quit each year, but only a fraction succeed. Your heroism derives from your willingness to set aside the gratification of the moment and to seriously consider the future results of the choices you make now.

- ✔ As a quitter, you're a living message of hope for others. For every quitter, plenty of wannabes exist. People will look to you as an example of what will power, inner strength, and decisiveness can do.

- ✔ Deciding to cut tobacco loose is a vote for life. You've been given an infinitely complex machine — your body — that's built to last a lifetime. If you take care of it, chances are it will take care of you. Imagine the fantastic interplay of cells and blood vessels and lymphatic ducts and organs and tissues, all working and playing together like a symphony. You are the conductor of this billion-member orchestra. You're on a voyage that can take you many places; the route you take depends to a certain extent on the navigational choices you make from moment to moment. You play an active role in where you go and what you do.

- ✔ Visualize the feelings and thoughts that come up as you get over the hurdle of Quit Day 1. You're likely to find that much of the discomfort arises from *anticipation* of continued success! In other words, you can think yourself right out of the success box. If you're preoccupied with concerns and worries — such as "What will I do when I'm working on this account?" or "What will I do at the end of a meal?" or "How will I handle all the studying I need to get done?" — you're psyching yourself out.

Deal with quitting from moment to moment. No matter what happens, and no matter how squirrelly you feel, remember that saving your lungs and clearing the air are the most important things right now. If everything else you're trying to accomplish goes by the wayside during the first few days of quitting, so be it. You can catch up later. You can't catch up on irreversible damage to your health.

✔ You are a scout on a dangerous expedition to the land of health. You may not have made this trek in years. At any moment, a tiger or fire-breathing dragon may appear and try to frighten you away. Or maybe it won't. Whatever happens, you're shouldering a great and wonderful responsibility.

✔ You are in a land without tobacco. You've taken a time machine into the past — or forward to the dim future — or you're a voyager into deep space. This is a wonderful adventure. You don't need a cigarette.

Chapter 9

Using Nicotine Replacement Therapies

In This Chapter

▶ Replacing tobacco with safer nicotine

▶ Patching up your health with over-the-counter quitting aids

▶ Making use of nicotine inhalers, aerosols, and lozenges

▶ Exploring prescription-only NRT options

▶ Conquering cravings with Zyban

▶ Combining NRTs and Zyban

This chapter discusses over-the-counter and prescription medications —
powerful tools that help smokers quit. Although these nicotine replacement therapies, or NRTs, contain nicotine, they are far safer than tobacco
and in the long run will cost you a lot less than cigarettes or other tobacco
products. Effective quit-smoking programs usually involve a variety of supports and tools, including NRTs, anticraving medications such as Zyban, and
counseling.

If you decide to use an NRT, especially an over-the-counter one, make sure to
read the package inserts and instructions very carefully. If used incorrectly or
by the wrong people, these products can have serious side effects.

Clearing the Air about Nicotine Replacement Therapies

A nicotine replacement therapy (NRT) is just what it sounds like: a therapy
that does its job by replacing the nicotine you'd normally get by smoking.
When you use nicotine replacement therapy, you are preventing and treating

nicotine withdrawal symptoms — but you aren't smoking. This is one of the great benefits of nicotine replacement therapy: You minimize the discomforts of withdrawal without having to smoke. No longer are you exposed to the irritating and disease-causing additives or the acrid smoke.

Replacement therapy is not unique to tobacco addition. In fact, one of the mainstays of many types of addiction treatment is the medical substitution of a substance or medication that's less harmful than the addicting drug.

Why use a replacement therapy? If you are a regular smoker and you stopped smoking cold turkey, you would experience uncomfortable nicotine withdrawal symptoms that could prevent you from functioning at work, home, or school — and could drive you right back to the very thing you were trying to get away from. These withdrawal symptoms include

- ✔ Fatigue
- ✔ Hyperactivity
- ✔ Anxiety
- ✔ Restlessness
- ✔ Difficulty concentrating
- ✔ Depression
- ✔ Irritability
- ✔ Preoccupation with smoking
- ✔ Wandering thoughts
- ✔ Excessive eating

Nicotine replacement therapies are healthier than tobacco because you eliminate the hundreds of toxic ingredients of smoke (except nicotine). Nicotine replacement therapies also contain far less of the byproducts of the combustion of tobacco — the particularly toxic free radicals and aerosolized polyaromatic hydrocarbons that can wreak havoc on cell growth and cause cancer. Plus, the NRT delivers a measured amount of nicotine to your body at regular intervals. Knowing how much nicotine you're taking in enables you to *titrate,* or carefully monitor and eventually decrease the amount of nicotine you're getting.

A 2002 report published in the *Journal of the American Medical Association* concluded that nicotine replacement therapy has not increased the rate of quitting since it became available over the counter. However, this study has been criticized because it was not conducted using rigorous scientific methods. The change to over-the-counter availability is relatively recent, so it's too soon to draw conclusions one way or the other regarding the impact on smoking cessation.

At the present time, we don't know whether one NRT is superior to or more effective than another. Likewise, we don't know whether one NRT has more or fewer side effects than another. We do know that there is no black-and-white formula that works for everybody.

There is no magic bullet for quitting smoking. Nicotine replacement therapy helps, but you may need to change your lifestyle and employ other tools such as counseling and group support in order to stay quit. (See Chapter 13 for more on support groups.)

Comparing Success Rates

The final word is not yet in on the "best" method of quitting smoking. Generally speaking, though, the more tools and information you have, the better your chances of succeeding. Quitting smoking is challenging. Many people have to make more than one attempt before they succeed.

Don't let yourself become a victim of statistic scare. Just because many people have a hard time quitting doesn't mean that you will.

At the same time, it isn't clear whether quitting all at once — cold turkey — or gradually tapering the amount you smoke is preferable. Different smokes for different folks, I guess. There are numerous ways to work out a tapering schedule. You may find that having your first cigarette a little bit later each day works for you. If you adhere to this method, you eventually get to the point where you first light up at lunchtime or in the mid-afternoon. By that time of day, you may start to wonder why you bother lighting up at all! Other people advocate the all-or-nothing approach: out of sight, out of mind. I wish it were that easy. You may decide to cut cigarettes loose completely, but chances are you will see others smoking and think of cigarettes with longing.

That's where NRTs (and other support measures) come in. Using an NRT simplifies everything. If you use an NRT such as the patch, gum, inhaler, or spray, you can't smoke. Period. Cold turkey is your method of choice (although with a nicotine replacement therapy, you experience more of a "lukewarm turkey" because it significantly reduces your cravings and withdrawal symptoms).

Statistics from available studies show that up to one in eight people can quit smoking on their own (without medicine) for at least six months. Between a quarter and a third of smokers using either Zyban (an anticraving medication discussed later in this chapter) or an NRT can stop smoking for at least half a year. Emerging evidence also suggests that success rates increase for those who use both an NRT and Zyban. Counseling, classes, and support groups further increase your chance of succeeding.

Playing It Safe with NRTs

Because nicotine replacement therapy, whatever form it takes, utilizes actual nicotine, you need to take certain precautions:

- ✔ If you have a history of heart disease, vascular (circulation) problems, chest pain, hypertension, thyroid problems, or diabetes, discuss your quitting strategy with your doctor.

- ✔ Do not use the patch if you have significant heart problems. Your doctor can advise whether NRT is safe for you.

- ✔ If you are pregnant, check with your obstetrician before starting any kind of nicotine replacement therapy.

- ✔ Don't use nicotine replacement therapy if you that know you aren't ready to stop smoking.

Remember that nicotine is a powerful drug that acts on the brain. If you take in too much nicotine — regardless of the source — you will experience a nicotine overdose. An excess of any drug that acts on the central nervous system can cause toxic reactions.

Using a nicotine replacement therapy such as the nicotine patch or gum and smoking at the same time is a perfect example of a way to overload on nicotine. You can also overload on nicotine if you use more gum, inhaler, or spray than is recommended. If you've ever "oversmoked," you know how nicotine toxicity feels.

Nicotine overdose can trigger the following symptoms:

- ✔ Dizziness
- ✔ Nausea
- ✔ Lightheadedness
- ✔ Irregular or pounding heartbeat
- ✔ Air hunger (feeling like you can't get enough air)
- ✔ Acute anxiety

Patching Things Up with Over-the-Counter Nicotine Patches

The nicotine patch is a common NRT — you probably see television commercials for this product every day. Four brands of patches are on the market today:

- ✔ Habitrol
- ✔ Nicoderm CQ
- ✔ Nicotrol
- ✔ Prostep

All four brands are available over the counter and by prescription. Some people prefer to have their doctors prescribe the patch because they save money if their health insurance will pay for it.

The patch is known as a *transdermal* nicotine delivery system because the nicotine on its surface is slowly absorbed through your skin into your bloodstream. (Cigarettes are the fastest nicotine delivery system. Within seconds of an inhale, the nicotine in cigarette smoke hits your bloodstream and then reaches your brain. With the patch, it takes a little longer.) A constant, albeit low, amount of nicotine is delivered to your body throughout the day. When you smoke, the amount of nicotine in your body fluctuates a great deal: It shoots up when you smoke and then decreases in the time between cigarettes. Falling nicotine levels cause withdrawal symptoms. The patch prevents these withdrawal symptoms from developing by providing a steady supply of nicotine while you wear it.

You place the patch on a clean, dry area of your skin somewhere between your neck and waist. You may find that placing it somewhere on your arm is most convenient.

The patch delivers its supply of nicotine over 16 or 24 hours. The 16-hour patch is preferable for light to moderate smokers (up to a pack a day) and has the advantage of not delivering nicotine during the night. If you're a heavy smoker (more than a pack a day), the 24-hour patch may work better for you. The potential downside of the 24-hour patch is that wearers can experience nightmares, insomnia, and sleep disruptions.

The patch comes in varying strengths as well. Manufacturers commonly offer three versions: one for light smokers (half a pack a day or less), one for moderate smokers (up to a pack a day), and one for heavy smokers (more than a pack a day). Generally speaking, you start with the patch that's right for you and wear it daily for six weeks. Then you drop to the next lowest strength for the following two weeks and then to the lowest strength for the final two weeks. Read the manufacturer's instructions for the specific product you choose to make sure that you use the product correctly and safely.

The recommended duration of use is up to three to five months, according to the Food and Drug Administration (FDA). Some people have used the patch successfully over a shorter period, such as six to eight weeks. Every four weeks, depending on your comfort level, you may taper your nicotine dose by using a lower-dose patch.

Be sure to consult with your doctor before using the patch if any of the following conditions apply:

- ✔ You have high blood pressure that's not controlled with medication.
- ✔ You are taking medication for depression.
- ✔ You are taking medication for asthma.
- ✔ You have heart disease.
- ✔ You have palpitations or some other form of irregular heartbeat.
- ✔ You have had a heart attack.
- ✔ You are pregnant.

Do not smoke or use any other tobacco product while using the patch. The nicotine from cigarettes or other tobacco products, together with the nicotine from the patch, results in dangerously high blood levels of the stuff. Too much nicotine can cause palpitations, blood pressure changes, anxiety, and other serious problems.

You may be wondering whether the patch has any side effects. *Any* medication can have side effects. The main side effects to watch out for with the patch are dizziness, rapid heartbeat or palpitations, insomnia, nausea, vomiting, headaches, and skin irritation. If you develop any of these symptoms, contact your doctor right away.

Some people find that skin irritation and itching diminish if they switch to a different brand of patch. Sleep disruption can be treated by switching from the 24-hour patch to the 16-hour patch. Using a lower-strength patch or a different type of nicotine replacement therapy altogether may diminish or eliminate side effects as well.

The patch is a just a tool. You still have to practice right thinking and use every other lifestyle strategy you have to beat smoking.

Keep these points in mind when using the patch:

- ✔ You can bathe or swim while wearing the patch.
- ✔ Never use more than one patch simultaneously.
- ✔ Don't let kids or animals touch or lick the patch.
- ✔ If the patch you're wearing falls off, put on a new one.

> ✔ Try to put on the day's patch at the same time each day in order to regularize your nicotine replacement therapy.
>
> ✔ Do not smoke or chew tobacco while using the patch.

Chewing Cravings Away with Nicotine Gum

Nicotine gum is a popular nicotine replacement therapy. Available over the counter, it is easy to use and provides regular, measured amounts of nicotine to the bloodstream. The gum is loaded with nicotine that's released slowly yet absorbed rapidly by the blood-rich mucous membranes of the mouth. As with the patch, the idea is to taper the amount of gum you chew over time until you no longer need it.

Nicotine gum (nicotine polacrilex) comes in 2 mg and 4 mg strengths. The manufacturer suggests that heavier smokers (25 or more cigarettes a day) and those who smoke first thing in the morning use the 4 mg pieces. If you smoke fewer than 25 cigarettes a day, use the 2 mg strength.

The original gum has a peppery flavor. (It now comes in orange flavor as well.) When the peppery taste becomes prominent, park the gum between your cheek and gums for a few minutes. When the peppery sensation is gone, you can begin chewing again. At that point, most or all of the nicotine has leached out of the gum, and you can discard the piece.

The manufacturer suggests that the gum squares be used as follows — see the package insert for details:

> ✔ Stop smoking before beginning to use nicotine gum.
>
> ✔ Don't have any food or drinks, especially acidic beverages like coffee, tea, juice, and soda, for at least 15 minutes before chewing, during chewing, and about 15 minutes after chewing. Some foods and beverages can absorb the nicotine from the gum and prevent it from getting into your system.
>
> ✔ Don't chew the gum the same way you would chew Bazooka or Juicy Fruit. The idea is to chew it intermittently, letting the wad rest between your cheek and gums between chews. Doing so permits the nicotine in the gum to diffuse into the capillaries of your cheek and from there into your bloodstream.

✔ Most people need up to 15 pieces a day to abate nicotine withdrawal symptoms. If you feel extra-strong cravings, you can chew an extra piece. Don't have more than 20 pieces in a 24-hour period.

✔ Try to chew approximately the same amount of gum each day for one month. After a month, start to lower the number of pieces you chew each day by one piece a day. After approximately three months, you can stop using the gum altogether.

✔ Keep in mind that you're chewing to avoid or reduce nicotine withdrawal. If you aren't experiencing withdrawal symptoms, you don't need to chew at that moment.

The upside of nicotine gum is that you have more control over the amount of nicotine you take in. You can chew it on a regular schedule or chew it only when you feel you need it. Typically, one or two pieces every hour or two does the trick.

Because the gum contains nicotine, a drug, it has potential side effects and downsides as well, including the following:

✔ Sore throat

✔ Nausea

✔ Unpleasant taste

✔ Tired or aching jaw

Note that some users get quite attached to nicotine gum — and I don't mean that it gets stuck to the soles of their shoes! Some successful quitters have kept on using the gum for a year or more after quitting. Most healthcare providers recommend a maximum period of use of six months.

Keep nicotine gum out of the reach of children!

Giving Nicotine Lozenges a Try

Nicotine lozenges are now available in the United States and have been available for some time in Great Britain. They work like nicotine gum does, delivering discrete amounts of nicotine as you consume them. The lozenges come in 2 mg and 4 mg strengths. One way to determine the right dosage for you is to consider the length of time between when you wake and when you have your first cigarette of the day. If you smoke immediately upon rising, it suggests that you need to get your blood level of nicotine right back up after a night's sleep (a night's worth of withdrawal from nicotine). If your smoking is more episodic and less predictable, you may be able to use a lower dose.

Evaluating other OTC options

- ✔ **One Step at a Time filters** are plastic cigarette holders that have a variable filtration system. The box contains four filters with different filtering powers. You start by using the filter that eliminates 25 percent of the nicotine and gradually work your way up to the one that removes 90 percent.

- ✔ **LifeSign** is a PDA-sized computer. You enter information about your smoking patterns and lifestyle, and LifeSign provides a customized withdrawal program based on the data you entered.

- ✔ **Nicotine lollipops,** which contain aspirin and a sweetener, have been manufactured by a number of pharmacies. Because of concern about accidental ingestion by children, the FDA has warned several pharmacies to stop manufacturing them.

If you use nicotine lozenges, be sure to keep them out of reach of children.

You use the lozenges for up to 12 weeks, on a tapering schedule. Although no set schedule is written in stone, the recommended frequency is one lozenge every one to two hours for the first six weeks, one every two to four hours for the next three weeks, and one every four to eight hours for the final three weeks. How frequently you use the lozenges will depend on your comfort level — just don't exceed the recommended maximum. You may find that you can go without cigarettes before 12 weeks have passed, so you may decide to stop using the lozenges sooner. Check the package for the recommended maximum daily dose.

As with nicotine gum, allow the lozenge to do its job. Keep it in your mouth for at least 20 minutes. Don't chew or swallow it. The lozenge works best when you avoid drinking or eating immediately before and after use.

Observe the following guidelines when using nicotine lozenges:

- ✔ Don't eat or drink for at least 15 minutes before using the lozenge. Foods and beverages tend to dilute or interfere with the absorption of the nicotine.

- ✔ Don't smoke when using the lozenges. If you do, you run a real risk of consuming toxic levels of nicotine.

Ariva is a tobacco-loaded lozenge that's manufactured not as a smoking cessation aid but as a source of tobacco for smokers who are in smoke-free environments. There is concern that children can mistake these lozenges for candy, so use caution if you bring this product into a home where children are present.

Talking It Out with Your Doc: Prescription-Only Options

Checking in with your doctor about your decision to quit smoking and how you plan to do it is always a good idea. He or she may have suggestions or advice based on your health status. Your doctor is the best authority on how much exercise and dietary change you can healthfully tolerate as you proceed with your attempt to kick the cigarette habit. Your doctor can also offer valuable input on the use and choice of a nicotine replacement therapy (especially because some therapies require a doctor's prescription) and can make you aware of potential interactions between nicotine, Zyban, and other medications you may be taking.

Considering nicotine inhalers

Like other kinds of inhalers, such as those used to treat asthma, a nicotine inhaler has a mouthpiece that pumps single aerosols of nicotine to the lining of the mouth. The mucous membrane of the mouth and throat is loaded with capillaries and easily absorbs medication. The inhaler can be used up to 16 times a day initially, but after two to three months, use should be tapered. It is not recommended that you use the inhaler for more than six months.

Comparisons of the inhaler and the patch show them to be about equally effective in promoting smoking cessation. However, one of the psychological advantages of the inhaler is that it approximates the feel of a cigarette — it's an object that you pick up and place between your lips. Not only do you get nicotine, but you simulate to a certain extent the action of picking up a smoke.

Using nicotine nasal spray

Nicotine nasal spray is a handy, highly accessible nicotine delivery system. Once it encounters the delicate mucous membranes of the nose, it is absorbed very rapidly. If you use it as intended, it will enable you to gradually reduce your daily nicotine intake without developing uncomfortable nicotine withdrawal symptoms. Spray users report satisfaction with this product because it provides an almost instantaneous fix for cravings and other manifestations of nicotine withdrawal.

Each squirt contains 1 mg of nicotine — the amount of nicotine you may get from one low-tar cigarette. The recommended dosage is between 8 and 40 squirts a day. You use the spray for about three months; two months after starting, reduce the dosage on a daily decremental schedule. Refer to the package insert for manufacturer's details on tapering the dose.

Because the device is so easy to use, some people begin to develop a nicotine nasal spray habit. The FDA suggests that it be prescribed for three months and not longer than six months. Side effects can include sore throat, coughing, sneezing, nasal congestion, tearing eyes, and irritation of the nose. If you have nasal or respiratory problems such as nasal polyps, sinusitis, allergies, or asthma, consult with your doctor about using a different nicotine delivery system.

Trying out anticraving medication (Zyban)

Zyban, also called Wellbutrin or buproprion, is an atypical antidepressant that's been used to treat depression and anxiety for a number of years. When used to treat these mood disorders, it usually takes two to four weeks to begin working. It is termed *atypical* because, unlike many other antidepressants, it does not seem to act on brain levels of serotonin. Instead, it may boost brain levels of dopamine. Dopamine, a neurotransmitter, has been implicated in the brain's reward system. It is, broadly speaking, a feel-good molecule. Scientists believe that euphoria, such as that following a good workout or the use of certain drugs, is related to increased activity of dopamine in the brain.

Some scientists believe that brain dopamine is involved in nicotine dependence. Zyban helps reduce tobacco cravings, perhaps by increasing dopamine in the reward circuits of the brain, thus bypassing the role of nicotine.

Although some people have concerns about taking an antidepressant to reduce or prevent cigarette cravings, the fact is that Zyban has been shown to have a fairly specific effect on nicotine cravings. Even if you aren't depressed, Zyban can curb your appetite for cigarettes. People who have manic depression (bipolar disorder) need to discuss Zyban with their psychiatrist before using it. Zyban and other antidepressant-type medications can overly "activate" people who have bipolar disorder.

Zyban comes in 75, 100, and 150 mg strengths. The usual practice is to begin with 100 mg twice a day and build up to a dose somewhere between 150 and 400 mg a day. Zyban is not nicotine, so its beneficial effect in countering tobacco addiction works by an alternate mechanism. Although most people do not experience side effects from this medication, some may notice headache, jitteriness, or insomnia. Zyban is better taken in the daytime, before bedtime, to avoid the possibility of disrupting sleep. The medication can be taken up to six months or longer — ask your doctor. Zyban is not habit forming and can be stopped at any point without withdrawal.

LaDonna's story

As a direct result of nonstop tobacco use — LaDonna being an extreme case, statistically speaking — a series of spiraling downfalls came her way. Her fingertips became so mottled with tar, with the black, unwashable stuff of polyaromatic hydrocarbons, that people in restaurants actually shied away from her, moving to the next counter stool or table. Unconsciously, perhaps, others would hesitate or even decline her offer to pass a dish or a piece of cutlery. So LaDonna became increasingly isolated by her habit. Once in graduate school, she returned to her apartment and noticed what felt like a cinder in her eye. She worked at the eye, poking her nicotine-blackened finger into the orb, which within seconds reacted angrily, growing red, irritated, and crisscrossed with bulging capillaries and watering copiously. The emergency room doctor sternly advised her to refrain from irritating her

eye like that in the future. After a hasty consultation with the hospital pharmacist, the doctor further advised her about various drops, emollients, and industrial-grade diluents that she could purchase to remove or at least bleach the telltale stains on her fingers.

Another time, LaDonna was dining with Nelson and his parents. Nelson, an accounting student whom she'd met on the steps of the student union, had invited her to meet his family. Little did she know that Nelson's quirky 12-year-old niece Caitlin would be there as well. Caitlin was on the brink of jamming yet another drumstick into her mouth when she noticed with ill-concealed horror the tobacco-stained stubs that were LaDonna's ruined fingertips. Caitlin gasped, choked, and flung the turkey from her as though it were a red hot poker. A terrible melee ensued. All because of cigarettes!

Consult with your doctor if you're taking any additional medication, because Zyban has potential interactions with some drugs. Overall, though, it's quite safe.

Combining Quitting Aids

Combining quitting aids is the cutting edge of "quit technology." In the not-too-distant past, people relied on self-discipline, self-exhortation, pep talks, scare tactics, and nagging from their family and friends. Now you have all these tools at your disposal, *plus* nicotine replacement therapies like the patch and nicotine gum, *plus* Zyban for cravings if your doctor thinks it's a good idea for you to take this medication. I've been saying all along that the more you do to quit smoking, the better. Combining quitting aids is where it's at. If you use a nicotine replacement therapy, you provide yourself with a gradual taper of nicotine — eliminating nicotine withdrawal — and hopefully you get a psychological boost from classes or support groups that you attend as well.

As our ability to treat smoking addiction with increasingly sophisticated tools evolves, it becomes clear that more people are succeeding by using combinations of NRTs. For example, you may find that a combination of the patch with Zyban works much better, reducing cravings and other nicotine withdrawal symptoms, than either one alone. Because physicians prescribe both of these NRTs, you need to get your doctor's input on your use of them.

Some very heavy smokers report that they're getting more mileage out of a combination of the 24-hour patch and the occasional (up to four pieces a day) piece of nicotine gum.

Chapter 10

Trying Alternative Methods for Quitting Smoking

. . . .

In This Chapter

▶ Finding fellow travelers on the quit-smoking path

▶ Going deep: meditation and health

▶ Exercising without tears

▶ Trying out methods like acupuncture and hypnosis

▶ Seeing quitting smoking as a spiritual leap forward

. . . .

Alternative methods to quitting smoking can complement more traditional methods, such as quitting cold turkey and using nicotine replacement therapies, and can augment each other as well. You want to find methods that boost each other's effectiveness, giving you maximum quitting power. For example, you can attend support groups (see Chapter 13), use the nicotine patch (see Chapter 9), *and* learn to meditate, which this chapter explains.

Some of the methods described in this chapter are not covered by most health insurance plans. Check with your insurer to find out what your particular plan does and doesn't cover.

Getting By with a Little Help from Your Friends: Support Groups

Don't talk about support groups too much. Attend them. My advice is to attend several. Ask around and shop around to find the group(s) in which you feel comfortable.

Support groups, technically speaking, are no-fee meetings in which like-minded people gather to hear about each other's experiences. Support groups do just that: provide emotional and cognitive support for your effort to quit smoking. If you've ever attended a group for therapy, a religious service, or even a town meeting, you know how much strength there can be in numbers. Groups of people focused on the same goal can be an incredibly powerful tool for change.

Nicotine Anonymous is the prototypical support group for smokers and ex-smokers. Like other 12 Step programs, Nicotine Anonymous is free and asks participants to surrender their will to a higher power and to rely on the accumulated wisdom of those who have been down this path before and have succeeded. You attend Nicotine Anonymous meetings and listen to other people describe their quitting efforts. You learn how other people have quit successfully. You may get a chance to speak about your own experiences with tobacco; most people who do so find it to be an emotionally rewarding experience. Check out Nicotine Anonymous's Web site, meeting_list@ nicotine-anonymous.org, which has an interactive "find your nearest meeting" feature.

Many other kinds of classes, workshops, and seminars focus on quitting smoking. Many of them charge fees. (Typically, a plate is passed around at the meeting. The funds collected are used to pay for refreshments, printing, and other costs of running meetings.)

Don't immediately dismiss a group or seminar that charges a fee. Think about the expense of tobacco. If you succeed at quitting, in the not too long run you will easily have realized your investment in the class many times over. Plus, investing some money in a healthy future is perfectly okay. If a quit-smoking workshop or seminar is right for you, go for it, even if you have to pay to attend.

How do you know whether a particular workshop is right for you? Talk to the people attending it. Find out if you can contact someone who has been through the program to learn what that person's particular experience has been like. Talk to the workshop leader, and find out about his or her experience. Be skeptical about success numbers, too. In my opinion, the feel of a group and the group leader's commitment to the spirit of the project are far more important than any marketing ploys the group may have.

You may be a private person who is loath to take that definitive step and put yourself out there. What is a cakewalk for someone else may be a harrowing experience for you. On the other hand, becoming more socially involved could be just the thing you need at this point in your life. You're taking a leap. You're cutting loose a very bad connection and reestablishing yourself on a firm footing with air (no laughing matter!), your body, and hopefully the rest of the world.

Most of the people seated around you in a support group feel as nervous and visible as you do.

Some of the people attending a quit-smoking support group may have already quit smoking. These people will be useful to you in your efforts to learn as much as possible about this brave new world of dignity and self-respect. That's right, dignity and self-respect. When you say good-bye to cigarettes, you say good-bye to a nasty habit that has cost you not only thousands of dollars, but also inestimable amounts of self-respect. Now you can look yourself in the mirror, look others in the eye, and, no matter what else is going on in your life, know that you're promoting your best interests (at least some of them).

When you go to a meeting, you may be fortunate enough to encounter one or more people who offer to be your sponsor or buddy. Depending on the arrangements at the meeting, you may have the opportunity to ask someone if he's willing to act as your mentor during your first few weeks of quitting. This could mean emergency phone calls in the middle of the night, but more often it just means that you have the comforting presence of a friend's phone number in hand.

Trying Hypnosis to Get Yourself to Stop

You may have thought about trying hypnosis in your effort to rid yourself of smoking. The temptation to look for something — a pill, a treatment, a hypnotic suggestion — that will forever rid you of the scourge of cigarettes is understandable. Most people look longingly at the prospect of a quick fix, whether it relates to getting rid of a toxic relationship, money troubles, or health problems. The idea that a magic bullet or elixir can wipe out the problem that's been hounding you all these years is tempting indeed. So it's easy to understand the appeal of hypnosis.

There is no trance as deep as that of nicotine addiction.

You may know someone who has tried hypnosis and even reported some success with it. Stranger things have happened! Even stranger is that when you delve into the history of hypnosis, it becomes less and less clear what hypnosis is and does. The practice of hypnosis has changed radically over the short time since it was introduced by Franz Mesmer, and scientists have very little understanding of or consensus on what happens during and after a person goes into the hypnotic trance.

Without going too far out on a limb, I'll say that it isn't always necessary to understand how or why something works in order for it *to* work. But if you talk to people who have been hypnotized, you don't get anything even approaching agreement about what their experience was like, what their state of mind was during the trance, and how far they were willing to go with the hypnotist's suggestions.

Nonetheless, many people try hypnosis in their effort to quit smoking. Some of them have succeeded. We will never know whether the hypnosis was the basis of their success. Perhaps you don't need to know. If you use counseling, the nicotine patch, and Zyban (see Chapter 9 for information about the latter two quitting methods), you'll never know which, if any, of these single tools made the difference. The important point is that you quit, and that you stack the odds in your favor as you approach and then reach that quit date.

Medical studies don't strongly support that hypnosis provides a specific benefit in quitting smoking. Still, if you're willing to spend a little time each day focusing your attention inward and focusing your energy on this monumentally important goal, consider *self*-hypnosis. Self-hypnosis is a form of meditation, and yet another way to approach yourself in a state of quiet and calm and reach a deeper and hopefully lasting understanding.

Contemplating Meditation or Self-Hypnosis

Imagine having a wonderful, beautiful place where you can go almost anytime you want — a retreat that shields you from the cares of the world, a harbor that knows no television, no newspaper headlines, no stress. Imagine being able to get there almost instantaneously, at will. With meditation, this place really exists . . . in your mind. Meditation is powerful stuff!

Self-hypnosis and meditation have so much in common that, to keep it simple, I'm going to refer to both practices as meditation.

Meditation is a passport to serenity. "How trite," you're probably saying. I understand. I'm not one of those people who spend their lives contemplating how to live, either. I'm caught up way too much in action, movement, and the frenzied dance of feelings and thoughts. Still, I know that meditation is a key part of living in this world.

I need to qualify the statement. What exactly *is* meditation?

At the risk of sounding vague and overinclusive, I'll say that meditation can be almost anything. There are many types of meditation, practically as many types as there are personalities walking this planet. Meditation can be your work. Meditation can be watching your child play or walking your dog. You can be consumed in tending your garden. For your needs — quitting smoking — the kind of mediation that can be done anywhere is the most suitable.

There is no single formula for meditation — or for quitting smoking. Try different approaches and use the one(s) that works best for you.

Formal meditation, as in yoga (discussed later in this chapter), is another level that complements the mindfulness of "being here now." If you're really living in the moment, you may not need much in the way of formal meditation training. Nonetheless, if you pursue training in one or more of the many schools of yoga and meditation, you'll find yourself on an incredible journey that requires time, patience, dedication, and skill. The formal mind and body techniques are best learned from experienced teachers in these disciplines.

Think — meditate — about the idea of "need." What do you need? Do you really need a cigarette? Do you need another pair of shoes? (Maybe you do!) Do you need a Maserati? As you get increasingly in touch with your feelings and with yourself, you may come to a whole new understanding of what you *really* need.

As a smoker, you already know how to hypnotize yourself. In fact, you already *have* hypnotized yourself. Each time you light up, you go into a trance. You are, in a manner of speaking, acting out a posthypnotic suggestion: *You will light up a cigarette even though everything in the world tells you that it's a bad idea.* You go into a trancelike state, where you turn off your regular concerns about your body, your health, and your future.

When you inhale, you achieve a state of mind that's relaxing and alerting at the same time. This is the sought-after quality of nicotine. The good news is that you can reach the identical state of mind by self-hypnosis or meditation. I don't promise that you'll achieve it immediately, but, as with any kind of exercise, the more patient you are, the better you'll get at it.

Learning to appreciate and control your breathing

Breath is the vital current of life. You've probably heard this before — so often that it sounds like a cliché. "Don't smoke" is a cliché, too. But facts of life that you ordinarily take for granted — such as your body, your breath, and your heartbeat — can become powerful allies or irritating reminders of mortality and limitation.

A great place to start with breathing is to appreciate it simply and directly. Although breathing is a miracle of the body's construction when it works well — which it usually does when you don't tamper with it — it can wreak havoc when it goes awry. If you've ever had a bout of the flu or, worse still, pneumonia, you know what I'm talking about. A persistent cough, a problem with the air supply to your body and brain, is no laughing matter. (See your doctor if you have a persistent cough!)

Meditation involves breath control, relaxation, and a state of "floating." While you meditate, the goal is to be aware of your body but not of your surroundings. You are aware of your body and breathing, and then slowly but surely you become unaware of your body and breathing. A great deal of evidence suggests that breath control, mind control, and the serenity that they lead to result, in turn, in healthful changes in your cardiovascular and immune systems.

Breath control is the opposite of smoking. With the breath control that you achieve through meditation, you take back control over your body.

Letting go: How to meditate

Meditation is an invitation to your own party. Take five minutes in the morning and five minutes before going to bed to meditate, to hypnotize away an eternity of smoking. You may want to start meditating two weeks before Quit Day 1, because when your mind and energy are exactly where you want them, the fun really starts. You can take it (your mind, that is) pretty much where you want it to go.

When you first start meditating, it may seem like work. The trick is to find out how to turn it into play. Find out how to make quitting smoking into play!

You may find it helpful to have a small sanctuary or retreat of sorts. A small area in your home or apartment (even the basement or attic) will do just fine. Just set aside a quiet place where you will be undisturbed for 10 to 15 minutes. Depending on your sense of drama, you can dress this meditation ritual up as little or as much as you like. Incense or colorful fabrics heighten the mood, but they certainly aren't required.

You may also find it helpful before you sit down to "ritualize" the meditation by lighting a candle, placing an object that means a lot to you nearby (such as a treasured photo), turning your chair to the east, lighting some incense, reciting a simple phrase such as "Now I am entering the kingdom of myself," or imagining a silvery curtain being drawn about your space that is impervious to sound and sight.

Sit in a comfortable chair, hands placed palms upward either on armrests or on your legs. Close your eyes. Concentrate on your breathing. Let all your thoughts become your breathing. The air that you're taking in is the vital energy that fuels your life. Feel it charging your life, your cells, with vitality and good feeling. As you exhale, feel all the tiredness and stress leave you, getting washed out of you into the air.

Let your abdomen (your diaphragm) breathe, not your chest. Inhale for a count of four, hold for a count of four, slowly exhale for a count of four, and then hold for a count of four again. Repeat the cycle. Controlling your breathing is one of the keys to meditation.

Another key to meditation is freedom from internal distraction. You achieve mind*ful*ness by achieving mind*less*ness. Still in your chair — hopefully still breathing — notice the sensations in your toes. Curl them. Notice how they feel when you uncurl them. Systematically tense and then relax each set of muscles on each side of your body, working up from your toes and ending at the top of your scalp. Once you've gone through this exercise successfully, your breathing will be on autopilot, your body will be very relaxed, and your mind will be very empty yet very alert — the way it is after a good hit of nicotine!

When you get really proficient at meditation, you may become able to turn off all thoughts and feelings at will, even the thought, "I'm not thinking anything!" Once you've cleared your mental field, you can go almost anywhere you want.

When it comes to meditation, practice makes perfect. Within a week, you can reach levels within that are quite inspiring.

You can use this superb point of focused mindfulness to visualize yourself and your world in exquisite detail, to see how you want it all to be once you quit smoking. Doing so will reinforce your determination to quit. Some people find that an emotionally charged decision, accompanied by repeated visualizations (of clear breathing and health), help bring about the desired result. This kind of mental self-discipline also results in increased powers of observation of yourself and others. You will sleep better, feel better, and probably have more interesting dreams, too.

You can get to very deep levels with meditation. The deeper you go, the greater its healthful effects. These practices have been shown to have powerful and lasting effects on sleep, mood, and overall health. So there's good reason to believe that achieving a state of mental and physical unity by means of mindfulness will move you toward and then beyond your goal of quitting smoking.

Meditation and breath control is not a touchy-feely thing. Although it requires sitting still, it is physically challenging and even heroic.

Because the practice of meditation is so varied, can be done effectively in so many different ways, and has such an interesting and complex past, I urge you to expand on the overview provided here if the practice interests you. Hundreds of terrific books, tapes, and Web sites are devoted to the subject. For example, see *Meditation For Dummies,* by Stephan Bodian (Wiley Publishing).

Exorcising Nicotine with Exercise

Believe it or not, physical exercise is a form of meditation. It is a way of boosting your well-being in a dependable, consistent, and healthy fashion. Vigorous exercise, the kind that gets your pulse pounding and your body sweating, is good for you (unless you have a medical condition that limits the amount and/or kind of exercise you can tolerate — check with your doctor first!). Exercise feels good. The right kinds of exercise kick off *endorphins* in the brain, which are the body's feel-good molecules.

Quitting smoking can be a double blessing for you. Not only are you getting rid of a life-depriving and financially costly habit, but you're also launching yourself in the direction of a number of awesome new possibilities. Which of the following activities have you dreamed of doing but couldn't because of limited stamina or lung power?

- ✔ Jogging
- ✔ Running a marathon
- ✔ Climbing a mountain
- ✔ Whitewater rafting
- ✔ Riding a bike
- ✔ Sailing
- ✔ Playing tennis
- ✔ Joining a baseball or softball team

You may be one of those fortunate people who are able to work out despite the fact that they smoke. But don't let this fool you into thinking that you can have it all. Once you quit smoking, your capacity to exercise and the enjoyment you get from it will increase exponentially.

Find a form of fitness that doesn't make you grit your teeth. Find a kind of exercise that actually becomes fun after you do it a few times. I remember the first few times I went running. I didn't look forward to the experience. As I trudged along, I looked askance at the other runners. Why were all these people doing this? What were they trying to prove? The fourth time I went out — yes, I had to force myself the first three times, propelling myself forward on the strength of friends' advice — I made it over the proverbial wall. I felt great. An oceanic feeling swept over me, and I knew once and for all why all these people were jogging and power walking. It is a healthy way to achieve focused well-being. You're sure to find the kind of exercise that achieves this state of being for you if you try hard enough.

Trying Acupuncture

Acupuncture, a 2,000-year-old system of Chinese medicine, is based on a theory that the body's energy flows in meridians. *Meridians* are considered to be the natural channels through which the body's energy flows. Acupuncturists treat a variety of disorders by accurately placing needles to stimulate these critical energy points. The treatments often need to be done regularly and can be costly because health insurance usually doesn't cover them.

One hospital center in the Bronx has a large addiction treatment clinic that uses *auricular* (ear) acupuncture as a mainstay of treatment for severely drug-dependent individuals. These patients have been smoking tobacco and marijuana and using cocaine and heroin as well. I met a number of these patients who swear that the acupuncture treatments are keeping them off the drugs. But it's difficult to know what to make of the experience of even hundreds of people unless the results are submitted to scientific study. (How would the patients do with sham acupuncture procedures done with incorrect needle placement, for example?) This work still needs to be done.

Nonetheless, alternative approaches such as acupuncture show promise and can complement nicotine replacement therapy (see Chapter 9), counseling, and sheer determination to quit. You can think of acupuncture as a kind of fast-food yoga: You get the well-being boost without having to do the work.

If you decide to try acupuncture, make sure that the practitioner is certified. If possible, talk to his or her other patients to determine whether they have had a good therapeutic experience.

Experimenting with Vitamins, Herbs, and Supplements

There's so much to say and learn about vitamins, herbs, and other supplements. Tread cautiously. If you choose to explore these waters, you can sink rapidly and deeply. Nutritional supplements can be costly as well as unnecessary — not a winning combination. Not to mention that too much of the wrong vitamin or supplement can also damage your health.

My acupuncture story

For all you skeptics out there: I was a skeptic, too. Still am, for the most part. But I tried acupuncture, and it actually did something for me. Here's my story.

It was the end of a stressful day at the office. I was working in Midtown Manhattan in an extremely busy practice — a pressure cooker, to be precise. Between the massive amounts of paperwork and the nonstop demands of patients, I found myself in a rarefied, if not stupefied, place by the end of the workday: tired, frazzled, and burned out. Chances are you've been there yourself.

In came one of my colleagues, who had just completed training in *auriculotherapy* — acupuncture of several of the key points of the ear. My colleague was eager to try out her new-found skill on me. I was eager to get through my mountain of paperwork and get home, so I heaved a sigh and said something like, "Okay, let's get on with it." She pulled out a little tray of not so little needles, sterilized them with alcohol wipes, and methodically inserted them at

specific points in the cartilage of my right ear while I remained seated at my desk. The process is slightly uncomfortable, but not terribly so. She stood back, admiring her work. I sat there as skeptical as ever. She departed (another guinea pig was waiting down the corridor), asking me to let her know how I felt a little later. I returned to the daunting pile of documents, discharge summaries, and insurance forms that lay before me.

Three or four minutes later, everything seemed to grind to a halt. All the noise in my head — the concerns about finishing the day's work, the replays of everything I had heard that day — were gone. In their place was a wonderful silence. Everything was quiet and peaceful. I felt light, buoyant, at my center. The newspaper I was about to read didn't seem that important anymore.

So, for my money, acupuncture did something for me. One person's experience does not a scientific statement make, however.

A normal diet supplies adequate amounts of vitamins and minerals. Supplements are intended to boost the amounts that you get from food.

There is a great deal of interest in the use of antioxidant vitamins like A, C, and E. They're called antioxidants because they work as cleanup molecules, attaching themselves to highly charged and potentially cancer-causing free radicals such as those that are found in cigarette smoke and food additives like nitrites. Many people believe that if they load up on these vitamins, they will dramatically reduce their chances of environmentally induced disease (disease caused by pollutants in air, food, and water). Antioxidants may prevent a number of diseases. Research is still being done.

You need to be aware that nutritional supplements present a spectrum of health risk. Certain vitamins, such as A and E, are *lipophilic* — that is, they dissolve in the fatty tissues of the body. Once you take them, they tend to stay in the body for some time. If you take too much, you can overdose. Overdoses of vitamins A and E can cause liver and other problems. Your best bet is to stick with the guidelines printed on the supplement bottle's label and to check with your doctor before taking any supplement.

Herbal supplements are beyond the scope of traditional Western *(allopathic)* medicine. You may know people who swear by the results they've obtained with store-bought herbs. Some people go to herbal doctors, homeopaths, or other nontraditional healthcare practitioners, and some of them not only live to tell about it but actually thrive. A key to recovery, to healing, is your belief in the practice and in the power of the person delivering the treatment. People have been healing each other since civilization began. (The juju man and the shaman arrived before the diagnostic radiologists got here!)

Exercise judgment as you shop around for quit-smoking tools. Nothing beats the dynamic duo of determination and common sense.

Getting in Touch Spiritually

How do you define *spiritual?* The word can have different shades of meaning, depending on whom you talk to.

Very often, the term *religious* is used to describe not only the inner commitment to a system of faith but also a set of practices that includes attendance at a church, synagogue, or some other recognized house of worship. *Spiritual* can refer to a system of beliefs that exists independent of an external faith. You may be a very spiritual person even if you aren't a card-carrying member of any of the world's major religions.

Spirituality can be your way of looking at and understanding things — your ability to appreciate the beauty and harmony inherent in things. You may even appreciate the chaos and fury at the heart of nature and find the flame of spirit abiding within it as well. My point is that spirituality covers a vast territory, and it can start with your decision to quit smoking. Really!

Quitting smoking is not a casual decision. It is a decision to align your judgment, your body, and "the forces of the universe" in your favor. I'm not here to tell you that you have control over most of the forces within and around you. Still, taking as much control as you can makes a lot of sense. The analogies that come to mind are numerous. For example, imagine that you're the captain of a seaworthy ship. Given the choice, would you prefer to have 30 percent, 50 percent, or 65 percent control over the rudder, the course, and the upkeep of the equipment? You would probably maximize your chance of a good passage!

The same idea applies to the body and the spirit. Why would you want to send messages to yourself that smoking doesn't matter? By analogy, then, it doesn't matter whether you get enough sleep, whether you have enough money in your pocket, or whether you get struck down by the next passing car. Of course, these are the thoughts of a depressed person. They could also be the thoughts of a person in denial. The "it doesn't matter" thoughts — rationalizations — can be symptoms of addiction. When you're addicted to tobacco (or to anything else, for that matter), you go in and out of different states of mind that don't recognize each other. These alternate states of mind are mutually exclusive. The smoking state of mind lobbies strongly for itself. Your nonsmoking state of mind would like to be rid of the smoking state of mind. Your healthy side, if you prefer to think of yourself this way, experiences the nagging urge to smoke as an intrusive and unwelcome presence — otherwise, you wouldn't be reading this book.

Get as much out of quitting smoking as you possibly can. A great way to take your mind off the seriousness of the task is to focus on other goals that you will achieve at the same time. Not only are you quitting, but you are also reaching for the person you were when you came into the world. The next time you hold a baby, remember that you were once one, too. The innocence and potential of health are built into the cells of your body and being. Your mission, should you choose to accept it, is to put that freshness and youth back into your heart.

Spirituality is about how you treat yourself. You are a micro universe within the larger physical universe that surrounds you. The more you care for yourself, the more your energy, your behavior, and the events around you will reflect your commitment to spiritual growth and health.

Checking Out Other Methods

Literally hundreds of therapies, interventions, and other methods for quitting smoking and promoting lasting health exist. You want to know about these other methods because people may recommend them to you as quit-smoking resources. If you decide to follow through with these or any other nontraditional methods, make sure to check the background, certification, experience level, and past successes of the practitioner(s).

T'ai chi

T'ai chi is a form of movement that helps you center your senses and focus your balance where it needs to be: within you. You have a vital connection to the Earth, and t'ai chi helps restore that link in a dynamic way. Those who practice t'ai chi feel that the benefits of the discipline stick with them throughout the day. After all, balance and focus are useful at all times. Quitting smoking is a supreme act of balance and focus.

If you're interested in giving t'ai chi a try, your local community center, wellness center, or continuing education program may offer classes.

Yoga

Yoga is an ancient practice of activation and release that involves deep concentration and breath awareness and control. You may think of yoga primarily as a form of exercise thanks to all the hype that fitness gurus have heaped upon it, but it's a great way to become *mentally* fit as well as physically fit.

Almost anyone can do yoga because yoga can be performed on the physical, mental, emotional, and/or spiritual levels. Physical, or body, yoga can be strenuous. If you have any concerns about your stamina or your ability to handle the yoga exercises, consult with your doctor beforehand.

Attempts to describe yoga briefly tend to come up short because a number of types of yoga exist. *Hatha* yoga, for example, is a set of practices that focus on the body. Through a variety of body- and mind-bending exercises, students stretch their physical shells. Other kinds of yoga focus on devotion, chanting, and energy.

Many kinds of yoga involve *mindfulness* — awareness of yourself and yourself in the world. Self-awareness is not a dreary philosophical exercise — far from it. As practiced by yoga students and masters, these explorations into the little-known byways of thought and feeling can result in fantastic control over mental and physical functioning. As a student of quitting smoking, yoga practice is an ideal path for you.

You can find out more about yoga from books, videos, and the Internet. *Yoga For Dummies,* by Georg Feuerstein and Larry Payne (Wiley Publishing), is a great resource. You can facilitate your learning by tapping into the greater experience of a teacher, but nothing is holding you back from giving yoga a try on your own.

Feng shui

Feng shui is a time-honored practice that applies to both your inner and your outer environments. It is a set of practices that are intended to spiritually cleanse and achieve harmonies between the inner and outer worlds. These practices can complement mainstream efforts to quit smoking. Whatever you do that involves dedicated energy, caring, and positive belief in the value of quitting smoking is a good thing! See *Feng Shui For Dummies,* by David Kennedy (Wiley Publishing), for more information.

Aromatherapy

Some people believe that aromas — fragrances — can act as healing forces. Many things around you can be healing forces, provided that you invest them with the energy to heal. So much of the world around you reflects the meaning that you give it.

Aromatherapy has not been the subject of much scientific study. The same can be said of many alternative therapies, such as *past-lives therapy* (understanding your present life through examining your supposed past lives) and homeopathy. *Homeopathy* uses minute amounts of medicine that are greatly diluted to treat many of the same symptoms that traditional Western medicine does.

 Fragrances are the stuff of life. Smell is one of the primary senses with which we make sense of the world around us. Because we are so highly evolved, we appreciate smells not only on the basis of their survival value to us but on an aesthetic basis as well. Not long after you quit smoking, you'll be rewarded with a restored sense of smell with which you can actively enjoy nature — the fragrances of the changing seasons, the odors of foods and flowers, and the thousands of other deeply gratifying essences that bathe you in this sensual world.

Part III
Sticking with Quitting

The 5th Wave   By Rich Tennant

"Oh, this? Since I quit smoking I just need something to do with my hands."

In this part . . .

*R*elapse prevention is the ultimate goal of quitting smoking. The first 24 to 72 hours of quitting can be challenging; you need to pay attention to internal and external triggers that can send you running for a smoke. Support for your decision to quit is all around you in the form of counseling, workshops, and support groups. This part helps you to amass many strategies to stay your course. Don't look back and don't look too far ahead: If you've quit, then you're already successful.

This part examines the complex relationship between moods and cravings for cigarettes. Mood dips and swings are usually fleeting, and your decision to quit smoking can outlast moment-to-moment emotional fluctuations. You may also be concerned about the possibility of putting on weight when you quit. Be assured that weight gain is not an inevitable consequence of quitting smoking; on the contrary, your health and physical appearance are likely to improve when you quit smoking.

Chapter 11

Fighting on All Fronts

. . . .

In This Chapter

▶ Formulating your quit plan

▶ Gathering your weapons

▶ Gearing up for the change

▶ Thriving, not just surviving

. . . .

Once you've decided to quit smoking, you need to come up with a concrete plan for how you'll go about it. Successful quitting involves not only determination and commitment but also a detailed plan of action that spells out how you will spend your time, energy, and money in the first few weeks, when cravings are still strong and temptations abound. The more comprehensive your strategy and the more tools you use, the better your chances of succeeding. This chapter helps you work out the minute details of your schedule as well as your mental and physical agendas.

An *addiction* is a habit or behavior that you keep doing even though it makes problems for you. Once you have that definition firmly settled in your mind and heart, you need to decide, to will yourself to take action, and then to quit. Then you need to decide *when* and *how*. These matters are not trivial; some people can launch themselves into a quit decision and lifestyle pretty quickly, while others need more time and planning to get off to a good and lasting quit. Going through the various exercises will help you define a style that's right for you.

Psyching Yourself Up to Quit

Quitting smoking takes not only the right mindset but also the right body set and environment set. In other words, not only do you need to be thinking,

"Yes, I can do this," but you also need to prepare your body for the change, and you need to make adjustments to your surroundings to give yourself the best possible chances to stick to your plan.

What do you think you need to do as you prepare to take the leap that may save your life? As you contemplate what it will be like without your old friend Smokey, visualize what you will need as you approach ground zero: Quit Day 1. In Table 11-1, list the lifestyle changes and personal arrangements you may need to facilitate to make quitting stick. Be as specific as possible, and add to the list as you come up with additional ideas. Actually scheduling your activities for the week leading up to Quit Day may be helpful, so I've structure the table such that you can write in specific strategies to tackle on specific days. Be as detailed as you can in the items that you list. Include exercise plans, dietary changes (if any), social plans, and even attitude changes that will anchor your quitting success.

Table 11-1	Pre-Quitting Strategy			
	Physical	*Mental*	*Environmental*	*Relationships*
Pre-Quit Day 7				
Pre-Quit Day 6				
Pre-Quit Day 5				
Pre-Quit Day 4				
Pre-Quit Day 3				
Pre-Quit Day 2				
Pre-Quit Day 1				

Creating a strategy for success

Using your best information and knowledge of yourself, figure out how much time you need to prepare. Choose a specific quit date, a day within the next four weeks. Make the day far enough ahead that you have adequate time to plan, but not so far that you can put off your decision indefinitely. Highlight your decision by circling the date on your calendar, recording it on your personal digital assistant if you have one, and telling friends and family members about your plan. You may prefer to pick a day that you are off from work. Or you may choose to quit on a day like any other day — business as usual. I would caution you to not overthink this move. Don't let indecision or procrastination hold you back from what you need to do!

Gleaning the wisdom you gain from this book, from your conversations with others who have quit, and from all your observations, work out as specific a strategy as possible. For example, can you take physical measures that will heighten your sense of physical well-being so that tobacco cravings are less severe? Regular exercise, particularly aerobic exercise that gets you breathing faster, makes you perspire, and increases your heart rate, releases endorphins — feel-good molecules — from your brain's pleasure centers. An added benefit is that a vigorous workout makes your lungs feel clean and clear and much less receptive to the toxic incursions of tobacco smoke. As part of your quitting plan, consider adding regular workouts to your schedule.

How about nutrition? Are there ways to help yourself feel healthier and more fit? Eating the right foods will go a long way toward this goal. Your physical engine runs much more smoothly and efficiently on a mix of proteins and fruit and vegetable carbohydrates than it does on fat-laden fast foods. Eating right gives you more energy (which is something you may have relied on cigarettes for).

If you're overweight or concerned about gaining weight after you quit smoking, excellent resources are available in the form of books, Web sites, and highly trained professionals. Nutritionists and dieticians can review your eating patterns and exercise schedule and help devise an optimal plan for you.

Mental strategies chiefly include picking the emotional stance you will have and maintain toward your quit decision. Remember that your choice to live tobacco-free is a heroic one and your decision to quit can take top priority over almost every other issue (at least during the first quit week!) Environmental strategies to insure quitting success include removing all triggers such as books of matches and ashtrays. To the extent that you can minimize your exposure to other peoples' tobacco smoke you are also improving your chances at success. If you are involved with anyone who is still smoking decide how much you can input their decision to continue smoking and then detach. Always keep in mind that your best ally in quitting smoking is yourself. Don't get overly attached to someone else's smoking issues.

I encourage you to be as specific and detailed as possible in your quit plans. Make check marks in the columns of Table 11-2, indicating which activities and therapies you will do during your first week off from tobacco. Spell out exactly how you will spend your time each day and night, filling up your schedule so that there's no time left for smoking or obsessing about smokes.

Table 11-2		Quit Plan, Week 1			
	Exercise	*Activity*	*Food*	*Entertainment*	*NRT*
Quit Day 1					
Quit Day 2					
Quit Day 3					
Quit Day 4					
Quit Day 5					
Quit Day 6					
Quit Day 7					

Sticking with your decision

Having an overarching motivation — the birth of a child, the loss of a loved one to lung disease, or the desire to be around for your family and friends for a good long time to come, for example — helps a lot. So does continually reminding yourself that quitting smoking is your *number-one priority*. During your first week free of cigarettes, practically everything else in your life takes a back seat. If you feel tired, exhausted, cranky, irritable, or in any way less than optimal, that's okay. It's par for the course.

Most people who stop smoking go through energy and mood changes in the first two weeks. Just let those feelings, as negative and annoying as they are, come and go. They will depart eventually.

A super-powerful physical and mental tool is meditation. Different types of meditation work for different people. Some meditators can take themselves to a safe and inviolable place by chanting. *Hatha yoga* is a physical form of yoga that practices and perfects breathing exercises during physical movement and postures. A devotional or mind-based type of meditation works excellently for many people. See Chapter 10 for more information about these methods.

Preparing Yourself for the Change

A great way to plan ahead and prepare for the changes in your life style is to anticipate smoking triggers/stressors that could lead to smoking. Although you may not be able to foretell the future you can with some reliability predict some of the things that may come up for you during your quit smoking induction period. In Table 11-3, list potential stressors that stand some tweaking in yourself, your environment, and your relationships. Write down changes you can make in each of these four areas as you approach Quit Day.

Table 11-3		Stressor Alert!		
Potential Stressors	*Physical*	*Mental*	*Environmental*	*Relationships*

Bear in mind that stressors, anxiety, and tension-builders, whatever form they may take for you, can lead to tobacco cravings and to lighting up. Build a mental or even physical wall between yourself and that stress. Decide ahead of time how you will handle things as they come up without relying on a cigarette.

Take a mental step back and notice one important thing: Cravings are not real in the sense that a safe falling on your head or an escaped lion from the zoo is real. A craving is a mental representation, a thought form fueled by strong desire. It is an idea — *I want a cigarette and I want it now* — dressed up and mightily empowered by thousands of repetitions and by the energy of desire. The wish for a cigarette is not a bland, theoretical, or cerebral abstraction. It is a strong and usually compelling urge.

No ifs, ands, or butts

I used to smoke a pack a day, usually with relish. (I say "usually" because there were plenty of times, such as first thing in the morning, or when I had a cold, or when I smoked too many, when the things tasted horrible.) I knew that I wanted to stop. As a medical student, I certainly couldn't justify my continued use of cigarettes given everything I knew about what they do to the lungs and the rest of the body. I had seen more people dying of chronic lung disease and cancer than I wanted to.

The breaking point for me came with the birth of our first son. This baby was new to the world, new in every sense of the word . . . new and healthy and wonderful smelling. The last thing I wanted to do was contaminate or compromise his physical well-being, his baby sweetness with the noxious fumes of tobacco. I quit the day our son was born.

What, after all, is desire? It is a variegated mental/emotional *thing* that lives only in your head. Undoubtedly, you've had many desires, some of them quite strong, at various times in your life. What has happened to these desires over the years? Has each of them survived completely intact? Do you have exactly the same strong wishes that you had 10 or 20 years ago? I doubt it.

The point is, desire comes and goes. Desire is a *feeling*. Feelings change. Sometimes you're angry, and sometimes you're happy. None of these states of mind is permanent.

Apply this knowledge to your desire for a smoke. Practice taking a detached stance from this desire. Watch it knock on your door, begging to be let in to your mental house. Your choices at this point are to swing the door wide open and welcome the beast into your living room, or to stand there watching Joe Camel. You can watch yourself watching Joe — while you do absolutely nothing but watch. Guess what? After you've practiced this detachment long and often enough to get really good at it, Joe starts to get less insistent about coming in. He somehow becomes less believable. His imperious knock — "YOU WILL LET ME IN!" — grows gentler, starts to fade, and eventually sounds more like a leaf rustling in the wind.

You are not your cravings. Your cravings come and go. Who, after all, is stronger: you or your cravings? If your thought forms and desires, overpower you, it's like Pinocchio becoming the puppet maker's master. It isn't right! Your thoughts and feelings should work for you, not the other way around.

All cravings are (or can be) transient and short-lived. You can choose to not endorse the craving. Seek a distraction and chances are the craving will go away.

As you move from what has been termed the *pre-contemplator* stage to actually quitting smoking, you will go through changes in a variety of areas: physical, emotional, mental, lifestyle, financial, social, and spiritual. Some of the changes are painful and involve some struggle and a good deal of commitment on your part; most of the changes are positive and excellent! You have a lot to look forward to as you move from the planning to the actual stage of quitting.

How your body may change

The physical changes associated with quitting smoking take place immediately and over the mid- and long-term as well. The acute or immediate changes can include depression, anxiety, restlessness, jitteriness, increased appetite, and diminished energy. Some people describe feeling wired or feeling simultaneously wired and tired. These are the average expectable withdrawal symptoms that many people who stop smoking experience.

From the moment of your last inhale, your body begins the work of repairing itself. Left to its own devices (that is, if you don't smoke again), your body renews and restores itself. White blood cells in your lungs and throat ingest and wall off as much foreign material (such as tar) as they can, while damaged cells are metabolized and replaced with new ones. The oxygen supply to your body increases as the red blood cells lose their freight of carbon monoxide and take on more oxygen. This boosts your stamina, your energy level, and your sense of well-being. Your chances of developing peptic ulcers and high blood pressure drop dramatically as the toxic, constricting effect of cigarettes on your blood vessels wanes. Statistically speaking, your chances of getting any of the dozens of smoking-related cancers plummets. Many of these excellent changes occur over the course of weeks, months, and years.

In the short run, you may experience nicotine withdrawal symptoms and increased appetite for food. One of the compelling reasons to consider using a nicotine replacement therapy during the first months of quitting is to benefit from the appetite-suppressing effect of nicotine.

How your emotions may change

Smoking has been bundled with a vast number of activities in your life, from eating to drinking to relaxing to working. You can add to the list by thinking about all the times you smoke, and infinitely expand the list by including your observations of all the things that other people do while they smoke. Although society puts a premium on the ability to multitask, smoking while doing something else is a place you no longer want to go. You have decided that the time has come to break the link between everyday activities and smoking.

Life goes on after smoking!

The principal psychological withdrawal symptom is *craving.* Long after the jitters, low energy, and mood swings have passed, you may have bouts of longing for cancer sticks. Cravings can take the form of flashbacks — nicotine nostalgia — including moments of actually tasting and smelling burning cigarettes. Cravings can take the form of ideas, romantic yearnings for the allure of cigarettes.

Rationalizations often accompany cravings. When you contemplate having "just one more," you are selling yourself a bill of goods. How often have you told yourself or successfully convinced yourself that

- This is the last cigarette ever.
- Lots of people smoke without harm.
- This is a bad time to quit.
- I want what I want when I want it.

✔ It's better to smoke than to gain weight.

✔ I've done so much damage already.

✔ One more won't matter.

See Chapter 12 for information about defeating rationalizations.

Surviving Your First Week

The first week of quitting smoking is very difficult for many people. But if you can make it through this milestone, your chances of cutting cigarettes loose for good improve considerably. As the preceding section explains, giving up smoking brings about a host of changes that you have to deal with, and sometimes it can be hard to cope. This section provides you with some strategies for making it through these crucial first few days.

Although it seems simple, one of the biggest issues that many quitters struggle with is all of a sudden not having something to do with their hands and mouth. During the first few days of quitting, and possibly longer, you may find yourself wanting an oral substitute. You may be tempted to replace cigarettes with food. If comfort food is what it will take to get you to quit smoking, go for it. I'm not endorsing a leap into the hog trough, nor am I suggesting that you arm yourself with barrels full of cookies, chips, and cake. Obviously, there's a hierarchy of acceptability and healthiness to what you eat.

Plenty of liquids are highly recommended. Some feel that the more (healthy) liquids you drink during your initial days of quitting, the better. Water, carbonated water, fruit and vegetable juices, and even diet soda are fine. Be careful with coffee and alcohol because they're often paired with smoking.

You can be as elegant and refined as you like with your substitute oral gratifications. Some newbie quitters find that it helps to carry around a bag of celery or carrot sticks to munch on throughout the day. Chewing gum is the old standby, over-the-counter replacement for smokes. If you enjoy cooking, this is your chance to invest the time and energy required to cook up the most varied and tasty dishes of your life. If you're somewhat less ambitious, treat yourself to some dinners out. The more delicious the food, the less likely you are to obsess about smokes.

The first 24 hours

It's Quit Day 1. First and foremost, don't smoke! Heed the following advice as well:

✔ Get rid of all tobacco products and accessories such as matches, lighters, and ashtrays.

✔ Be as active as possible. Now is the time to exercise, engage in your hobbies, and spend as much time as possible with other people. If certain activities are particularly relaxing or rewarding for you, by all means pursue them. And if certain activities are particularly stressful and usually mean reaching for a smoke, avoid them as much as possible during your first quit week, and especially on your first day as a non-smoker.

✔ Modify and improve your environment so that it's comfortable, supportive, and facilitates your new life. This super-important task will be a major boost to your efforts on Quit Day 1.

The first 24 to 72 hours are the toughest, most challenging period of quitting smoking. This period features big-time physical and psychological withdrawal. However, you are equipped with enough tools and know-how that you'll be able to masterfully avoid trigger situations, soothe and comfort yourself, offer yourself alternate activities and oral substitutes for cigarettes, and win! The list of available resources and activities that will make this decision to quit stick is as long as this book.

Nicotine withdrawal is real; it's not "all in your head." Do whatever it takes not to smoke (within reason).

Working on your environment

If you've read this chapter up to this point, you are very much aware of your internal environment. You can engage in a process that I like to think of as interior redesign. Interior redesign has to do with consciously choosing your priorities and goals for both the immediate and short-term future. As you proceed with making over your inner world, and as you move toward shedding addictive and putting-off behaviors, consider what changes in your external environment will move your ambitions closer toward reality.

Your environment matters. Set it up or change it to support your smoke-free lifestyle.

Dedicated smokers are surrounded by the appliances and appurtenances of smoking. You may be surprised to find how much of your home is adorned (or cluttered) with ashtrays, cigarette lighters, matches, and other fixtures of the smoking lifestyle. Take a moment in your car or living room to close your eyes and take a deep breath. How riddled with the odor of stale tobacco smoke are your surroundings? How many such compromises are you willing to make in order to accommodate your habit?

That's not all. Can you recall all the times you've made allowances — set doors ajar, left windows open, aired out rooms — in order to dilute and dispel the tell-tale traces of tobacco smoke? How many correcting and undoing and cleansing actions do you have to perform before you feel that enough is enough?

Your environment is a reflection of you. You can't help but notice how some people have very orderly, neat surroundings, while others are surrounded by piles of paper, chaotic belongings, unmatched socks, and the like. The good news is that as you decide to change, the world around you will parallel those changes. As your nose and head clear and the smoke settles, so to speak, you can enjoy the universe of fragrances that are really powerful and primary and moving if you only let them in.

You can set up your place to support your quit smoking decision. You may find it comforting or meaningful to set up an area in your home that's dedicated exclusively to the pursuit of your goal to quit. A special space devoted to your spiritual pursuits could be considered an altar or a small personal temple. You can set up such a space almost anywhere at home — perhaps even in a private part of your office or in one of your favorite out-door spots, such as a beautiful park — provided that the area is undisturbed and fairly private most of the time. Elements for an altar or sanctuary could include photographs that mean a great deal to you, keepsakes or special belongings that have a great deal of personal value, incense, candles, or per-haps jewelry or a small sculpture or other type of artwork. The idea is to create a space that's hallowed with positive thoughts and energy. Some people find the idea of a brief but focused daily ritual helpful in the pursuit of their dreams and goals. Set aside five or ten minutes at the beginning or end of each day in which you spend time at your personal altar (whether it's inner or outer) and recite an oath or prayer on the theme of personal health and fulfillment.

You can get as elaborate as you want with this kind of ritual. If you follow one of the traditional religions, you can incorporate your wishes for cigarette sobriety and improved health into your regular prayers.

There are many ways to modify your environment so that you feel a sense of renewal and fresh purpose. Rearranging the furniture in your home or a room can make all the difference in how you feel about yourself and your ambitions. Entire volumes and workshops have been crafted on the application of *feng shui,* which is the art of aligning yourself and your surroundings with the forces of nature. Once you really start to believe that your body is sacred, that your body is a temple entrusted to your care for some undetermined but hopefully long period, you can approach it as the sacred house it truly is. In the old reli-gions, nothing was more sacred to the people and the religion than the temple. The temple was the house of God. The temple was the place on Earth where God or his symbols resided and made contact with man. Desecration of a temple, whether built of marble or flesh, is a spiritual sin. Imagine receiving a brand-new shiny Lamborghini and applying hot blasts of tar and other staining chemicals to it every hour of every day. No one in their right mind would do that to a car. How about the chariot known as your body?

Actual physical relocation, even temporary — as in a vacation to a pristine, awe-inspiring spot — can help turn the tide as well. If you commit heart and soul to quitting smoking and decide that you need to be out of your usual surroundings with their predictable levels of pressure and stress, then by all means go for it. If you have the time and the money, go on a retreat. Find a spot in the woods, deep in the heart of the mountains, or somewhere along a beautiful beach strand and allow yourself to go back into yourself and your past until you get to the point where you started . . . with clean lungs and a pure spirit.

Working on your relationships

To some extent, your relationships with other people are influenced by smoking. Like attracts like, as the saying goes. When people are trying to meet other people, their descriptions of themselves include their status as smokers or nonsmokers. So if you never considered smoking an essential part of yourself, think again! After all, smokers spend a lot of time pursuing their habit, and that habit leaves traces and signatures everywhere.

When someone is trying to find out what someone else is like, "Do you smoke?" is a reasonable and important question. The individual asking the question wants to know about the other's habits, environmental needs (such as privacy and open windows), health, and values.

Tobacco tragedy number 3,413,918

I know a man whose plans were very much in the direction of health and beauty and nature, but were tragically cut short by a smoking habit. This gentleman, a well-read, good-natured spirit, a scholar who nonetheless could and did talk to everyone, a person whom people naturally gravitated toward because of the sweetness and depth of his heart, worked as hard as a dog (how hard do dogs work, actually, aside from the ones you see on TV pulling sleds?) for 40 years, running not only a highly successful dental practice but taking on weekend and overtime work whenever possible. He had a gorgeous wife who was devoted to him. His greatest dream — the reason he worked so hard — was to save up to buy a retirement home in the Seychelles, where his wife was originally from. One weekend, he and his wife were home, the phone rang, and he was about to go out on an emergency dental call, when suddenly his face became contorted with pain. He dropped the telephone receiver, clutched ineffectually at his chest, and dropped to the floor, pale as a ghost. He never woke again. He had fallen victim to a massive heart attack at the young age of 52.

His brand: Camels.

When you acknowledge that you smoke, what are you saying, aside from the fact that you smoke? You may be revealing that you enjoy cigarettes, that you have a live-for-the-moment philosophy, that you don't care about the consequences of smoking, that you have a habit that you can't control, and that you don't mind rank, fetid odors.

The connection between smoking and relationships doesn't end there. The interaction between you and your significant other, whether spouse or partner or special friend, is colored by the presence or absence of tobacco. During routine activities, such as meals or work, cigarettes can become a dominant theme in your mutual lifestyle.

Working on relationships is a lifelong project. You hopefully get better at it as you go along. Quitting smoking is an excellent incentive to refine and be increasingly selective about how you relate not only to yourself but to others.

Remember the adage about people, places, and things that people in recovery frequently espouse. To the extent possible, avoid situations that usually involve reaching for a smoke. Be prepared to say no if offered a cigarette.

You've made it through the week!

Congratulations! You've survived your first week of quitting smoking. Welcome to the beginning of the rest of your hopefully healthy life. I'm not going to tell you that *everything* will be perfect from here on in. Nonetheless, you have the extreme pleasure of knowing that you have much more control over what happens to your health and your appearance than you ever had before. The nature of tobacco addiction is such that cravings and withdrawal symptoms may continue to appear from time to time, but they will gradually and definitely subside to the point where they're infrequent and nowhere near as compelling as they were during your first quit week. This is the time to congratulate yourself, feel proud about your accomplishment, and consolidate the terrific gains you have made. Do so by keeping on target with your exercise routine, good nutritional habits, positive relationships, and environmental strategies.

Ex-smokers in the maintenance stage need to remain wary of relapse warning signs such as rationalizations and cravings.

If and when you find yourself subject to stinkin' thinkin', you can have a conversation with yourself, reminding yourself of your crucial priorities; pick up the phone and call a friend for quit smoking support; then take a walk and ten deep breaths. Breath is a gift.

Chapter 12

Staying Clean

. . . .

In This Chapter

▶ Recognizing rationalizations

▶ Identifying relapse triggers

▶ Handling self-blame and guilt

▶ Avoiding past mistakes

. . . .

*A*t some point in your effort to quit smoking, it happens. Just when you think you're doing so well and accomplishing so much, you have a relapse. You give in and have that cigarette after dinner. You're feeling guilty, weak, and angry with yourself for giving in.

Relapses are common, however, and even the most resilient people have them. The important thing is not to give up and not to quit quitting, so to speak. In this chapter, I share my knowledge on what to do when you have a relapse, how to handle cravings, and how to deal with other smokers in your life as you're trying to quit.

Practicing Early Relapse Prevention

Relapses are wakeup calls, not swan songs. Surrendering to the impulse to smoke can be disastrous if it leads to renewed smoking. However, relapses can be opportunities to find out more about your triggers and how to handle them better the next time around. You don't want to have a relapse in the first place if you can help it. Relapse is a sad, guilty place littered with the corpses of your best intentions. Relapse prevention is the most important ingredient for cutting cigarettes loose for good.

I have plenty of good news about relapse prevention. As succeeding generations of potential smokers have turned their backs on Joe Camel and the Marlboro Man, more people are quitting smoking than ever before. People have gotten smarter and done better at preventive efforts. Former smokers know more about handling cravings, recognizing triggers, and substituting healthy habits for nicotine. Systematic research demonstrates the positive impact of prevention efforts on smoking behavior. As you go through these strategies for staying clean, try them out and see which ones work for you.

More is better. The more skills and healthy habits you acquire, the less likely your chances for a relapse. You can breathe a sigh of relief.

Assessing your relapse risk

The first step to practicing early relapse prevention is to find out how close you are to relapsing. Identifying your risk for relapse and avoiding these high-risk situations can help you on your journey to recovery.

Your risk for relapse is on the rise when you

- ✔ Have just recently quit.
- ✔ Feel so confident that "just one more can't hurt."
- ✔ Buy a pack "just to have around."
- ✔ Don't discard that last pack.
- ✔ Expose yourself to people, places, and things formerly associated with smoking, such as bars, smoke-filled restaurants, and friends who smoke.
- ✔ Are in high-stress situations that usually lead to a smoke, such as family conflict, deadlines, or social obligations.
- ✔ Are in low-stress situations that invariably lead to smoking because you want to maximize your relaxation, such as a vacation.

If you can relate to any of these points, you're at risk for relapsing into the habit.

Recognizing relapse rationalizations

Relapse readiness is the opposite of quitting readiness. Does that sound confusing? Actually, it's quite simple. Basically, your risk for relapsing to smoking may be triggered by any number of rationalizations that you use to let yourself off the hook so that you can slip back into the habit. Smokers who relapse generally share some common rationalizations, some of which may be very familiar to you. Even if they aren't, watch out for them anyway! Even the mighty have fallen as a result of buying into these illogical messages. If you're aware of these rationalizations, you can practice early prevention and stop yourself from getting back into the smoking habit.

- ✔ Despite all my resolutions, I just smoked. I'll never do it again.

- ✔ Just one more won't make a difference. The damage to my health is already done.

- ✔ There's no need to quit right now. I can always start fresh tomorrow (or next week or next year).

- ✔ Everyone else smokes — and they look fine. I'm in great shape, and I have plenty of time before I need to quit.

- ✔ I'm dealing with so many other problems that I just can't take this one on right now.

- ✔ I worked/played hard and earned this cigarette. I deserve a break.

- ✔ Low-tar/low-nicotine cigarettes are not as dangerous as regular ones.

- ✔ If I don't inhale deeply, my lungs won't be damaged.

- ✔ I simply don't care. I'm going to smoke.

- ✔ I broke my vow by smoking this morning. There's no point in trying to get back on track now.

I was a one-pack-a-day man for many years before I quit. I can remember jogging through the last half-mile of my afternoon run. My main motivation to finish was the sheer pleasure of lighting up the moment my workout was over. Talk about insanity!

Picking up: Cycling from rationalization to relapse

Most people prefer to think of themselves as unique — as people whose behavior is spontaneous, interesting, and perhaps even creative. The sequence of relapse behavior, on the other hand, is as predictable as a formula.

Wannabe quitters light up after buying into one or more rationalizations or after getting exposed to a compelling *trigger* (anything that reminds them of smoking). The pleasure and utter familiarity of those first puffs are tainted by a cascade of guilt and self-blame. You may think, "Oops, I did it again," or, "I'm pathetic, I have no control over myself," or, "I'm a slave to my habit." These feelings of helplessness and self-loathing earn compound interest. The more you've tried to quit, the worse you feel about each subsequent failure.

If you're not smoking right now, you're succeeding. This breath is the first fresh one of the rest of your life. It doesn't matter how many times you've failed in the past. Most successful quitters have three or more quit attempts behind them.

Nailing stinkin' thinkin'

Rationalizations? Anyone who has tried to quit smoking has them by the dozen. I call these thoughts stinkin' thinkin'. These cravings, delusions, and enticements will come knocking on your door, but the good news is that you don't need to invite them in. Are you flooded with rationalizations, ensnared by smoky dreams, or at high risk for relapse? The next time tobacco nostalgia strikes, try one of these liberating moves.

If you've just recommitted to abstinence ("I'll never do it again!"), good for you! This book is filled with tips on what to do, where to go, and who to contact in order to stay smoke-free. (If you need help, see Chapter 13 to find programs and support groups.)

Here's what to say to yourself when you find yourself making the following excuses:

- ✔ **"One more cigarette won't hurt me."** The fact is that each additional cigarette does make a difference. Every additional puff (or chew of tobacco) increases your exposure to tobacco's toxic wasteland. The damage to your health is cumulative. Even if you smoked earlier in the day, a walk outside, a drive, a shower, or a glass of juice is way better for you than that next cigarette. In a spirit of jest, would-be quitters may say that it's too late to quit, that the damage is already done. Not true. The damage to your health from smoking is always cumulative. The more and longer you smoke, the more grievous the effect on your body. Less cigarettes are better than more. And none is best of all.

- ✔ **"I can start fresh tomorrow."** Well, like they say, the road to hell is paved with good intentions. Although you should have your recovery planned out from hour to hour, don't put your health and lung liberation on hold. Accumulated tomorrows add up to *never*. Turn to Chapter 7 right now.

- ✔ **"I look and feel great."** Appearances can be deceiving as can the rationalization that other smokers look fine. Although the smoker in the jogging suit looks to be in the pink of health, you have no idea what his chest X-ray looks like. Nor are you there in the morning when he's hawking up gobs of bronchitic phlegm. Visualize your own insides, clean and healthy and energized. Imagine each breath filling you with vitality and power and calm.

- ✔ **"I'm too busy to tackle that now."** Sure, you have a lot on your plate. If you feel that you have so many problems that you cannot take on staying smoke-free, take a paper and pen and list them. Assign each of them a number. Which problem takes priority? Is your current and future health somewhere on the bottom of the list? Is it possible that quitting smoking may actually empower you to master some of the other challenges you face?

✔ **"I deserve a break."** Sure, you do, but, don't reward yourself by giving in and having a cigarette. When you give up a compelling habit like smoking, you need to substitute other gratifications. You need to have other goodies to look forward to. What if you went shopping, or cooked a great meal, or had a massage next time you really wanted a smoke? Find health-promoting ways to please yourself.

✔ **"It's just a low-tar/low-nicotine cigarette."** Thinking that low-tar or low-nicotine cigarettes are okay is one of the more dangerous rationalizations. In fact, low-tar and low-nicotine cigarettes are every bit as dangerous as the regular ones, because people who switch to them end up smoking more and inhaling more deeply. Try carrot sticks, other fresh vegetables, sugarless gum, and lots of liquids instead.

✔ **"I don't inhale . . . really."** Inhaling less? Though you think that inhaling less won't damage your lungs as much, you still need to think about mouth, tongue, and throat diseases that result from exposure to tobacco and tobacco smoke. What is the most delicious taste or fragrance you can think of? Mint? Citrus? Pepper? Imagine this aroma replacing the rank odor of tobacco on your breath . . . anyone you kiss will thank you!

✔ **"I don't care about my health."** Many smokers claim that they don't care about their health because they don't care about their future, but is this really true? How many things do you do each day that are geared toward the future? Each of these actions demonstrate that you're planning on being here tomorrow. Take the money you would have spent on smokes today and set it aside for a future treat. (See Chapter 22 for ways to use that extra money.)

✔ **"I already blew it today, so I may as well have another one."** Lose that perfectionism! Just because you broke your nonsmoking vow doesn't mean that it's all over. All-or-nothing thinking gets you right back where you don't want to go. Are you so harsh on yourself in any other areas of your life? Why be this way about an issue that ultimately is so important, an issue where each day's — each moment's — decision to not smoke is a victory?

Feeling worse or guilty or giving up are powerful triggers too. Don't be a self-blaming relapser. Understanding what caused the slip is different from getting down on yourself. Don't surrender to these negative feelings. When you're feeling low, any of the rationalizations (*"I'll never be able to stop," "What difference does it make if I smoke? I have no self-control anyway,"* and the classic *"I'm a loser"*) may kick in and cause you to pick up the habit again.

Handling Relapses

One struggling smoker said, "Quitting? No problem. I've done it a thousand times." Sound familiar? Losing momentum, losing hold of your best intentions to quit, and losing control is what relapse is all about. This section can help equip you with a set of tools and strategies that empower you to handle your relapses.

Losing the battle, but winning the war

The effort to quit is a life-and-death battle for your health, your dignity, and your future. If you're fully committed to this struggle — if quitting is your number-one priority — then this is war! Relapsing — surrendering a beach-head here, taking some casualties in a skirmish there — is a process of learning and then putting that knowledge to use.

If you pick up, practice immediate damage control. Don't finish the cigarette (and by all means, don't finish the pack!). Limit the amount of physical and psychological exposure you have to the smoke.

 Get into the habit immediately after a relapse of turning toward other (non-smoking) activities. Get out of the house. Take a walk. Call a friend. Go to the gym. Take a shower. Put as much distance between you and that cigarette as possible. You also need to place a lot of psychological distance between you and the relapse. Don't fall prey to self-condemnation, self-blame, and self-pity. As you have seen, these negative states are potent relapse triggers themselves. Do try to understand what led to the lapse, try to avoid setting up similar situations in the future, and continually remind yourself that you're succeeding if you're not smoking right now.

Catastrophizing

Relapsed smokers face many temptations. Think of these temptations as fire-breathing dragons: They're big, they're scary . . . and they are figments of your imagination. So is *catastrophizing* — when you make a mountain out of a mole-hill, such as when you convince yourself that you'll never quit because you've slipped. When you melt down because of a slip, you're acting as your own worst enemy.

One of the most important things to remember in order to handle relapses is not to start catastrophizing. If you pick up, you've surrendered to the same will-numbing impulse that has bested you and your good, healthy intentions. You're not alone. Millions have been there before. And millions of people just like you have gotten beyond relapse, too.

If you pick up:

- ✔ You're not a bad person.
- ✔ All your intentions, choices, and decisions are not spineless or ineffective.
- ✔ You can still succeed at quitting.

Think it through. In the course of your life, you've made hundreds, if not thousands, of decisions that have stuck.

Picking up doesn't mean giving up. All it means is that on this particular day, at this particular time, you picked up. That's it. (Not the end of the story.) A small defeat doesn't have to lead to even larger failures. (Imagine if FDR, considering Allied losses during World War II, had decided not to invade Normandy.) Each tobacco-free moment is a fresh and healthy start. Each cigarette-free day is another victory. An accumulation of smoke-free moments, days, and eventually weeks is what makes for success.

If you've picked up after deciding to quit, view the experience as a slip rather than a full-fledged disaster. If you surrender to feelings of disaster, you're more likely to throw up your hands in disgust and say, "The heck with it, I may as well smoke."

If you occasionally give in to a craving and light up, put out the cigarette immediately. Don't finish it. The more nicotine that enters your system, the more the balance is tipped in favor of further smoking and a deeper, more serious relapse.

When you're craving a cigarette — or after you've had one — is the best time to launch all your best quitting strategies:

- ✔ Get out of the house or office.
- ✔ Call a friend.
- ✔ Read more deeply in this book.
- ✔ Call a buddy who's quitting.
- ✔ Take a shower or bath.
- ✔ Go out to a movie.
- ✔ Take a walk in the park.

Do whatever it takes to immediately start reaccumulating good, healthy quit time. Throw away whatever cigarettes remain. You can lose the battle and still win the war!

Tackling Triggers

Triggers, or relapse cues, often take the form of "people, places, and things." Avoid at all costs situations where picking up a smoke is a reflex. Which of these events or triggers pull your chain (or starts you chain-smoking)?

- ✔ After a meal
- ✔ After sex
- ✔ First thing in the morning
- ✔ After working out
- ✔ In social situations, such as in bars, at parties, or at conferences
- ✔ When you see another smoker puffing away
- ✔ When you see a cigarette ad
- ✔ While watching a movie where the hero or heroine lights up at a dramatic moment
- ✔ When you're hungry
- ✔ When you want to lose weight

Rome, as they say, wasn't built in a day. Likewise, your quit-smoking program takes planning and sophisticated strategizing, as well as serious commitment on your part. The first step is a cognitive one: You need to know what kinds of things make you reach for a smoke. Undoubtedly, you can add your own tobacco triggers and smoking precipitators to the preceding list. Identifying your triggers can be a real eye-opener. It's humbling to realize how often you act in reflexive, highly predictable ways.

Take the analogy a step further: Consider the dogs in Pavlov's experiments, trained to associate the taste of meat with the ringing of a bell. Eventually, the animals salivated to the stimulus of the ringing bell alone. It's the same with smoking. Cigarettes, cigars, and other forms of nicotine are highly — extremely — reinforcing. The most primitive parts of our nervous systems respond in a basic way to the rush of adrenaline, of alertness, to the taste of tobacco, especially when tobacco has come to be associated time and time again with other pleasurable events such as meals, sex, celebrations, and parties.

Smoking sobriety, like other kinds of sobriety, works one day at a time. In the first weeks of smoking cessation, you may be disgruntled or even disgusted with your low mood and low energy, as well as your increased thoughts about food, drink, and sleep. (I speak more about mood swings and weight gain in Chapters 14 and 15.) You may feel lazy or wired or both. It's okay. These feelings are par for the course. As long as you don't smoke, you're succeeding.

Putting smoking cues on disconnect

Your mission, should you choose to accept it, is first to recognize your smoking triggers and then to disconnect them from positive associations. For example, you can practice enjoying a meal or a good conversation without a smoke. As with most newly acquired skills, practice makes perfect. The first few times you sit through a four-course dinner — or hold your own during a conversation at a social gathering — you may feel twinges of anxiety and that creeping sensation that alerts you to the fact that *this is one of those times I smoke.*

It's just a thought. An impulse. Impulses come and go. Like all thoughts and impulses, it will — given time and sufficient detachment — evaporate and be replaced by others.

Impulses have nothing inherently commanding or irresistible about them. Everyone has impulses that they consciously choose not to surrender to all the time. How many times have you considered telling your boss or teacher what you really think of them? How many times have you thought of killing the alarm clock and sleeping in? Chances are, you decline these choices and instead do what you need to do. Some people find it helpful to actually replace the smoking reflex with other, less destructive, rituals. Chewing on a toothpick, flossing after a meal, or eating a piece of candy, though perhaps not envisioned or desired as permanent habits, can substitute for smokes during the first few weeks of abstinence.

Learning from your (and others') mistakes

People who are trying to cut loose addictions and other self-defeating behaviors often share war stories of their struggles. Knowing that others have been in your shoes can be helpful and sometimes inspiring. Support — whether offered informally from friends or in quit-smoking groups such as Smokenders — validates your experience, reduces your feeling of isolation, and provides valuable lessons from the front-line experience of others. I talk more about support groups in Chapter 13.

However, a fine line separates therapeutic talk and nicotine nostalgia. The latter occurs when smokers' tobacco tales — of how they would walk a mile (or a continent) for a Camel, how good that first hit in the morning tastes, or how nothing beats a hot cup of coffee and a smoke — act as triggers themselves. At some point, the speaker's and listeners' nostalgia turns into active craving. You may find it helpful to note some mistakes you've made in the past, during previous attempts to quit. Once you've created this kind of inventory of trial and error, you'll have an easier time spotting slips or focusing less on your part in the future.

Identifying common relapse mistakes

Another way to tackle smoking triggers is to identify common relapse mistakes, such as avoidance. With the best of intentions, people put off what they need and really want to do. New Year's resolutions are great on paper, but they come only once a year. An alternate approach is to ask yourself, "If I'm not quitting now, then when?"

On the other hand, a sudden (or impulsive!) decision to quit may undermine a later, more committed attempt. You need to be psychologically, physically, socially, and perhaps even spiritually prepared to jump this hurdle. You need to feel that this task is the most important one in your life right now, and that despite transient discomfort and lack of gratification, you're ready to do what it takes to reclaim your health. The decision should involve those around you — family, friends, and even coworkers — because your behavior during the first week may affect them.

Another frequent mistake involves taking on too many healthy resolutions at once. When you get the wakeup call — which can take the form of "Oh my goodness, I've been abusing my body all these years, and I have to do something about it right now!" — the temptation is to wipe the slate clean and cut loose every ingrained self-defeating habit at once. Success at quitting is driven by a commitment to reality, which includes a recognition of personal limitations. No one is Superman. Doing a mega-makeover on yourself overnight is difficult, if not impossible. As much as you may want to quit smoking, stop overeating, start exercising, take that second job, and write that book, you can't do it all at once.

Understanding recidivism and denial

Any meaningful discussion of relapse, relapse triggers, and recidivism (*recidivism* is literally "quitting" quitting) is ultimately about denial. *Denial* (not a river in Egypt!) is the unspoken or even overt willingness to ignore either your own or another person's addiction. Denial can be insidious, pervasive, and even all-consuming. It's one of those terms that you hear everywhere. It's a meaningful, useful word, a specific term for blindness to addiction and the problems it causes. Denial is the engine that drives your continuing use of tobacco.

Those who state that they choose to smoke deny the massive dependence they have on nicotine and minimize their awareness and concern about the eventual health-robbing effects of their habit. Others smoke without thinking twice. They think, "Why think something to death — especially if it may end up killing me someday? Why spoil the pleasure of a smoke by worrying about something that may or may not happen down the road? For that matter, why bother to point out that an elephant is sitting in your living room?"

This is exactly where it's at with smoking. Each puff you take is more money out of your pocket; another step closer to emphysema, hypertension, cardiac disease, and possibly cancer; and another nail in the coffin of your self-confidence and self-esteem. Yet, like many others who have thought about quitting but aren't quite there yet, you're playing a game with yourself that involves lying, distortion, and manipulation of the truth, practically around the clock, in order to spare yourself the pain of awareness. Going back to smoking is a prime example of denial of work. If and when you contemplate picking up that cigarette, you put the blinders on to reality. The relapser tells himself, "I can always quit tomorrow," or, "Today is not a good day to stop. I have too much on my plate," or, "My health is fine. I'll think about quitting when I don't feel well."

What about long-term chronic smokers who awake each morning to a symphony of chest-wracking, gob-producing coughs? The level of denial operative for those people may take the form of "I don't care."

Even people who have been smoking for years can halt and often reverse the progression of lung and other physical damage.

A wealth of evidence indicates that smoking-induced damage reverses over time. Within weeks of quitting, the paralyzed cilia in the respiratory tract begin moving again, helping to wash and sweep clean the airways. White blood cells ingest and contain foreign debris, such as tar and other pollutant chemicals. Over time, new cells replace tired and/or dying ones. If you don't tamper with your body, it usually takes great care of itself.

Staying Focused

Your success at staying clean hinges on your ability to remain focused on the task. Quitting smoking is not a casual project. It's not a hobby. The decision to quit is a decision to make abstention from tobacco the main priority in your life. Typically, the first few days or week following smoking cessation are a difficult time. Newly abstinent smokers are bombarded with distractions, nicotine craving, episodic bursts of energy (and valleys of fatigue), anxiety, insomnia, and even depression. To a certain extent, the reaction to cutting nicotine loose is individual. You may face some, all, or none of these difficulties.

Holiday time, especially around Christmas and New Year's, may be the wrong time for you to quit smoking. This time of year abounds with triggers and motivators to light up. On the other hand, you may be one of those people who are truly and highly motivated by New Year's resolutions. Go for it! Just make sure that you think about when is the best time for you to quit.

The challenge is to stay on target. With the aid of right thinking, exercise, plenty of liquids, and perhaps nicotine replacement therapies such as the patch (see Chapter 9), you'll be equipped to handle even the most unpleasant of rides — provided that you're committed to seeing the process through.

I can't say it enough: Stay focused. Think of yourself as you want to be, free of a habit that has and will continue to drag you down. Think of yourself scouring the house for a butt, an ashtray, or a match. Remember your first puff ever, and how sick it made you feel. Ever smoke too much? Can you recall feeling your stomach tied up in knots, your head pounding, and your resolution at the time to never smoke again? Those feelings were real. You've made a decision for health — a decision to take the high road — and remaining focused is what will keep you where you need to be.

Focusing your energy on other things

When your thoughts start to wander, drifting nostalgically toward your old "friend" tobacco, do the following:

- ✔ Get up and change your surroundings: Change rooms or get in the car.
- ✔ Think of those who have succumbed to the urge and where they are right now.
- ✔ Imagine that you are a child smelling tobacco odor for the first time.
- ✔ Visualize your healthy pink lungs after the tar and other particles have cleared out.
- ✔ Have a substitute gratification such as gum, a beverage, a piece of fruit, or some vegetables.
- ✔ Get some exercise.
- ✔ Make a list of all the things you can buy with the money you save on cigarettes.

One of the main relapse culprits is excessive focus of your thoughts on how you feel or how much better you might feel if you lit up to the extent that you can direct your awareness outward to the people and world around you — you're better able to stay on track An alternate approach sometimes works: Sharply focus your energy on your body, your breath, and your muscles. Notice how they feel working synchronously, calmly together . . . and remember how disruptive and jarring each hit of smoke is, slamming the beautiful and delicate orchestration of your body into screeching high gear.

Which state do you prefer?

Taking charge: You are king of your thoughts

In the so-called Perennial Wisdom — across innumerable schools of thought, religion, and philosophy — one teaching is universal and may even be true. One version of this teaching is related in the Kabala, which began as the mystic branch of Judaism and has since gone through many transformations. The teaching is "You are king of your thoughts."

The idea is also expressed in terms of the *macrocosm* (the universe at large) and the *microcosm* (the subjective universe, your world within). Schools of wisdom teach, "That which is above is as that which is below." This statement can be interpreted in a number of ways. Many spiritual schools use this statement to promote the notion that the world is either a direct expression or reflection of the Maker, of God, of the Supreme Being. Similarly, you can think of your body as a direct reflection of your mind.

Your body — your organs, your health, your outlook, level of energy, and vitality — flows directly from the output of the mind, or brain. The mind is the emperor, or king, or master gardener — use whatever metaphor works for you — and the body is the kingdom, or garden, or empire. Whatever seed is planted now will spring to life later . . . for good or for ill.

This causal relationship between mind and body has even been extended by some into the realm of the physical world. Some people hold that obscure or unseen linkages occur between your thoughts and the world around you. People invoke these connections when trying to explain why some individuals seem to have all the luck, while others live their lives as though under a perpetual dark cloud. C. G. Jung, one of the most prominent thinkers in psychology in the early 20th century, believed that a collective unconscious connected everyone through the world of dreams and symbols and archetypes. Other sources that tap into these ideas are medieval alchemy, the Western hermetic or occult tradition, and the tarot. If you look at the so-called major arcana of the tarot deck, you can see that many figures play important roles in this dynamic between conscious mind, physical body, and external world.

Whether you're an ineffectual, tired, sickly person or a whirlwind of ideas, ambition, and activity, you are king (or queen) of your thoughts.

Your health and your thoughts

Bad, unbidden things happen all the time. It's usually not your fault if you come down with a serious illness or you're in a bad accident. Nonetheless, many situations seem to develop or accrue as a direct outgrowth of numerous and repeated and persistent messages to the self about where, who, and how you want to be.

I can flesh these ideas out somewhat — put some meat on the bones of these somewhat abstract concepts.

Cognitive therapy is a school of healing that trains people to identify thoughts and feelings that may contribute to depression, anxiety, and negativity. Scientists know that in stress reactions, the brain goes on red alert and prepares the body for fight or flight. In states of meditation and deep calm, significant chemical and electrical changes occur in the central nervous system. Science has not yet identified the immediate consequence of specific thoughts and feelings, although progress is being made in that direction. Recent imaging studies, for example, show which parts of the brain become active (light up) under varying emotional conditions.

You can safely and definitely assume that your thoughts and feelings have consequences for ill or for health. Although scientists may not yet know all the intimate mind-body connections, it makes sense to act as though your kingly pronouncements — your thoughts, emotions, and feelings — are translated into hormonal, electrical, and chemical signals that trigger many other physiologic responses. Depression and chronic stress impair the functioning of the immune system. People with depression are more likely to have heart attacks, other cardiovascular disease, and peptic ulcer disease. It makes sense to likewise assume that positive states of mind cause healthful states of the body.

What would it really mean if your thoughts and feelings are that powerful? What are the real life implications of "the word made flesh" (in other words, that your thoughts may "go somewhere" and that they work toward either health or decline)?

Your smoking habit and your thoughts

Every time you pick up a cigarette, you're giving yourself a set of very negative messages, which may include the following:

- ✔ I live only for the here and now; I don't believe in or care about the future.
- ✔ My health is already so far gone that it doesn't matter how else I abuse my body.
- ✔ I don't deserve to have clean, healthy lungs.
- ✔ I don't care about how I feel or look.
- ✔ My parent (or wife, or best friend) smokes, so I may as well smoke, too.
- ✔ I don't deserve the best that life has to offer.

You get the idea.

Likewise, every decision to not pick up a cigarette is accompanied by a corresponding idea and message to yourself and your body:

> ✔ I am working on having a healthy future.
>
> ✔ I deserve to feel well.
>
> ✔ I care a lot about how I look and feel.
>
> ✔ I believe that I have power over what happens to me.
>
> ✔ I am on good terms with my body and want to continue in a happy, healthy, and long-term relationship with it.

Seeing the Big Picture

Although quitting smoking is a daily struggle — at least in the beginning — this major step you're taking to make your life better is not a battle so much as a war, a massive and ongoing campaign and crusade to have the most vigorous, energetic life you can. The goal is superior well-being, and you get there one day at a time.

Always keep the big picture in mind. Your big picture may be hanging in a huge gilded frame among Rembrandts, da Vincis, and Michelangelos. Or you may be the kind of person who sees herself as a sleek glass- and chrome-trimmed modernist sculpture, the centerpiece of a trendy downtown gallery.

What do you want? Your vision of yourself is all-important. A decision to quit smoking can also be part of the big picture. At the very least, you're painting a wishy-washy canvas whose outline and direction are uncertain and murky. If you can't decide, if you can't see what you want for yourself, then the colors are gray, half-tones, and changing all the time.

Clarity and specificity — concrete goals for the immediate and longer term future — are what work.

In the most specific terms possible, use Table 12-1 to record how you see yourself in the next week, month, and year.

Table 12-1	What I Want: A Wish List		
	Next Week	*Next Month*	*Next Year*
Clothing (What are you wearing?)			
Weight			
Energy level (1 = low, 10 = Superman)			

(continued)

Table 12-1 *(continued)*			
	Next Week	*Next Month*	*Next Year*
Activity level			
Work (How many hours per day?)			
Exercise (How many hours per day?)			
Free time (Where are you spending it and what are you doing?)			
Self-esteem (1 = abysmal, 10 = sky-high)			

Reframing Relapse: A Day without Nicotine Is a Successful Day!

Rome, as they say, wasn't built in a day. Neither is healthy tobacco-free living. Freeing yourself from the shackles of smoke is a laborious, time-consuming process that requires a more or less steady input of energy and resolve over an extended period of time.

The path toward liberating your lungs is usually not a smooth one, although many have been able to simply stop and never pick up another cigarette again. More typically, people proceed in the direction of smoking sobriety in fits and starts, with periods of success (abstention) interrupted often erratically and/or unpredictably by "relapses."

Relapses are par for the course. If despite your best intentions you surrender to the impulse to smoke, your next move must be to exert immediate damage control. It's much better to smoke one cigarette and then fire up your renewed resolve, jump back on the wagon, and pick up exactly where you left off. What you don't want to do is use the slip as an excuse, a kind of flabby justification, for a full-blown relapse.

The rationalization may take the form of "Well, that proves it. I just can't stop, so I may as well go ahead and have as many as I want."

Wrong. Dead wrong. The less you smoke — and the sooner you reclaim your intention to quit forever — the better you feel. Not only will your throat and lungs and cardiovascular system feel immediately better, but so will your self-esteem and dignity. You'll probably enjoy a heightened sense of self-confidence, of empowerment. You were tempted, were swayed momentarily by an errant impulse, gave in — and then got right back on track.

Another thing: Many, if not most, smokers who are just starting out can have a fair amount of physical and especially emotional discomfort, especially during the first several days of not smoking.

Some new quitters complain of pervasive tiredness, lethargy, and an inability to focus or concentrate. Others have these feelings and feel wired, too pumped up, as well. Newly abstinent ex-smokers often feel that they're miserable and useless and can't get anything accomplished. Their minds are in a blur.

That's fine. A day without tobacco is a successful day, regardless of how little or how much you accomplished — provided your number-one priority for now is quitting smoking. The investment now in time and energy — even if it means reduced productivity or fatigue — is going to pay off in major ways in the near future. You'll have excess energy and drive and will further benefit from eliminating all the distraction and time and expense that went into getting smoking supplies and taking the innumerable smoke "breaks" that interrupt so many smokers' work and home and recreation lives.

This message bears repeating. It doesn't matter how you spend the day — even if you spend the entire day in bed — provided that you kept that healthy distance between you and the cigarette. Your effort to quit is aided by numerous adjunctive resources, such as meetings, support groups, meditation, exercise, and medication interventions such as the nicotine patch and Zyban.

Keep in mind that the path you're on has been trod by millions of others before you.

Quitting smoking, though not easy, is possible. It's a reachable goal, a concrete and specific health, lifestyle, and even spiritual aim that you can create and achieve for yourself over time.

Handling Secondhand Smoke When You're a Quitter

Secondhand smoke (smoke that is passively inhaled from others' cigarettes) has become a major public health issue. Not too long ago, secondhand smoke was a non-issue. You could light up in restaurants, in bars, and even on buses and trains. Areas set aside for nonsmokers in cafes and hotels were the exception, not the rule.

All that has changed drastically in the past five years. Many states are now enacting legislation that makes it illegal to smoke in public places except in specially designated areas. (Now, when you dine in a restaurant, you can ask to be seated either in the dining room or in the humidor . . . .) This legislation comes up at the same time as a number of major class-action suits against tobacco companies, some of which have already resulted in awards of billions of dollars to smokers whose health was irreversibly damaged as a result of their tobacco use.

Clearly, times have changed. I know how I feel when I go into a restaurant and someone sitting near me lights up: discomfited, irritated, and annoyed that another person has so little consideration for the people sitting and eating (and trying to breathe) around him.

If your spouse or roommate is a smoker, you and your intention to quit face a special challenge. Depending on the level of support, you may encounter variable willingness on her part to alter her lifestyle to accommodate yours.

The issue is definitely worth talking about, so discuss your goal with family and friends. Nice. Many partners and family members of quitting smokers are willing to go all the way to facilitate their loved ones, even to the point of quitting themselves. You can arrange compromises, such as not leaving cigarette packs around the house or only smoking outside of the house or car, that also are tremendously helpful and need to be explored.

Consider the increasing evidence that secondhand smoke is actually toxic and may result in physical injury and illness. The estimates on the amount of physical damage actually caused by proximity to tobacco smoke vary tremendously, although some authorities have put the health-care costs of passive exposure to smoke in the (again) billions of dollars. One source estimates that as many as 50,000 die each year as a result of secondhand smoke.

A related issue is that of fetal exposure to nicotine and the hundreds of other chemical compounds in cigarette smoke. The intrauterine environment offers no alternatives, unlike secondhand smoke situations where you may be able to avoid further contact and inhalation of smoke. (After all, you can always choose another table or simply decide to leave.) The developing fetus doesn't have a choice.

Conquering the Dragon: Cognitive Skills for Success

You have a powerful set of tools at your disposal to succeed at quitting. One is this book. Another is your body, which will respond to your careful and loving attention by feeling better and giving you the green light for your continued and greater efforts to live healthy, eat right, exercise, and breathe clean air.

Your social network, including supportive family, friends, coworkers, and your doctor, are (I hope) all poised to help you as much as necessary. (If you want their support, you need to tell them what you're doing.) Your doctor may prescribe one of the nicotine replacement therapies such as the patch, gum, or inhaler — see Chapter 9. Another terrific and powerful source of support from people are support groups, which can be informal or organized national networks such as Smokenders. Chapter 13 has more information about these groups.

Last but certainly not least is your mind. Your mind is your greatest ally in your effort to quit. Make no mistake: It can also prove to be your worst adversary. Laying the mental and emotional foundations for success involves frequent reminders to yourself that are positive and forward-looking and that examine the daily events in your life in a temperate, rational, and caring way.

As you prepare to quit, revisit the following thoughts frequently:

✔ I can quit smoking. Millions of people have quit smoking before me.

✔ I've overcome other big obstacles in my life.

✔ I have many important reasons to quit. I count. My health counts.

✔ The future is real. The future will arrive. To a certain extent, I have a hand in what happens to me down the road.

Once you've quit, invoke these ideas as often as necessary:

✔ I may feel shaky or tired or miserable today, but what I'm going through is temporary. It will get better every day.

✔ Even if I don't feel great, I'm having a successful day because I'm not smoking.

✔ Quitting smoking is a loving, caring thing to do for myself. I deserve it. I would certainly encourage anyone else I care about to take this step.

✔ I don't have to surrender to the impulse to smoke. I can do something else instead. I will feel much better about myself tomorrow knowing that I didn't slip.

Taking the High Road: Will Power versus Kill Power

What is will power? This is one of the oldest and thorniest problems in philosophy and in life. Do you or do you not have control over your behavior, your decisions, your fate? The question has been argued since time immemorial and the consensus is far from being in.

Some of the world's major religions are based on the central notion of free will — that you make your own choices, you choose the high road or the low road, the morally right or the morally reprobate path — heaven or hell. Another major religion states as dogma that people are born as either saved or as sinners — that they're fated to an eternity of following one or the other way. The addiction field, at least at a superficial glance, looks divided on this question as well. Addiction scientists and biologists are constantly finding new evidence of the robust transmission from one generation to the next of addiction liability. Of course, your heredity for most traits is not an all-or-nothing situation. Many of the traits you inherit (short of features like eye color or height) are actually responsive to a host of different variables — particularly behavioral traits, like smoking or drinking. Does that mean you have a choice over whether to pick up the very next cigarette? Ask a roomful of people and you'll get a surprisingly wide range of responses. One of the central tenets of Alcoholics Anonymous and other 12 Step-based self-help groups is that the addicted person recognizes that he or she is powerless over the substance and the hold it has on his or her life. The concept has always seemed a little fuzzy to me, but the important idea is that you *can* decide whether to buy a pack of cigarettes, whether to go the health club, whether to avoid people, places, and other triggers to smoke.

Rather than getting hung up on whether free will exists, I suggest that you live as though it does and then go right ahead and make the preferred choices. (You can worry about the philosophical fine points later, when you're breathing free and clear.)

The other point with free will is that the free will you do have has actually been eroded by nicotine dependence and cigarette addiction. This book and other programs that you might try to quit smoking are meant to bolster your free will and support you in ways that you may not be able to achieve on your own. Activity, being among people, distracting yourself even more than usual with family, work, hobbies, volunteer work, charity, rest, self-care are all different but synergistic ways of amplifying your choices and diverting your path from reflex behavior (picking up a smoke) to behavior that's wider and freer in range and gives you more choices and more control.

Chapter 13

Getting Help from Support Groups and Programs

Although the battle to quit smoking may seem lonely at times, it doesn't have to be. By means of the numerous support groups, meetings, classes, and Internet resources that are out there, you can join a growing number of people who can help you reach your goal. Excellent quitting resources are available locally and nationally. You may even want to start your own campaign to educate people about smoking and prevent the spread of this social contagion. Sometimes the most devoted advocates of health are reformed smokers. If getting on the health bandwagon and convincing others helps you quit and stay quit, go for it.

Finding a Quitting Buddy

They say that you're more likely to stick with an exercise program if you find a buddy to work out with you. (See Chapter 15 for more on the importance of making regular exercise a part of your quit-smoking plan.) The same can be said for quitting smoking — you're more likely to succeed if you team up with someone who's in the process of quitting, or who has already quit and can be there for you throughout your effort to kick the habit. A quit buddy is yet another form of support — a social and emotional tool — that can help make the difference between a lukewarm effort and a resounding success.

You will find an extraordinary array of personalities among those who have quit smoking or are in the process of quitting. Some people approach the task in a determined yet understated way, while others become cheerleaders and coaches for others in order to keep themselves motivated. No single personality type guarantees success at quitting.

If you succeed in quitting on your own, that's terrific. On the other hand, you may benefit from feeling like you're part of a team — a winning team that makes a healthy lifestyle its top priority. Part of the skill of team-building involves identifying people who can help you make your quit attempt work. At the same time, you can almost always learn from the experiences of others.

You can learn from others' failures as well as from their successes. An essential ingredient of quitting success is learning what _not_ to do.

Perhaps you're most comfortable with people who are similar to you. You may feel most supported when you're among people who live in your town, city, or county. On the other hand, you may want to have a fresh start and find your support among people you don't shop, work, or go to school with on a daily basis. Plenty of Web sites can hook you up with faraway quit buddies through online chat groups — see the section "Locating Helpful Web Sites" for details.

You may be most motivated by people who are extroverted and are clamoring to be heard — people who try their hardest to get their message across to as many others as possible. You'll find ardent supporters of the quit-smoking cause, among them a range of types from mildly detached to rigidly doctrinaire. In addition, some people find that working with a quit buddy of the same gender is less demanding than working with someone of the opposite sex.

The important thing is to find a quit buddy whom you feel truly supports you. Support groups, classes, and meetings may team you up with a quit buddy as part of their approach, as later sections of this chapter explain.

Making Networking Work

How are you at networking? If you're like most committed smokers, you're probably highly skilled at it. After all, _networking_ has a lot of meanings. One accepted meaning for the term is "the ability to get around." When you've run out of smokes and needed to bum one, you may have surprised yourself with the depth of your resourcefulness. How many cigarette war stories, how many narratives of nicotine fits, do you have? Any regular smoker has had times when he would have gone to China and back for a smoke.

Managing multiple addictions

The Anonymous program is applicable to most, if not all, addictions. Cocaine Anonymous, Pills Anonymous, and Narcotics Anonymous are other groups that target recovery from substances of abuse. You or someone you know may wonder what to do with a double or multiple addiction — concurrent use of, say, alcohol, nicotine, and marijuana. This scenario is not uncommon. The consensus among people in the field is that you do what you can. You work on each addiction as though it were a life-or-death matter, which it usually is. Moreover, there's so much overlap in the approach of each group — and so much overlap in the problems that arise as a result of each addiction — that you really can pick up the right approach, attitude, and self-change behaviors from any of the groups.

You can apply the same networking talent, the same ability to track down resources, to your quitting campaign. You are incredibly resourceful. Evidence of this fact is your involvement at this moment with this book. You will gather further evidence of your capabilities and talents when you talk to others who have or who are now quitting smoking.

The more help you have, the better. The network of people and programs out there that are poised, ready, and able to help you is vast.

Supporting Your Success with Nicotine Anonymous

Nicotine Anonymous is a self-help group for people who are quitting tobacco. It's based on the 12 Step philosophy that has become a way of life for millions of recovering addicts. Unlike most quit-smoking programs and Web sites, Nicotine Anonymous is a nonprofit, supported mainly by members' contributions. Nicotine Anonymous meetings are held all over the world, usually on a frequent basis. Often, people start their own groups as the good word is spread.

The 12 Steps are the core philosophy that drives the various Anonymous groups, including Nicotine Anonymous. In this program, you pledge, or admit, that you have lost control over your life and your use of tobacco. At the same time, you try to believe that something bigger than you, a power greater than yourself, can help. Having come this far, you're asked to turn your will and your life over to "God as we understand him." This qualification is important because it clearly identifies Nicotine Anonymous as nonpartisan, nonaffiliated, secular group. You use whatever works for you as a notion of God or a higher power to steer your way to a better place, without addiction.

Recovering smokers are encouraged to find sponsors who are there like guardian angels to smooth the way to abstinence and recovered health. You can call your sponsor 24/7, and he or she will guide and encourage you just when you're about to reach for a Virginia Slim or a generic or anything else in the ashtray that even remotely resembles a brown leaf.

Overcoming your fears of fitting in

If you're considering a support group such as Nicotine Anonymous, you may be struggling with the issue of how well you will fit in. What if you see someone you know? What if, on the other hand, the support group turns out to be a room full of strangers?

There may be more than one group in your area. (Visit the Nicotine Anonymous Web site, www.nicotine-anonymous.org, to find out where meetings are held.) People in recovery agree that, given a choice of meetings to attend, you need to shop around and find the group (within NA) that works for you. You may find that you fit in better and feel more comfortable with one group than with another.

The best source of information about any support group is someone who attends or has attended the group. Ask around!

You may find yourself grumbling about the necessity of attending a support group at all. To these objections, I can offer the following:

- ✔ You don't know whether a particular support group will work for you until you've tried it.

- ✔ There is power in numbers. If you've studied group psychology, you know that a group, beyond a certain minimal size, takes on an identity and cohesiveness of its own. Enthusiasm and other feelings are amplified and become contagious when refracted and reflected among large numbers of people. Recovering addicts in groups like Nicotine Anonymous routinely report that the most helpful or therapeutic aspect of their experience was belonging to something that was bigger than them. When you join a group, to a certain extent you hand over some of your individual characteristics and choices, but think about how much you get in return: validation, appreciation, immeasurable amounts of support, kindness, and good humor from others. These ingredients can make your attempt to quit smoking a lasting success.

How Alcoholics Anonymous got started

Alcoholics Anonymous, the prototype of Nicotine Anonymous and all other self-help groups, started in the 1930s. Legend has it that Bill W., the founder of Alcoholics Anonymous (AA), was a totally out-of-control drinker. His alcoholism had ruined his life. Legend has it that he even went to see Carl Jung, the famous Swiss psychoanalyst . . . and Jung told Bill that his situation was utterly hopeless. At the end of his tether, Bill returned to America only to dream one night of a worldwide fellowship of recovering alcoholics. The dream included a visual of people "in recovery" holding hands, stretching the net of support literally around the globe.

Learning to scrutinize your behavior and its effects

As a Nicotine Anonymous member, you are asked to scrutinize your behavior — to perform a "fearless moral inventory" to see where and when you have let yourself and others down as a result of your addiction. This self-examination can be a disturbing experience because it may result in your becoming aware of harm that you may have done to people as a result of your smoking. Self-examination can rattle your cage. The 12 Step solution is to make amends wherever possible to those you have harmed; to continue to appeal to your higher power for energy, strength, and guidance; and to try to bring this healing message forth to others who may wish to quit smoking.

You may find this language, this approach, a bit Draconian or severe. You may wonder what role, if any, personal failings play in acquiring a nicotine addiction. What's the role of self-scrutiny when all you really need to do is quit?

If you could have quit on your own, you already would have.

You need tools, support, and resources — as many as you can get. Nicotine Anonymous may be one of them. If you rankle or feel somewhat uncomfortable with part of the Nicotine Anonymous approach, don't sweat it. Take the best and leave the rest. Your mission as a recovering smoker is to find out as much as you can about what help is available and to cram your calendar and your spirit with as much enthusiasm for the work as you possibly can. Don't become so choosy about meetings that you rationalize away your need to attend.

Adjusting to the group mentality

I've worked with hundreds of people recovering from addictions to tobacco, alcohol, and other substances, and I know that the program works. It doesn't work for everyone, though. Nicotine Anonymous, like other 12 Step programs, is based on *groups*. Meetings are the lifeblood of the organization. You may need to attend meetings frequently, if not daily, if Nicotine Anonymous is available on a daily basis in your area.

You may have a difficult time working in groups. (On the other hand, you may really like it. Being able to speak your heart in front of others is an incredibly liberating experience.) You may feel pressured or self-conscious, or you may object to attending meetings with many other people. You may object to what some have described as the rigid or doctrinaire approach of Nicotine Anonymous. You may even agree with some of the critics of this approach who say that Anonymous meetings are a cult, a virtual religion.

They aren't meant to be. They're meant to be secular. Although the higher power concept is prominent in the 12 Step philosophy, members are encouraged to use whatever higher power works for them. Your higher power may be God, money, love . . . it doesn't matter, as long as it works for you.

I know people who cling to these meetings like a drug. I know people who feel that they need to make it to meetings as often as possible, even two or more times a day. As extreme as this may seem, Nicotine Anonymous and other meetings won't harm you the way smoking does. If you must think of these meetings as a substitute addiction, that's fine. You'll do far better to attend 1,000 meetings than to keep lining your lungs with carcinogenic soot.

You can taper your meeting attendance as your recovery progresses.

Embracing the 12 Step (or some other) approach

One of the most fascinating things about 12 Step meetings is that they can be embraced as a way of life. Many people in "the program" (you'll find that Nicotine Anonymous meetings involve a complete language and a common set of aphorisms and approaches to life) promote the idea that smoking and other addictions are the tip of a spiritual and emotional iceberg. The idea is that smoking is a symptom of an incorrect approach to yourself and to life. I view the program as a launching point for self-mastery, self-exploration, and self-control. There are many paths to serenity, and Nicotine Anonymous is one of them.

Another interesting thing about the Anonymous program is that, as a direct result of the insistence upon confidentiality — anonymity — you can't study the outcome. Because people in Anonymous programs can't and usually shouldn't identify themselves, scientifically scrutinizing this approach to determine whether it works is just about impossible. If it works for you, then it works. If chanting or deep-sea diving works for you, then those approaches are effective — *for you.* You may drop out of a 12 Step program; you may relapse to smoking while attending. In that case, it obviously doesn't work for you. Or the meetings may work for you at a different point in time. The take-home lesson is to be open-minded and to use as many tools at your disposal as possible. This one is essentially free (aside from the time and energy you devote to it) and should definitely be tried — along with exercise, healthful substitute gratifications for smoking, and possibly nicotine replacement therapy (see Chapter 9).

The more active approaches you take to quitting smoking, the better your chances of quitting for good.

Sampling Smokenders

Smokenders (www.smokenders.com) challenges you to "Quit Smoking Forever! Stop Smoking for Good!" The program is well known and has been praised by a number of celebrities. Smokenders offers a seminar as part of an educational kit that you can review at home. It is a commercial (for-profit) venture and will cost you money — but so will continuing to smoke! As with other quit-smoking tools, the idea is to pile on the weapons in order to win the battle.

Smokenders operates in many different countries, and many multinational corporations have used it to assist its employees in quitting smoking. Its smoking cessation program boasts an 81 percent success rate. Smokenders tries to help its members not only quit but also enjoy their new and continuing freedoms as nonsmokers. The program involves a sequence of educational sessions that cover

✔ Basic material on tobacco dependence, behavioral strategies, and addiction in general

✔ Group sessions, including buddy groups

✔ A set of assignments that essentially gets you to put more time and thought between your impulse to smoke and the moment of lighting up

✔ Written and other materials to reinforce learning

Smokenders permits gradual, stepwise withdrawal from tobacco and emphasizes a number of complementary approaches rather than promoting a single doctrinaire tactic. Smoking rationalizations are challenged, and motivational supports are provided. Quitting smoking is an excellent thing to do for yourself, and Smokenders emphasizes motivational support — increasing your awareness of all the great results of kicking the habit.

Smokenders, like Nicotine Anonymous, religion, and meditation (see Chapter 10), works for some people. The only way to find out whether it will work for you is to try it out.

Starting Your Own Support Group (or Finding Peace by Keeping to Yourself)

Consider starting your own support group. You may already know enough people who are quitting or seriously considering quitting to have a quorum.

All it takes to start a support group is two or three like-minded people.

In a support group, you can find dozens of ways to boost each other's resolve and rally around the cause. For many people, being as active as possible during the first quit week is a key component of success. The more you have to do, and the more you focus your energy outside of yourself, the better your chance of eluding the smoke fiend within. It wants you to light up. Your compulsion to throw all rational considerations (and the future) to the wind wants you to have that gratification right now! If you force yourself to be around other people, to be busy and active at constructive tasks — or at having fun, playing sports, seeing movies, or cooking meals — you'll win.

Of course, I know other people for whom the opposite formula seems to work. You may be one of them: a person for whom socializing seems like work, for whom privacy and solitude bring peace and relief from stress. If you're among this group, do what works for you. Set up a tranquil environment that takes you away from the everyday cares and worries that "cause" you to light up. A change of surroundings can result in a change in your frame of mind.

Discovering Sources of Inspiration

Think of quitting smoking as a personal statement. Think of it as something you're doing to express your deepest wishes for yourself and those around you. Quitting smoking is a growth step, a necessary part of your development. There's something beautiful, natural, and necessary about a caterpillar shedding its cocoon and bursting free as a butterfly. Remember Patrick Henry, who said, "Give me liberty or give me death?" Smoking — any kind of addiction — is a terrible form of bondage. When you break free, you'll find it hard to believe that you put up with the shackles for so long. You'll amuse yourself with the miles-long list of justifications and rationalizations that you probably came up with to keep on smoking.

Sources of inspiration to stop smoking are all around you.

If you're a nature lover, take an extra-hard look at the plants and animals reaching for the sun and the sky. They live to eat, breathe, and grow. There is nothing less natural than smoking. If you're religious, it may be difficult to convince yourself that God intended for you to smoke. Buddha didn't smoke. Christ didn't smoke. Neither did Lao-tse or Moses. Smoking is nonessential as far as your life is concerned. Smoking is not a luxury, either (except perhaps in the old days, when few people were aware of the life-threatening implications of the habit).

Take a walk along the shore. Spend some time with a baby or a puppy. Spend an hour concentrating on the fragrances that blow through the air, arising from stores, food, and women wearing perfume. You can cut cigarettes loose and call it a day — or you can feel free and cherish every single freedom and healthy moment you're lucky enough to have.

Have you ever heard of the *Tibetan Book of the Dead*? This ancient document was written as a guidebook, meant to provide instruction to those who were about to pass from this life to the next world, wherever and whatever it may be. The *Tibetan Book of the Dead* describes in great detail a state called the *bardo:* the transitional state between this world, or this incarnation (depending on your beliefs), and the next. The dying are instructed to be very careful of their reactions to what they experience during the bardo state. Hallucinations and frightening visions are said to emerge, and these are distillations of negativity from the person's lifetime: a gruesome collection of terrible, sad, angry, and destructive feelings and images. The book instructs you to pass these visions by and not get caught up in their seductive imagery.

My inspiration is that the bardo is *right here and now.* You are what you think. If you let yourself become captivated and led astray by a never-ending preoccupation with smoking and the desire for a cigarette, you will become that desire. And that desire will materialize sooner or later as a cigarette in your hand. Your thoughts, especially those that are charged with strong feeling, color and eventually create your world. Don't be a Jackson Pollack of the spirit. Make your inner and therefore your outer world an orderly and beautiful scene, touched by wisps of green and azure and earth.

The Cigarette Papers

You may need a different kind of inspiration than nature and the spiritual. Some people find motivation in the fact that there is, in essence, a huge conspiracy to get people to smoke, and to keep the truth about the harm of smoking from the public.

If you got turned on by Watergate or Whitewater, this scandal may be just the ticket to anger you into quitting smoking. Back in May 1994, a parcel containing literally thousands of pages of "classified" documents from the tobacco industry appeared in the office of a professor at the University of California. The papers, which turned out to be an insider's narrative of the corporate hijinks of the Brown & Williamson company, were shocking. (Brown & Williamson is owned by British American Tobacco, a bedfellow in scandal.) You can see the documents yourself on the Internet by clicking on to the Brown and Williamson Collection (www.library.ucsf.edu/tobacco/).

The Cigarette Papers (edited by Stanton A. Glantz, et al, University of California Press, 1996) is an impressive collection of self-damning documents from the tobacco industry. The book takes a critical look at these papers and provides a much-needed perspective on the industry. The essence of the book is its irrefutable corroboration of double-dealing on the part of Big Tobacco. Within the industry, as these documents show, tobacco-related addiction, disease, and death have been acknowledged for decades. Despite this awareness, the tobacco companies have engaged in double-speak, promoting their products and attempting to dispel any public concern about the dangers of the weed. These underhanded and devious tactics are what would now be called *misinformation* (which used to be called *lies*).

The Passionate Nonsmoker's Bill of Rights

This book, written by Steve Allen and Bill Adler, Jr., is a compendium of advice on quitting smoking. It's also a call to action for the public, providing detailed information about dealing with tobacco industry misinformation, recognizing friends and foes in the war against smoking, and setting up anti-smoking activist groups.

Steve Allen, whom you may remember as a television comic and host, is himself an antismoking activist. The book is somewhat unique in stance on its public health and practical and hands-on political concerns. Allen and Adler also discuss what it takes to set up a smoke-free workplace and deal effectively with the media if and when you decide to get involved in antismoking efforts.

Locating Helpful Web Sites

You're probably familiar enough with computers to be able to get on the Internet and do some research. If you don't have a computer at home, your public library probably has one that you can access for free. If you can point and click a mouse and type with one finger, you're on! (And by the way, you can buy a brand-new computer with the money you'll save after a year of not smoking.)

Once you log on to a Web browser, such as AOL, Mindspring, or Earthlink, simply head to your favorite search engine (Yahoo!, Excite, or Lycos, for example — I prefer Google) and type in your search term.

This is where the fun begins. As soon as you enter your search term, you will undoubtedly be presented with numerous choices. If you enter **smoking**, for example, you'll find literally hundreds of options. One site I found promises you that you can quit smoking in seven days. Another sells cigarette papers.

One of my all-time favorite sites for detailed information about addiction is the National Clearinghouse for Alcohol and Drug Information (NCDAI), an information geyser from SAMHSA (Substance Abuse and Mental Health Services Administration), at `www.health.org`. This giant federal agency is responsible for education, prevention, and research efforts. NCADI gives viewers access to Webcasts and to targeted facts on specific diseases, substances of abuse, and programs. The Web links, calendar, and archives on drugs are terrific sources of knowledge on addiction biology, healthcare, prevention, and community resources.

Make your Web search selective. Don't go off on in a blind alley when you're looking for specific information. Try flexing your Internet muscles (and breathing muscles) by doing enough Web surfing to complete Table 13-1. Find out where and when support and educational meetings take place in your area. See if you can find enough scheduled meetings to fill in a complete week's calendar. Fill in the locations of each meeting. Maybe you can find some that I missed in my search.

Table 13-1		Schedule for Staying Smoke-Free			
Time	*NA*	*Smokenders*	*ALA*	*ACS*	*Other*
7:00 a.m.					
8:00 a.m.					
9:00 a.m.					

(continued)

Table 13-1 *(continued)*

Time	NA	Smokenders	ALA	ACS	Other
10:00 a.m.					
11:00 a.m.					
12:00 p.m.					
1:00 p.m.					
2:00 p.m.					
3:00 p.m.					
4:00 p.m.					
5:00 p.m.					
6:00 p.m.					
7:00 p.m.					
8:00 p.m.					
9:00 p.m.					

For example, suppose you live in Westport, Connecticut (or want to attend quit-smoking meetings there). You want to find out as much as you can about the nearest support groups and meetings. By logging on to the Internet and searching for five minutes, I came up with the following information:

✔ Nicotine Anonymous meetings were available in Greenwich, Bristol, and Norwich, among other locations.

✔ I could sign up for a trip on the world's first smoke-free cruise ship, arranged by Manchester Community College, the American Lung Association, and Carnival Cruise Lines.

✔ The Freedom from Smoking program (tuition fee involved) has clinics in New Haven, Stamford, and New London, as well as at other sites.

✔ The American Cancer Society (ACS) has an office in Wilton, Connecticut, reachable by phone or fax. ACS also has organized a smoke-free New England Campus Initiative as well as a program for business leaders promoting a smoke-free New England.

Much more information is available for this region and for your region as well.

You can visit a number of highly informative Web sites to find out more about smoking prevention, the consequences of smoking, and health and health-care in general. Many of them are interactive and give you a wide range of choices. Depending on your time, availability, and interest, you can get a narrowly focused search on a particular topic, or you can educate yourself broadly and achieve a refined and sophisticated understanding of many inter-related topics from these sources.

The American Lung Association

The American Lung Association's Web site has an incredible amount of information that's relevant to anyone who wants to stop smoking. The site (www.lungusa.org) is complex, multilayered, and well organized. Visitors can choose from an extensive and varied menu that includes a veritable course on quitting smoking; a series of Lung Profilers, such as Asthma Profilers and Small Cell Lung Carcinoma profilers, enabling you to log on to an interactive program that offers customized advice and up-to-date scientific information about these specific diseases. In order to access this useful support for those who have to make treatment decisions, you need to log in.

The site also features a Wall of Remembrance, which gives you a chance to post written memorials to those who have been struck down by lung disease. In addition, it has sections on data and statistics, advocacy, occupational health, and school programs, as well as an A-to-Z list of lung diseases. You'll also find sections on tobacco control and air quality. The ALA offers an online smoking cessation clinic as well as books and articles on the life-or-death project of quitting smoking.

You can contact your local chapter of the American Lung Association to get involved in educational, preventive, and public health efforts in your community.

The American Cancer Society

Talk about a full menu. You may be reluctant to take a look at the American Cancer Society's Web site (www.cancer.org), but if you do, you'll be highly rewarded for your time. The site has buttons that you can click if you're a cancer patient or a family member of a cancer patient. Other buttons are designated for professionals, survivors, and ACS supporters. You can educate yourself about cancer, coping with cancer, and some of the newest data on treatment and research. The site also offers a bookstore, as well as detailed information about early detection, prevention, and statistics. Yet other buttons lead you to scientific news, stories of hope, and community calendars (you type in your zip code and the program does the rest).

The ACS also maintains a Web site specifically designed to help people quit smoking. The American Cancer Society's Complete Guide to Quitting (www.quitsmokingsupport.com) is packed with information about your number-one priority. It touches on many of the issues covered in this book. Visitors can read archived articles, view photographs of diseased lungs, pick up tips and strategies for quitting, and even go interactive, clicking on bulletin boards and chat rooms for further support. (I visited the chat room, introducing myself as Joe Camel, a 50-year-old doctor who lives in the Northeast. Unfortunately, I was the only person in the room at the time.) The sophisticated site also has an extensive list of useful links and is definitely worth checking out.

Other great sites

Many other Web sites offer resources and support for people who are in the process of quitting smoking. Here are some additional sites you may want to visit:

- ✔ **Campaign for Tobacco-Free Kids** (www.tobaccofreekids.org): I really like this site. The campaign's home page features special reports on the tobacco companies' settlements with the states, on how corporate tobacco is still reaching out and addicting kids, on the industry's massive efforts at buying political influence, and on international efforts to achieve tobacco control. There's a feature on Kick Butts Day, as well as a series of buttons that you click to get lots of information about research and facts, tobacco advertising, federal and state initiatives, and ways for youths and adults alike to take action.

- ✔ **Medscape.com** (www.medscape.com): Medscape.com is an interactive Web site. You enter your particular area of interest, and Medscape does the rest. The home page features a menu that includes health news as well as spotlights on various specialties within medicine, such as cardiology and pulmonary medicine. Subscribers who log in can access expert areas on various topics, including baldness, allergies, and clinical immunology. Medscape also provides conference coverage of recent medical meetings and conventions. Another nice feature is an archive of articles from the top medical journals (*CHEST, American Heart Journal,* and so on). The search tools MEDLINE and Medscape Search Info are also available. I also found textbooks like the *Manual of Lung Transplant Medical Care* offered here (for subscribers who log in).

- ✔ **QuitNet** (www.quitnet.org): QuitNet, rated among the top ten online healthcare sites in *Online Health Care For Dummies* (also published by Wiley), offers an impressive array of information, interactions, and tools. The home page gives you the option to start a quit plan right then and there, asking you to provide some facts about yourself. I said that I smoked 40 cigarettes a day and had my first smoke of the day within five minutes of waking (hard core!). I received the following set of responses: "The Nicodemon is stealing you blind! You are not alone. 15% of QuitNet members smoke their first cigarette of the day within five minutes of waking up." According to the QuitNet calculator, I would save $4,380 a year by quitting and would add three months, 21 days, and 12 hours to my life per year by quitting. My nicotine withdrawal? "After quitting," said QuitNet, "your cravings and/or other physical withdrawal symptoms could be intense." I'm glad I no longer smoke!

✔ **QuitSmoking.com** (`www.quitsmoking.com`): This interesting and highly informative site offers browsers a quit-smoking diary. With it, you can keep a running record of your trials and tribulations as you make progress with quitting. You also can read about the experiences others have had. The site does have a commercial slant; a fair amount of banners and product offers are there to help smokers quit. Free articles on quitting are offered as well.

✔ **Tobacco Information and Prevention Source** (`www.cdc.gov/tobacco/`): The Centers for Disease Control's Tobacco Information and Prevention Source (TIPS) is really cool. It's organized in a straightforward and easy-to-access format. You can quickly get an overview of the topic, quitting guides, and an enormous amount of research and epidemiological information. The Surgeon General's reports and campaigns and events in which you can participate are listed as well. You can log on to a page featuring model Christy Turlington and other antismoking celebrities cautioning against the perils of smoking. If you enjoy scholarly research, the site includes a new listing of citations each week — recently appearing articles on tobacco and the consequences of its use.

✔ **WebMD** (`www.webmd.com`): WebMD has levels for healthcare consumers — the public — as well as physicians. You'll find a search tool, buttons to click if you've been newly diagnosed with a condition, message boards, and sections on living with various illnesses. That's not all. Sections on health and wellness, a medical library, and additional components on drugs, herbs, and symptoms are available. This site also has a body mass index calculator for those who are concerned about their weight. The day I logged on, one of the News in Depth items portrayed how a smoking ban in a small town in Montana saved lives.

✔ **WhyQuit.com** (`www.whyquit.com`): WhyQuit.com has an attractive home page featuring a large menu of choices. Some of the items meander into the grisly zone, such as "Kim's Missing Lung" and "If You Could Spend a Day with Me," by Dr. Werner-Wasik, Oncologist. Heavy-handed? Maybe. But deservedly, too. The subject of smoking is deeply morbid, after all.

As if that weren't enough, the popular online services Yahoo! and AOL provide search capabilities and information about healthcare topics, too. The National Institutes of Health (NIH) and the National Institute of Drug Abuse have excellent in-depth coverage on many topics related to breathing, tobacco, addiction, and smoking.

You must remember this . . .

If you're losing your resolve and wondering why you're reading this chapter — wondering why you need to bother with support groups, nicotine replacement therapy, or any of these concerns — remember that

✔ Women who smoke are at much higher risk of heart attacks and lung cancer.

✔ Children of smokers are much more likely to become smokers themselves.

✔ U.S. medical expenses related to smoking top $50 billion a year.

✔ The federal government foots a large part of the healthcare costs of smoking-related illness — by using your tax dollars.

✔ Most smokers want to quit at some point.

✔ The annual death toll in the United States from smoking exceeds that from cocaine use, murder, suicide, and auto accidents.

✔ More women die each year from lung cancer than from breast cancer.

✔ The brown stuff that leaches out of wet cigarettes — tar — lines smokers' lungs. The amount of tar accumulated in a smoker's lungs in one year can exceed a full quart.

Joining in the Great American Smokeout

Have you heard about the Great American Smokeout? This event takes place annually, on the third Thursday in November. The idea is simple: You take part by "simply" not smoking for 24 hours. Easier said than done! You wouldn't be reading this book if quitting smoking were that easy. Nonetheless, thousands of people do manage to "kick butt" for at least one day every year. Knowing that you're participating in a national event (under the auspices of the American Cancer Society, the event went national in 1977) may give you the extra boost that takes you over the wall. All it takes is the first step. Once you've shown yourself that you can stop smoking for one day, you'll start to wonder why you smoke at all.

Many successful quitters have achieved freedom from tobacco by putting off their first smoke of the day for consecutively longer periods. If you're accustomed to smoking first thing in the morning, then you cut back by delaying that first cigarette until 30 minutes after rising. The second day, you put off the first smoke until an hour after you get out of bed. Eventually, your first puff will be after lunch, and you'll increasingly wonder why you smoke at all. The point is, if you can do it for one day, then you can do it for longer. Think about the statistics. Think about 50 million Americans not smoking for one day. That's a lot of unused cigarettes and a lot of reclaimed air.

On the Great American Smokeout day, you can join dozens, if not hundreds, of your neighbors in an important and fun event that may change your life. All you have to do to participate is be there. The activities are sponsored by the American Cancer Society. An example of activities: One franchise gave out "cold turkey" sandwiches to anyone who traded in half a pack or more of cigarettes. Newborns at a hospital in Washington got tiny T-shirts reading, "I'm a Born Nonsmoker."

If you choose to quit permanently from that day on, you can look forward to continued support from people you meet on this day and from community health groups that you may learn of during the Smokeout. If you pick up a smoke the next day or after, at the very least you've shown yourself that you can stop smoking for a while.

Chapter 14

Self-Medicating Mood Swings

This chapter describes mood and anxiety problems that may cause you to reach for a smoke. It's important to understand these varieties of mood disorders because they occur more frequently among smokers than among nonsmokers. Also, many people with depression, bipolar disorder, or anxiety disorders self-medicate with a variety of substances, prominent among which is nicotine.

Safe and effective treatment for depression, mood swings, anxiety, and panic attacks are available. There are far better and healthier solutions to emotional highs and lows than lighting up.

Deciphering Depression

Depression has to be one of the most commonly bandied-about words in the English language. The term (when it's not referring to the economy) refers to a gamut of different mood and feeling states. When people speak of depression, they may be referring to any or all of the following:

- ✔ Stress
- ✔ Moodiness
- ✔ Irritability
- ✔ Low energy
- ✔ Loss of interest or pleasure
- ✔ Low self-esteem

✔ Difficulty concentrating

✔ Agitation

✔ Anxiety

Quite a menu! Not too long ago, people even used the phrase *nervous break-down* to describe extremes of a scattered, low, or even wired mood.

In recent decades, psychiatrists and other mental health professionals have made giant strides toward better understanding and characterization of depression. As a result of hundreds of studies involving surveys, self-reports, and clinical trials of medications and other treatments, depression is now seen as a family of related disorders differing in severity, duration, and features.

Depression is one of the most common disorders in the United States. Although it's very treatable, it needlessly accounts for a great deal of suffering and debility. If you think you're depressed, please reach out and get some professional help. See the section "Managing Mood Swings" at the end of this chapter for information about treatment options.

Situational (reactive) depression

Situational (reactive) depression is a mood swing in the low direction that typically occurs following an upset or an adverse event. Perhaps your boss or teacher criticized you (unjustly, of course!) or you received some bad news. Perhaps someone you care about is ill, or you recently lost or separated from someone.

The hallmark of this type of depression is its reactive nature. A trigger event gets the depression going. The decline in mood and energy can be swift, severe, and even debilitating, although, because they are reactive, these fluctuations more commonly are truly transient, meaning that with the passage of time (usually a day or two) or with further changes in events (the boss or that girl you fancy finally smiles at you), your mood rebounds.

Situational depression can take on a life of its own and become more severe, but this development is exceptional. More often, your mood bounces back to where it's been, and you're back to your familiar, resilient self.

Some people are more susceptible to these reactive lows than others. In part, you are the inheritor (or victim) of your own nature. You relate to others and to the world in a somewhat circumscribed set of ways. You have specific personality traits that come up again and again in particular situations. You may have a sunny disposition, or you may be permanently disposed to gloom. If you are optimistic and tend to see the good in most situations, you're less likely to have these reactive depressions. If you do fall victim to this kind of depression, it's likely to be very temporary.

Major depression

Major depression is depression that has become autonomous. It takes on a life of its own, no matter what you do, think, or say. Major (also referred to as *clinical, biological, chemical,* or *endogenous*) depression is quite different from reactive depression.

Although major depression may start out identical in appearance and severity to situational depression, the depression hangs around, no matter how many pep talks your family and friends give you. It's a "gift" that keeps on giving.

The distinguishing features of this type of depression are duration, severity, and so-called *vegetative* signs. When you're having a major depression, your body, your hormones, and your fight-or-flight system are all in high gear, essentially overreacting to dangers that may not even exist. Sleep is disrupted, as is appetite for food and for life in general.

Symptoms of depression must last for at least two weeks in order to qualify for a diagnosis of major depression. Psychiatrists use *The Diagnostic and Statistical Manual* (DSM) to diagnose depression and all other mental illnesses. The manual is constantly updated and refined as knowledge about mental disorders accumulates. Actual diagnostic labels and definitions of illness change over time.

Major depression is currently defined as including many of the following characteristics:

- Depression lasts for at least two weeks
- Mood is depressed and doesn't improve with positive changes in the environment
- Insomnia or hypersomnia (too much sleep)
- Anorexia (loss of appetite) or hyperphagia (eating too much)
- Marked weight gain or loss
- Impaired concentration
- Loss of interest and pleasure in usual activities *(anhedonia)*
- Diminished libido (loss of interest in sex)
- Feelings of guilt
- Low self-esteem

Extreme depression can feature hallucinations (hearing voices, seeing things that aren't there), delusions (often of a persecutory nature), and thoughts of suicide. Individuals who have these symptoms should consult with a doctor, because major depression is a significant cause of work loss, stress, and suicide. Even if you don't have the full-blown syndrome, any one of the symptoms of depression can be uncomfortable and can interfere with work and relationships. If you have a symptom that's making problems for you, consult with a professional.

Even the most severe and disabling depression is treatable. See the later section "Managing Mood Swings" for details.

Unipolar and bipolar mood swings

The most recent approach to mood disorders distinguishes between unipolar and bipolar disorders. *Unipolar* mood swings are those that occur in only one direction — usually that of depression. *Bipolar* mood swings involve both highs and lows. Bipolar highs — also called *mania* — involve heightened energy, reduced need for sleep, nonstop thinking, spending sprees, and rapid, pressured speech. Some people have "mixed" states that feature either rapidly cycling moods or simultaneous highs and lows.

The pattern and severity of these mood disorders vary almost as widely as the people who have them. Unipolar disorder may occur once in a lifetime, seasonally, several times a year, or with increasing frequency over time. The same is true for bipolar disorder, or manic depression. Manic depression is further complicated by the usually unpredictable presence of upward mood swings (highs), downward mood swings (lows), or concurrent highs and lows.

A variant of an upward mood swing that people with unipolar and bipolar depression experience is the moderate high, or so-called *hypomanic* state. Interestingly, many people who experience periods of hypomania actually enjoy them and feel that they're able to work better and longer and in general have more energy and creativity when they're hypomanic. Understandably, these people may be reluctant to relinquish these highs and may be opposed to taking medication (other than nicotine!) for their disorder. The main reason certain medications are suggested for sustained elevated moods of bipolar disorder is that whatever goes up eventually has to come down.

All too often, bipolar highs are followed by a crash, which can take the form of a profound and disabling — even life-threatening — depression. Appropriate treatment of these roller-coaster moods leads to an evening out and stabilization of the highs and lows. The highs aren't as high, and the lows certainly aren't as low.

Everyone enjoys experiencing a natural high from time to time. There is nothing abnormal about it. In fact, a terrific personal goal is to train yourself to achieve states of well-being, alertness, and brisk energy without the use of substances . . . especially nicotine.

Do you recognize any of the features of mania or hypo-(mild)-mania in yourself?

✔ Rapid, pressured speech

✔ Racing thoughts

✔ Reduced need for sleep

✔ Diminished appetite for food

✔ Increased impulsiveness

✔ Spending sprees (tear up those credit cards, fast!)

✔ Preoccupation with sex

✔ Irritability

✔ Mood swings

✔ Extreme bouts of anger

✔ Increased self-medication with alcohol, cigarettes, or other substances

Creative, hard-driving people often have some of these traits and may be reluctant to give them up. In fact, several studies have demonstrated that mood disorders are actually more frequent among writers and artists than among the general population. So if you have any features of bipolar disorder or depression, consider yourself in good company! The challenge is to come up with ways to feel well and stay well, to remain productive and creative, without the burden of mood swings and the accompanying risk of debilitating and severe mood disorder.

Alleviating Anxiety

Anxiety often accompanies depression and vice versa. Like depression, it has many other names, such as stress, "nerves," and agitation. Anxiety is an ordinary part of life. Flipping through this month's stack of bills can be quite stressful. So can crossing the street! But there are limits to how much anxiety is normal. As with depression, the threshold for concern — the signal that you should consult with a professional — is when the anxiety interferes with your life.

Anxiety is the inner or subjective counterpart of a perceived danger. The key word here is *perceived*. Your body and brain are hard-wired to react instantly and effectively to danger signals around you. You're crossing the street and suddenly, seemingly out of nowhere, an 18-wheeler comes bearing down on you: the classic fight-or-flight situation. Your muscles tense, your heart pounds, you hyperventilate. Inside your body, adrenaline and cortisol prepare you to react swiftly and effectively. Your pupils widen to maximize your awareness of the environment. Bear in mind that all this happens way out of proportion to any real danger in your environment.

Take a mental step back and imagine if this were happening to you in the comfort and safety of your living room. People with anxiety disorders have continuous bouts of fight-or-flight reactions.

The causes of these responses are multiple. Some people inherit a tendency toward anxiety or panic or a predisposition to the syndrome. For others, catastrophic, violent life events trigger the anxiety. People with post-traumatic stress disorder (PTSD) undergo episodes of severe anxiety along with other problems.

If you've ever had anxiety symptoms, you'll be quick to recognize these features:

- ✔ Dry mouth
- ✔ Sweaty palms
- ✔ Racing pulse
- ✔ Quick, shallow breathing
- ✔ Intense sense of foreboding and impending doom

Even when they're transient, anxiety symptoms are extremely unpleasant. Perhaps you've had the occasion to speak in public and found your stomach tied up in knots, your thoughts confused, and your heart racing. This is called *performance anxiety*. A related experience, social anxiety, occurs when you are in a crowd, at a party or meeting, for example. In these situations, your nervous system may go on overload and pump out stress hormones as though your life were truly on the line. Knowing this, it's no wonder that nicotine, with its antianxiety effects, is so difficult to kick!

The problem (aside from the extreme unpleasantness of the sensations) is that ongoing stress reactions are damaging to your health. Studies have shown that unchecked stress responses, including anxiety, essentially wear down the immune system and thus make you more susceptible to infections and to the effects of injuries.

It makes sense to ask yourself if you experience anxiety to a disabling degree. Do nervous feelings restrict your ability to interact with people or limit your ability to work, study, or otherwise function? Are the nervous feelings present around the clock? Do you have episodes or attacks that wake you from sleep? Is the anxiety severe, with sweaty palms, dry mouth, heart slamming against your ribcage? These symptoms suggest that the anxiety is severe and should be treated.

Effective treatments for anxiety and panic are available — see the section "Managing Your Mood Swings" at the end of this chapter for details. Very often, appropriate doses of an SSRI-type medication (such as Paxil, Effexor, Prozac, or Celexa) with or without behavioral therapy can diminish or even eliminate these symptoms.

Most lists of anxiety symptoms fall short of being all-inclusive. Even if you don't have major symptoms such as a pounding heart, sweaty palms, and a feeling of impending doom, you may have low-level or chronic anxiety. Mild to moderate anxiety can cripple careers and relationships. Countless people don't reach their personal best because social situations and asserting themselves cause them too much anxiety. Treatment for anxiety is usually very effective and can make the difference between marginal and top-notch functioning on your part.

Putting down panic

Panic is a frightening word. The experience itself is far worse.

Panic, or *anxiety attacks,* is a pronounced form of anxiety that arises episodically. It's like a fire alarm going off in your brain. Anyone who has experienced an attack will tell you that it's far and away one of the worst experiences one can have.

The episode typically last from one to five minutes. It involves a feeling of impending doom, a sudden rush of desperate fear, and a sudden and compelling need to escape. Quite often, the attack occurs in a closed space such as a car or an elevator. Sometimes panic attacks occur in public places, such as supermarkets or other stores.

It's not unusual for people to *generalize* from their first attack. If someone has his first panic attack in a shopping mall, he may develop an intense aversion to shopping malls — and decide to never visit one again. Likewise with cars, buses, or elevators. It's not too difficult to see how one panic attack can snowball into full-blown *agoraphobia:* fear of open spaces.

Anxiety under the microscope

Extreme anxiety is the equivalent of a fire alarm going off in your brain. The *locus ceruleus,* a tiny brain center with intimate connections to the rest of your nervous system, fires off the neuro-transmitter *norepinephrine* in what are, relatively speaking, huge amounts. This sudden flood of norepinephrine turns on all kinds of other warning systems in the brain and in the rest of the body, resulting in physiological bells and whistles and the urgent message to all body systems: "Fight or flight!"

People will try almost anything to prevent the recurrence of panic. "It's a feeling that comes over you like you're going to die," a mother in her early 30s explained. "All of a sudden, your heart is pounding in your chest like a jackhammer, your mouth is dry, and all you can think about is, 'How can I get away from here?'" The problem, of course, is that "here" is really the person's mind and body . . . and you can't escape from yourself.

Naturally, panic sufferers attempt to understand where these attacks come from. With the help of professionals such as psychiatrists, psychologists, and therapists, they try to figure out why their attack occurred at a particular place at that particular point in time. From time to time, they may be able to put together a reasonably coherent explanation, taking into account what that particular trigger situation means to them emotionally and psychologically. Other times, there simply is no explanation. The attack seems to come like a bolt out of the blue.

 What does all this have to do with smoking? Plenty. Smokers "self-medicate" anxiety, including panic attacks, with cigarettes. Although small amounts of nicotine act as a stimulant, greater amounts exert a sedative effect. The sight of a harried, stressed-out person reaching for a smoke is so familiar that it has become a cliché. Also, because nicotine is a stimulant, it can actually provoke greater anxiety and further panic attacks.

If you have round-the-clock anxiety, or panic episodes, effective treatment is available. See a professional to get the help that you need.

Understanding the Principle of Drug Karma

Do you smoke or chew tobacco to stave off or reduce anxious feelings? If you have recognizable anxiety, the answer to this question is likely to be *yes.* But you need to know that all drugs that affect the brain cause rebound. I call this phenomenon the Principle of Drug Karma. Whatever goes up has to come down, and whatever goes down has to come up.

Consider another sedative, alcohol. The first drink or two makes you feel relaxed and helps you unwind. You may feel more comfortable and sociable around people after you've had a drink. Several hours later, however, the picture is quite different. Instead of feeling loose and relaxed, you may begin to feel uptight. Your nerves may be on edge. If you've had too much to drink and fallen asleep, you may wake a few hours later feeling wired and anxious.

This is your brain going into rebound. Once the alcohol — the sedative — has been metabolized and is out of your system, your brain overreaches in the opposite direction like a spring that has been compressed and then released.

The Principle of Drug Karma applies to stimulants such as nicotine as well. After some minutes of increased energy, alertness, and excitement, the only direction to go is down. Following the nicotine rush (which you notice especially when you have your first cigarette of the day or when you abstain from smoking for several hours and then light up), you experience a physical letdown. You're tired, probably more fatigued and played out than before you had the cigarette.

Don't despair. You can do plenty of things, many of them on your own, to combat anxiety, as the following section explains.

When you do cut back and eventually completely cut out cigarettes, you may have a temporary increase, or rebound, of anxiety symptoms. To get through rebound (nicotine withdrawal) anxiety:

- ✔ Remember that the anxiety is only temporary.
- ✔ Engage in physical activity such as walking or jogging.
- ✔ Consult with your doctor if the anxiety is severe enough to interfere with your functioning (if the anxiety is disabling).
- ✔ Keep a log of your well-being. Chances are, over the course of the first quit week, you will see a dramatic reduction in the amount of rebound anxiety you experience.

Managing Mood Swings

Treatment of mood disorders and anxiety takes a variety of forms, depending on the problem at hand. To get help, you first need to recognize that the problems exist. If you have symptoms that are interfering with your ability to function from day to day, seek professional help.

These days, less stigma than ever is attached to mental illness, and plenty of helpful community resources are available. Most cities and towns have a community mental health center, and most have a nearby medical center that includes a department of psychiatry. Locating good therapists, psychologists, and psychiatrists who are in community practice is relatively easy. Often, the best way to get a referral is by word of mouth: If someone you know and trust has had a good experience with a doctor or therapist, chances are that you will, too.

The following additional resources are available for directories and referrals of mental health experts:

- ✔ Your local or regional mental health association
- ✔ The American Psychiatric Association (www.psych.org; 703-907-7300)
- ✔ The American Hospital Association (312-422-3000)
- ✔ The American Psychological Association (www.apa.org; 900-374-2721)
- ✔ The National Association of Social Workers (www.naswdc.org)

Practitioners differ in their treatment recommendations. Some recommend cognitive or another form of talking therapy for mild to moderate mood problems, while others feel that medication offers the fastest and most dramatic relief of symptoms. Moderate to severe depression and anxiety are best treated with medication with or without talking therapy. When medication (not nicotine!) works, the patient usually spends significantly less time and money than would be involved in ongoing talking therapy.

Undergoing cognitive therapy

Cognitive therapy may be helpful for mild to moderate anxiety and depression. It's based on the idea that beliefs determine feelings. The things you tell yourself throughout the course of the day create and then reinforce how you end up feeling and functioning.

For example, a depressed person tends to be pessimistic. If you're depressed, you're likely to interpret events — even neutral events, such as the weather — in negative ways. A depressive wakes up to an overcast sky and reads it as proof that his life and future are dark and will always be that way. It's possible, even likely, that these interpretations (of which dozens, if not hundreds, occur in the span of a day) trigger emotional and even physical reactions that are ultimately destructive.

The first step in cognitive therapy involves identifying the self-statements that you make all the time. The next step involves singling out the negative, irrational statements and holding them up to the light of day. For example, is your belief that you will never be able to stop smoking really true? If you think about it, haven't literally millions of others been able to stop? What is it about yourself that you think will stand in your way?

Having identified the worm in the apple, so to speak, the next step is to chuck it and replace it with a more logical, constructive belief. For example, you may believe that you can't or will never quit. When you re-examine this belief, you may be able to reframe it in a more positive way, such as, "I used to think I couldn't quit. Millions of people have quit. I probably can, too."

Combating panic and depression with medication

Effective pharmaceutical treatments for anxiety and panic are available. Mild, moderate, and severe anxiety and mood disorders usually respond quickly to medication.

The SSRIs and other medications used to treat depression, panic, and anxiety these days are truly wonder drugs. They are safe, easy to use, and effective for most people with anxiety and/or depressive symptoms. These medications are thought to modify the amount of particular brain chemicals (neurotransmitters such as serotonin) that are intimately involved in mood, appetite, and overall well-being.

Table 14-1 lists the medications commonly used to treat depression; Table 14-2 lists those commonly used to treat anxiety; and Table 14-3 includes medications used to stabilize moods.

Table 14-1	Antidepressant and Antianxiety Medications	
Brand Name	**Generic Name**	**Typical Daily Dose**
Celexa	Citalopram	10-80 mg
Effexor	Venlafaxine	37.5-300 mg
Luvox	Fluvoxamine	25-200 mg
Paxil	Paroxetine	5-80 mg
Prozac	Fluoxetine	5-80 mg
Zoloft	Sertraline	25-200 mg

Table 14-2	Antianxiety Medications	
Brand Name	*Generic Name*	*Typical Daily Dose*
Ativan	Lorazepam	0.5-4.0 mg
Buspar	Buspirone	10-90 mg
Klonopin	Clonazepam	0.5-8.0 mg
Valium	Diazepam	5-30 mg
Xanax	Alprazolam	0.25-4.0 mg

Table 14-3	Mood Stabilizing Medications	
Brand Name	*Generic Name*	*Typical Daily Dose*
Depakote	Valproic acid	250-1500 mg
Lithium	Lithium carbonate	300-1500 mg
Neurontin	Gabapentin	300-2400 mg
Tegretol	Carbamazepine	200-1200 mg

For easy reference, Table 14-4 reviews the various mood and anxiety problems, their symptoms, and how they are usually treated. Note that *cognitive therapy* is a talking therapy that focuses on the kinds of thoughts you have in the here and now. *Psychotherapy,* generally speaking, is a talking therapy that looks at the present as well as some of the past life stressors that may have contributed to the way you feel now.

If you believe that you may be suffering from any of these conditions, please seek professional help.

Table 14-4	Treatments of Choice	
Condition	*Description*	*Treatment*
Anxiety	"Nerves," persistent fear, fear of social situations, fear of open spaces, avoidance of people or particular settings, fight-or-flight symptoms including dry mouth, racing pulse, sweaty palms	Antidepressant medication, antianxiety medication, mood stabilizers, cognitive therapy/psychotherapy

Condition	Description	Treatment
Panic attacks	Extreme brief bursts of panic, feelings of doom, feeling an overwhelming need to escape	Antidepressant medication, antianxiety medication, cognitive therapy/ psychotherapy
Unipolar depression — mild	"Blahs," low energy or mild loss of interest or pleasure in things, decreased spontaneity and curiosity	Antidepressant medication, psychotherapy
Unipolar depression — moderate	Same features as mild unipolar depression, plus sleep and/or appetite loss or excess, with weight gain or loss; feeling that life may not be worth living	Antidepressant medication, psychotherapy
Unipolar depression — severe	Same features as moderate unipolar depression, plus agitation, pronounced jitteriness, or profound loss of energy; detachment from reality	Antidepressant medication, antipsychotic medication
Bipolar depression	Same features as unipolar depression, plus personal history of one or more upward mood swings	Antidepressant medication and/or mood stabilizers
Hypomania	Euphoria or irritability, grandiosity, decreased need for sleep, increased interest in sex, spending sprees, talkativeness	Mood stabilizers
Mania	An exaggerated version of hypomania, with markedly increased energy, pressured speech, suspiciousness, protracted wakefulness, racing thoughts, grandiosity	Mood stabilizers and/or antipsychotic medications
Mixed-mood state	Both depressive and manic moods, either alternating rapidly or co-occurring	Mood stabilizers and/or antidepressants and/or antipsychotic medication

Beyond the Bell Jar

You can't be a psychiatrist, psychologist, or therapist without having heard of Sylvia Plath and her book *The Bell Jar*. A bell jar can be many things. It can be a vacuum tube containing an electron or X-ray arc. It can be a terrarium containing a world in miniature. Or it can be the cover you have to lift to get at the cupcakes inside.

I finally had my personal encounter with *The Bell Jar* several months ago. As usual, my preconceived notion — that the book would be a precious, self-pitying, overrated exercise in self-indulgence — proved wrong. The book is anything but that.

In the book, heroine Esther Greenwood (an alter ego of Plath) is adrift in the glamorous world of 1950s Manhattan. She tastes life. She is a wry observer, a perennial outsider. While an intern at a fashion magazine, she becomes the romantic target of an uptight, self-righteous, morally limited Yale student and becomes the victim of an increasingly intense and pervasive depression.

Esther is so depressed that she gets herself committed to an insane asylum and goes through several courses of shock treatment. Her doctor, her family, her boyfriend, and her mentor, an older woman who is also a writer, try to reach her and bridge the yawning chasm of her depressive isolation. Except that she is truly in hell.

Esther walks the walk and talks the talk — she is an incredibly articulate and likable narrator, her intelligence the kind that makes you like her despite her most ferocious attempts to put you off — but she is dead inside. Her inner world holds no joy, no charm, no pleasure at all. Her elitist posing is the very best she can do. Her feelings are *dead*.

Sylvia Plath the author grew up outside Boston. From early on, she wrote and drew. As a teenager, she published writings in *Seventeen* magazine and *The Christian Science Monitor*. She graduated from Smith College with the highest honors and went to Cambridge, England on a Fulbright scholarship. She produced an acclaimed body of work, including a number of powerful novels and disturbing but beautiful poetry. And she killed herself on February 11, 1963.

What, you ask, does this story have to do with smoking?

The Bell Jar is among the most powerful testimonials from the other side. Those who haven't been there, who haven't had to wrestle with the angels and demons of depression, have no idea how fortunate they are. Those who have lived with depression will be astonished by the heroism of Plath, Virginia Woolf, or anyone else who manages to survive and even create under the soul-crushing weight of despair.

I maintain that the same applies to anyone lucky enough never to have been tainted by the habit of nicotine.

Depression, anxiety, and other psychiatric disorders are pandemic. So is smoking. No family is spared from the challenge of emotional and addictive disorders.

People who master their lives and habits are heroes. Not only do they master their addictions, but they go on to live admirable, courageous lives filled with dignity and achievement. This is the kind of bell jar that begs to be smashed open. Beyond its glass wall is the real world, filled with life-giving fresh air.

Chapter 15

Getting the Skinny on Weight Gain and Healthy Living

*P*art of the truth about smoking and weight gain, if any universal truth exists, is that you may put on a few extra pounds shortly after you quit. However, this problem is eminently solvable compared to having irreversible lung disease. As millions of people can attest, a combination of healthy diet and exercise can slow and reverse weight gain.

I believe that quitting smoking needs to be your (and every smoker's) number-one priority. If you eat a little more for a period of weeks or even months, that's okay. Granted, no one wants you to pork up and have to trade in your wardrobe for a piano crate. That would be trading in one set of problems for another set of equally serious ones.

This chapter gives you the information you need to manage your diet and weight while quitting smoking. As you probably know, many people defer or permanently decline quitting smoking because of the fear that they'll substitute boxes of cupcakes for packs of cigarettes. This chapter reassures you that you can quit smoking and stay at your present weight.

The Truth about Quitting Smoking and Weight Gain

Tobacco use and eating are intimately related. For starters, many, if not most, smokers use tobacco after meals. Many smokers use tobacco before meals, too!

Smoking after a meal has become a social and biological reflex: It's just what we do. In some parts of the world, smoking after a meal has become as natural a part of the day as setting the table or lighting dinner candles. The cigarette-after-meal connection may relate to the fact that nicotine acts as a stimulant. After taking a meal, particularly a large meal or a meal accompanied by alcoholic beverages, people like to alert themselves with a smoke. Part of successful quitting is working out a new behavior pattern for after meals and every other time you're accustomed to having a smoke.

Plenty of smokers actually substitute tobacco for food. "Why not?" you might ask. "Who couldn't stand to skip a meal or two?" Simply reaching for a cigarette instead of sitting down for a meal may seem convenient. These days, most people are so busy that they find themselves reaching for whatever cures those hunger pangs the fastest as they rush from one work, school, or family event to the next. If you could see what smoking does to your body from the point of view of your arterial walls, intestinal lining, and cardiac and lung chambers, though, you would never think that a cigarette is an acceptable substitute for a meal.

You may have a fear (or even an outright horror) of gaining weight, and you may prefer to take on whatever damage the cigarettes are doing. I've heard people say this. You've probably heard people say that they're willing to pay the piper, too. However, you know that it's possible to stop smoking and watch your weight at the same time. You don't have to be a movie star to take care of your body inside _and_ out.

Maybe you've experienced the strange cycle of food avoidance. Not eating causes peculiar physical and mental changes that can be both unpleasant and rewarding. The "rewards" can be a change in appearance and a change in state of mind. If you recognize yourself in this description, you understand that a _change_ in the way you feel is sometimes preferable to no change at all. Sometimes a change for the worse is preferable to staying where you were.

One technique that dietitians use to help compulsive eaters overcome their problem is to have them record all the foods they consume. The same idea applies to cigarettes. Imagine taking all the cigarettes you consumed in the last six months and laying them out in front of you. You would be stupefied!

At least food is either metabolized, eliminated, or stored as fat. The waste products of tobacco combustion are stored in the linings and cells of your throat and lungs — not a good place for toxins.

An interesting exercise is to take all the excess food that people eat and imagine it wrapped up like a cigar. My point is that like a Macanudo or a Camel, you reach for foods mechanically, reflexively, and without thinking. Remember that you are in charge of what you eat, what you drink, and what you smoke. If you're feeling out of control about eating and/or smoking, put yourself right back in the driver's seat. The person you are now is the sum of all your previous decisions, and the person you will be in the future is the sum of all the decisions you make today.

As you quit smoking, these after-eating strategies may help you stay away from cigarettes:

- ✔ Make a phone call.
- ✔ Get right up and take a walk.
- ✔ Read to your children.
- ✔ Walk your dog.
- ✔ Kiss someone.
- ✔ Have a mint or a stick of gum.
- ✔ Go out.
- ✔ Read a section of this book.
- ✔ Take a shower.

You have to eat. You don't have to smoke. Don't let a fear of weight gain keep you from putting your health first.

Understanding Obesity and the Factors That Cause It

Medical scientists, nutritionists, and clinicians around the world are still trying to understand why people overeat and keep on gaining weight. The obesity problem is pandemic. In the United States alone, two-thirds of the population is overweight. A large number of them are *morbidly obese* — that is, their body mass index (BMI) is over 40. (Your BMI is calculated from your weight and height. Normal BMI is in the range of 20 to 25.) If your BMI is in the morbid or stratospheric range, you're at risk for a number of problems (and you've probably been struggling with severe obesity for most, if not all, of your life):

✔ Arthritis, especially of the weight-bearing joints

✔ Coronary artery disease

✔ Diabetes

✔ Hypertension

✔ Hardening of the arteries

✔ Low self-esteem

✔ Sleep apnea and other respiratory disorders

✔ Social isolation and stigmatization

✔ Fewer social, career, and romantic choices

The more you weigh, the greater your risk for these unhappy situations.

Genetics or environment: Which makes you fat?

A raging debate in the science of obesity is whether the acquisition of fat is genetic or environmental. This question is especially tricky because separating genetics from environment is nearly impossible. A developing fetus, expressing its parents' genes, is also in a physical environment: the womb. As soon the baby is born, it's in another environment, where it's either underfed, adequately fed, or overfed.

As a part of my practice, I work with hundreds of patients who undergo gastric bypass surgery. We review in meticulous detail their life histories, their food histories and attempts to diet, and their struggles with weight loss and gain prior to surgical intervention. The vast majority of these people — mostly women, as it turns out — have been overweight since childhood. They feel that they were born overweight. At the same time, many freely acknowledge that they reach for comfort food — particularly carbohydrates, and particularly at night — as soon as they feel tired, hungry, lonely, or stressed. Sound familiar? You may reach for a smoke in these same scenarios.

Neither a cupcake nor a cigarette is going to help you overcome fatigue, hunger, loneliness, or stress. You need to address these issues by finding lasting and meaningful substitute activities, such as walking, working out, and conversation, that will serve you way better in the long run.

Some of the most recent thinking on these matters suggests that people are born with different set points in their *lipid,* or fat, metabolism. Those who have higher set points have more trouble metabolizing fat, which predisposes them to weight gain. Other researchers believe that if you start taking in excessive amounts of food early on in life, you permanently alter your set point; your body becomes used to getting more food and insists on a continued larger influx of food.

The good news for people who struggle with obesity is that medical scientists are actively researching a group of hormones called *leptins* that may send chemical messages to the body regarding fat retention. The hope is that greater understanding of how these messenger molecules work will lead to the development of drugs that outsmart the body and expand our pharmaceutical options when it comes to weight control.

Saying bye-bye to bingeing

You may not be a party to the habit of bingeing on food, but in times of high anxiety, or when they are lonely or needy, many people reach for a box of donuts or a bag of chips for solace. If you've been a slave to cigarettes or cigars, you certainly can't discount the power of habit. Simply put, bingeing is a loss of self-control. This lack of power is continually reinforced by returning to the use of breakfast pastries or salty, fatty snacks or cigarettes, whichever it may be.

Bingeing and anorexia are concepts that apply equally to eating and smoking. Anorexia nervosa — an extremely serious eating disorder characterized by episodic refusal to eat, obsessive concern with what goes into the body, and ruminations about being thin — has a fatal outcome 20 percent of the time. I maintain that "uncured" smokers — to adopt the vernacular of the alcohol allergy movement — may find themselves in much the same position: Should they smoke or shouldn't they? If you have not yet quit smoking or often take a long time pondering the decision, you may be stuck on the wheel of overthinking.

Don't get sidetracked by obsessions. If you find that you're preoccupied with this kind of thinking when you're in quit mode, you may be but a stone's throw away from lighting up.

Mouthing off on quick-fix foods

I've said that eating foods that are bad for you isn't nearly as bad as smoking, but there is a limit. You can find a wealth of information about calorie intake, food groups, the best time of day to eat or not eat, and even the ideal state of mind while taking your meals and snacks. I urge you to read, talk to nutrition experts, and avoid at all costs fast foods and high-sugar foods such as candy.

Counting calories, not cancer sticks

Sometimes obsessing is a good thing. God, as they say, is in the details. If you're concerned about gaining weight after quitting, why not put your energy to good use and learn as much as you possibly can about nutrition, weight control, and exercise? Focusing your thoughts and efforts in this direction will not only distract you from the desire for tobacco, but also inform you of the better world that's within your grasp.

High-fat foods such as those you get at drive-thrus and pizza joints are the gastrointestinal equivalent of smoking, as far as I'm concerned. In recent years, fast-food chains have been forced by statute to post the "nutritional" content of their meals in publicly visible areas, and let me tell you, it's not a pretty sight. A burger can have 20 or more grams of fat, not including the extras, such as a slab of cheese. Pizza and similar foods are no bargain if you're watching your weight or your cholesterol.

The best foods to eat, whether it's Quit Day 1 or Quit Day 1,000, are high-protein, low-fat, low-carb foods, such as chicken, fish, and tofu. Other foods that are generally healthful are "slow-burn carbs" that are high in fiber, such as vegetables and fruits.

The things of value in this life, such as health, longevity, and continued good looks, don't come easy. You have to work at and invest in them. The good news is that the down payment is quite low: a pack of cigarettes. Don't stop there, though. Once you quit smoking, you will want to keep boosting your feelings of wholeness and well-being. Lifestyle changes such as eating better and healthier foods and getting more exercise pay off big time.

Getting a Handle on Weight Gain

Weight gain is not a unique situation for you or anyone. Being overweight is a fact of life for the majority of Americans, whether or not they smoke. The way to reverse weight gain — or, better yet, to prevent it in the first place — is to make a solid long-term commitment to your health and your appearance. One of the many fascinating aspects of eating and living right is that as your lifestyle takes a permanent detour for the high road, your tastes actually change.

Quitting smoking is a trade-off. What you give up is negligible compared to what you get in return. For example, soon after you quit smoking, you'll begin to notice finer and subtler flavors and aromas around you. Similarly, if you've become accustomed to chips and other famously unhealthy snack foods but start replacing them with more sophisticated and refined items, your taste buds will become more aware of the complex and less strident personalities of grains, leafy green vegetables, and more subtly prepared foods. Think of how something prepared delicately after steeping in a tender marinade versus a food being thermally blasted by a flame thrower!

Managing weight gain medically

Medical approaches to countering weight gain are out there. The good news is that many insurance plans will pay for you to consult with a weight management specialist if your weight exceeds a certain plateau. The local group that my office works with has a staff comprised of physicians, nutritionists, nurses, and physical therapists who perform complete evaluations of patients' lifestyles, nutritional profiles, exercise tolerance, and overall stamina. With this information as a baseline, the nutritionist and doctor can create an action plan that has multiple components.

Medically supervised weight loss generally includes the following elements:

- ✔ An exercise regimen
- ✔ A customized diet
- ✔ Nutritional supplements, including high-protein meals and vitamins
- ✔ Charts of daily activity and food intake
- ✔ Medication

For some people, stimulant medication is helpful in their effort to shed pounds. Newer classes of medication that prevent the absorption of fatty foods are also being used today. The key is to work with medical professionals to engineer a plan that works for you.

Doing your part by exercising regularly

The keys to losing weight are regularity and consistency. Start exercising now, and do it every day. I recently advised a patient who was concerned about weight gain to work out daily, and she panicked. "Every day?!?" she exclaimed. Yes, every day! You must be dedicated to your goal in order to succeed.

Talking to the experts

Dr. Jonathan Fine, Associate Director of Pulmonary Medicine at Norwalk Hospital in Connecticut, makes the point that successfully quitting smoking is based on appealing to the person's stated priorities. "When I have this conversation with a patient in the office," Dr. Fein states, "I find out where they want to go — *why* they want to quit. Armed with this knowledge, I can really help them quit."

Dr. Fein makes other terrific points. If you are using nicotine replacement therapy such as the patch, make sure that you are using enough. Sure, the nicotine in the patch (and the gum, inhaler, and aerosol) is a real drug: too much will harm you. But not enough can lead to craving and smoking relapse. Evidence shows that part of nicotine replacement success is using the right amount of nicotine replacement — roughly the equivalent of the amount you used to inhale.

Understanding why you smoke may help you quit. Part of the reason (aside from the mental and physical dependence) may be that smoking is a way of showing that you are brave, that you can flaunt being alive: a kind of denial of death. Smoking is like flipping the bird to the grim reaper.

A slew of books have been written about lives devoted to and marred by struggles with smoking. One example is *Conversations with Zeno* by Italo Svevo, which documents in painstaking detail the exploits of a poor wretch who grapples with his soul in order to stop smoking. Richard Klein's *Cigarettes Are Sublime* is another book worth checking out. Klein takes a counterintuitive tack, describing cigarette smoking as a heroic career, as a passionate challenge to mortality and all of life's limitations. Nonetheless, he ends up encouraging readers to quit.

Margaret Haggerty, RN, MSN, and Program Coordinator of Pulmonary Rehabilitation at Norwalk Hospital, agrees. You have to go to where the person quitting is. You can't impose your own agenda on the person. One approach that works with some people, she says, is to have them wrap their cigarettes up in aluminum foil. The foil puts an additional obstacle in the way of smoking. She suggests that when you go for a smoke, you write down the time of day and what came up that may have caused you to reach for a cigarette. She also finds that getting people to add up the number of puffs they take per day can be a daunting exercise. "Ten puffs per cigarette, 20 cigarettes per day: That adds up," Haggerty says. She emphasizes that smoking cessation is a multimodal project that is best achieved when you are highly motivated and well informed. One of the many poignant encounters in her work involved a man who kept a small photo of his daughter lodged in the cellophane of his cigarette pack. Each time he reached for a smoke, he saw her beautiful shining face.

Regular exercise feels great. No kidding. Find the kind that works for you, and you'll be eager to stick with it.

Daily exercise sounds like a tall order. I understand. But how often do you smoke? Imagine smoking only three times a week! Physical exercise kicks off endorphins in your brain that make you feel euphoric. Endorphins are the bliss molecules of the body. Like many people, I often have to drag myself to the gym, especially at the end of the day. But without exception, at the conclusion of each workout I'm glad I went. Exercise makes you feel terrific not only immediately afterward, but usually for the rest of the day.

It doesn't matter whether you join a gym, hire a personal trainer, or slog it out in your basement. What matters is that you work out regularly.

The kind of workout you choose depends on your preferences. The duration and frequency are more important than the activity itself. If you have health problems and/or are older, consult with your doctor before you begin any exercise regimen.

Eating right

During the fragile transitional days and weeks when you first cut tobacco loose from your life (congratulations!), you may want an oral substitute. Try the following suggestions:

- **Chewing gum:** Gum, particularly sugarless, may be helpful.
- **Raw vegetables:** Carrot and celery sticks are great because they are practically calorie-neutral and are extremely portable.
- **Low-calorie beverages:** Many people are big fans of bottled water, and you still see lots of people toting around cans of diet soda.

You may not have the time to become a world-class gourmet cook — after all, you're quitting smoking, not opening a four-star restaurant — but with half an hour's research, you can find healthy shopping or even takeout food near you.

Keep a bottle of spring water on hand. It's filling and delicious.

Supporting Your Health Habit

How do you maintain a healthy lifestyle? You have to want it badly, for starters. You have to want clean, healthy lungs and a clear conscience enough to put in the time and energy right now to ensure a better tomorrow. Don't be one of those patients who hitch their pack to their tank of oxygen!

Exercising your way to a new you

Working out is great. Just like quitting smoking, it is one of the best things you can do for yourself. It is not something to shudder over, dread, and put off. Don't delay incorporating exercise into your lifestyle.

Many people I talk to have an immediate rejoinder about exercise: "Exercise, oh, sure. I walk every day." Right. You breathe every day, too! There's a difference between walking and true exercise (not to denigrate real, concentrated walking as a way to stay fit). Bear in mind that almost any kind of physical activity done with focus and consistency can be good for muscle and mind tone. Also bear in mind that any exercise advice or decision has to be made in the context of your overall health. If you are overweight or have other medical problems, discuss them with your physician before making any modification to your daily physical activity.

Staying in good shape is not only possible without smoking; working out on a regular basis actually *promotes* staying away from cigarettes. One way it works is by boosting your body's endorphin levels. Endorphins are the feel-good molecules that provide a sense of well-being — that inner glow, that sense of release and relaxation, that is so vital to continued health and high energy. How you choose to stay fit is not as important as the fact that you do choose to stay fit. These days, you actually have to work to avoid staying fit. Calorie counts practically hit you in the face wherever you go: in restaurants, on food packages, in magazine ads. And stress busters, nutrition tips, exercise tapes, and stay-fit programs are everywhere. So hop on board!

Practicing self-care

Self-care is the most important theme in quitting smoking. Although what you're doing is called quitting smoking, you can think of it in a more positive way, as embracing health or life.

What is self-care, anyway? It is

- ✔ Paying attention to details of who you are and what you like.
- ✔ Maintaining a sense of dignity.
- ✔ Enjoying yourself.
- ✔ Remembering that tomorrow always comes.
- ✔ Knowing that others like and count on you.
- ✔ Remembering that you deserve kindness and health.

Think of it like this: You deserve at least the level of kindness that most people would show to a dog or a goldfish. Minimal self-care extends to shelter, adequate nutrition, and clothing. Adequate self-care includes paying attention to what you put in your body. And good self-care pays attention to emotional and spiritual input as well.

Part IV
Looking at Special Groups

In this part . . .

Smoking and tobacco are nearly ubiquitous in modern culture. Tobacco-related health, social, and financial problems do not discriminate between demographic groups. Young people, for example, have been studied as tobacco targets. Teenagers and pregnant women need to be aware of the specific impact that tobacco products have on their growth and development and on the growth and development of a baby. This part talks about those effects and gives you information about helping a teen or a pregnant woman give up smoking. It also helps you help someone you care about — a spouse, a friend, or a coworker — quit. Regardless of your age, sex, or educational background, quitting smoking is an excellent decision.

Chapter 16

Focusing on Smoking, Fertility, and Pregnancy

In This Chapter

▶ Finding out about smoking's effects on fertility

▶ Previewing a normal pregnancy

▶ Looking at the devastating consequences of maternal smoking on a fetus

▶ Recognizing the effects of smoking after pregnancy

Getting pregnant, carrying a baby to term, and raising a healthy, loving child are unequalled among life's positive experiences. If you smoke, your habit puts all these things — your ability to conceive, your chances of carrying your baby to term, and your child's health — at risk. This chapter looks at the processes of conception and pregnancy in order to help you understand the negative effects of smoking on mother and child (and on Dad, too!). It also provides tips and strategies for supporting a pregnant woman's effort to quit smoking.

If you are pregnant or thinking about getting pregnant, it is imperative for you to quit smoking. Your health is at stake — and so is the health of your baby.

Monitoring Mom's Health

You need to be at your physical and emotional peak at the time of conception and during pregnancy to optimize your baby's health. One enormous step you can take for yourself and your baby is to stop smoking as soon as possible. If you're pregnant and still smoking, choose a quit day soon. Even better, actually quit soon!

Keeping an eye on other health factors that could harm your baby

Some maternal illnesses can affect the developing baby and need careful medical monitoring from the prepregnancy stage until delivery. If you're pregnant, keep your eye on

✔ Diabetes

✔ Heart disease

✔ HIV/AIDS

✔ Hypertension (high blood pressure)

✔ Kidney disease

✔ Liver disease

✔ Lupus

✔ Rheumatoid arthritis

✔ Sickle cell and other anemias

✔ Syphilis

✔ Thyroid disease

The adverse medical consequences of smoking are not related only to your baby. Smoking moms can develop a host of health problems as a result of continued tobacco use, including the following:

✔ Cancer

✔ Chronic obstructive lung disease

✔ Hardening of the arteries, which can lead to strokes, high blood pressure, and heart attacks

✔ Pneumothorax (outside air takes the place of healthy lung tissue)

✔ Sleep apnea (a type of breathing problem that occurs during sleep)

See Chapter 5 for much more on the health effects of smoking.

Nicotine is very addictive. As few as four cigarettes a day can lead to chronic nicotine addiction. There's no such thing as casual smoking — especially if you're pregnant.

Smoking and Sex

Despite the glamorous appeal of swaggering cigarette-mongers like James Dean and Humphrey Bogart, the reality of smoking is quite different. Tobacco can be a real turnoff to partners or potential partners. Many smokers prefer for their partners — and even their casual dates — to be nonsmokers. (Ask any dating service manager.) Serious life choices are made on the basis of whether you are a smoker. Ms. or Mr. Right may have just walked into your life and then walked on out because you were puffing away on a cigarette.

Who, given the choice, would want their romantic partner to have mustard-colored fingertips, stained teeth, and chimney breath? You might even say that smoking is an indirect form of birth control.

When it comes to sex, smoking has medical and biological effects, too. For example, impotence can result from long-term tobacco use. (Although this term is often confused with problems involving sex drive, arousal, and ejaculation in the male or orgasm in the female, *impotence,* strictly speaking, refers to erectile dysfunction — the inability to attain or maintain an erection. Performance is what all the fuss is about.) An erection results from a properly and sufficiently maintained pool of blood in the penis. Blood is pumped from the heart through the arteries to the various end organs, including the genitalia. If the arteries are constricted as a result of high blood pressure, fatty buildup, diabetes, or smoking, the plumbing doesn't work right.

Impotence is much more common among men who smoke. I worked with Dr. Helen Singer Kaplan for a year, evaluating and treating cases of sexual dysfunction. We saw a number of men who couldn't rise to the occasion because of damage to their vascular systems and blood vessels brought about by years of smoking. Worse yet, the problem is very difficult to treat. Is smoking really so great that you would risk giving up sex for it?

Smoking and Fertility

Cigarette smoking has a significant negative impact on fertility. A variety of toxins, including those arising from cigarette smoke, can impair a person's ability to conceive. And it's not just active smoking that reduces fertility. Exposure to secondhand smoke can do it, too.

Long-term tobacco use may result in reduced fertility or fertility problems in both men and women. Tobacco doesn't discriminate between the sexes in this regard.

✔ **Women:** Conception takes longer (more menstrual cycles) for smokers than it does for nonsmokers. As with many of the health-related consequences of tobacco use, this effect on fertility depends on the number of cigarettes the mother-to-be smokes: The more she smokes, the more likely fertility (and health) problems will result.

Even in very low amounts, cigarette smoking can significantly reduce your ability to become pregnant.

✔ **Men:** Paternal smoking is no walk in the park as far as baby-making is concerned, either. Compared to nonsmokers, men who smoke have fewer sperm. The sperm they do have are less motile than those of nonsmoking men, and movement is an essential function of sperm. It's also possible that the chemicals in tobacco smoke can alter the chromosomal makeup of male genetic material. This damage can be passed along to the developing fetus, resulting in a variety of physical abnormalities or even subtle changes in the brain and behavior that emerge later in life.

Smoking during Pregnancy: Everyone Loses

The best way to understand the potential impact of smoking on a pregnancy is to understand the flow of events in a normal pregnancy. From the union of male and female genetic material through the extraordinarily complicated development of the fetus, pregnancy is an amazing sequence. It's best left to its own, to proceed untampered with by substances such as nicotine. Of course, some women develop obstetric problems during pregnancy, and these problems need to be monitored and treated, if necessary. For most women, however, the sequence of events in pregnancy unfolds predictably and consistently.

Conception results from the fusion of the DNA of the father's sperm and the mother's egg. Initially, a single-celled *zygote* is formed. The chromosomes of this "parent" cell proceed to divide until literally billions of cells exist. On the way, through a miraculous process that scientists don't completely understand, the cells begin to *differentiate*, with groups of cells becoming specialized and forming the body's various organs. What start out as *pluripotent* (they can develop in any direction) cells turn into skin, eyes, muscles, brain, and other organs of the body.

Cigarettes and oral contraceptives

Smoking and oral contraceptives don't mix. Women who use birth control pills and smoke have a greater chance of having a stroke or heart attack. Women who are older than 45 have an even greater chance of developing one of these potentially catastrophic illnesses. Ask your doctor for advice on this issue.

Smoking, menopause, and aging

Smoking causes more than just fertility problems in women:

✔ Women who smoke have up to a four times greater risk of developing cervical cancer than nonsmokers do. The more you smoke, the higher your risk.

✔ "The change" (menopause) occurs earlier in smokers. The more and longer you've smoked, the greater your chance of having an early menopause.

✔ Evidence suggests that long-term smoking causes many of the manifestations of aging. It may cause wrinkles, for example. Your insides age more rapidly, too.

If you're a smoker, think about giving your heart, lungs, skin, and immune system a break. They are on your team. Be a good coach! One of the most exciting aspects of quitting smoking is that almost as soon as you quit, your body begins to heal itself. Some of the changes induced by smoking are reversible to a certain extent. Your body is constantly cleaning out the old and bringing in the new. Help it along with a healthy diet, regular exercise, and "right thinking" habits.

After further increases in cell size and number, the zygote becomes a *blastocyst,* which firmly implants itself in the lining of the uterus. Five days after conception, the blastocyst gives rise to the inner cell mass destined to become the *embryo* as well as the *placenta,* a complex nest of cells that protects the fetus and facilitates the exchange of nutrients, oxygen, and carbon dioxide between mother and developing baby.

Genetic material — DNA — serves as a template that directs the cells to manufacture proteins that carry out the various tasks of life, such as metabolism (burning energy), recognizing foreign matter (fighting off infection), reproduction, and movement. Hazardous materials such as the carcinogens in tobacco smoke can seriously damage the chromosomes and cause them to mutate. Their reproductive timing deteriorates, and they may begin to divide like crazy. These deviant cells may lose their ability to function properly. The delinquent cells — cancer cells — may be recognized by the body for what they are and be destroyed, or they may escape the body's surveillance system and take on a life of their own, forming a tumor that can keep on growing. Healthy cell division and the elimination of unhealthy or deviant cells are part of normal fetal development.

Good prenatal care, including regular visits with the obstetrician and childbirth classes for the parents, is crucial to the health and well-being of both mother and baby.

Monitoring meds

If you're pregnant, you need to discuss any drug you are taking with your doctor. (Doctors prefer that pregnant women take as few drugs as possible.) Because nicotine is a drug, it can interact with other drugs you take. Drug-drug interactions take a variety of forms. Often, one drug increases or lowers the potency of the other. If you're taking two drugs that are known to affect each other's blood levels, discuss the situation with your doctor. Sometimes it's possible to monitor the levels of medications you take by means of blood tests.

Reviewing the risks to the fetus

The first three months of pregnancy, known as the first *trimester,* is the most critical period of development for a growing fetus. During the first three months of growth, the organs and tissues are especially vulnerable to toxic and traumatic influences. Many things can go wrong. The good news is that most of the time, they don't. Nonetheless, the last thing a growing fetus needs is a steady supply of poison coming downstream from Mom. Any substance or drug that Mom takes in can end up passing through the placenta and into the fetus. Exposure of the fetus to most, if not all, drugs — including tobacco — can result in significant or subtle damage to the unborn child, particularly during the first trimester.

Recent research reveals that smoking can have the following physical effects on a growing fetus:

✔ Children of mothers who smoke during the first trimester of pregnancy have a somewhat greater chance of being born with a cleft palate.

✔ Children of mothers who smoke more than 15 cigarettes a day during pregnancy have more illnesses during their first months of life. Some of these illnesses are serious, such as stomach, breathing, and skin problems for which the infant may need to be hospitalized.

✔ Pregnant women who smoke have almost twice the risk of giving birth to a low-birth-weight baby. Smoke may reduce the blood supply to the placenta, which may result in fewer nutrients reaching the developing fetus. A low birth weight can complicate the care of the infant during the first months of life. Babies who weigh less than 5½ pounds at birth face a greater risk of illness and even death during infancy and the toddler years.

If you quit smoking during the first trimester, you increase the chance that your baby will be born at a normal birth weight.

✔ Evidence suggests that maternal smoking raises the chance of the baby arriving sooner than expected. Babies who arrive preterm tend to be smaller and weigh less than full-term babies. Babies born at less than 5 pounds may have an increased likelihood of complications such as cerebral palsy, mental retardation, and behavioral problems.

✔ Maternal smoking has been correlated to chronic low blood flow and oxygen to the fetus, more frequent tremors, abnormal muscle tone, and excessive startle response in infants.

✔ The toxins in tobacco smoke may play a role in disrupting normal fetal development, especially if the pregnant mother smokes heavily, and especially in the first eight weeks of pregnancy, when developing organs are extremely sensitive. Numerous factors cause mental retardation, including exposure to birth-defect-causing agents such as tobacco, especially in the first eight weeks of pregnancy.

Many expectant parents wonder how to optimize the intrauterine environment in order to create the healthiest, smartest, and most talented child they can. No one has the exact recipe for an Einstein, a Shakespeare, or a Mozart, but not smoking during (and after) pregnancy goes a long way toward giving your baby the chance to grow up healthy, smart, and well adjusted. Exposing a child to tobacco, whether during pregnancy or as secondhand smoke, throws unnecessary physical obstacles in the child's way.

Looking at smoking-related complications to the pregnancy and the mother

Not only does smoking put the fetus at risk for all sorts of health and mental problems, but it can also put the entire pregnancy — and sometimes the mother's life — at risk. *Miscarriage,* or spontaneous abortion, occurs more frequently among women who smoke. Generally speaking, pregnant smokers have a higher rate of other kinds of problems in pregnancy and delivery as well, including

✔ Bleeding during pregnancy, sometimes severe

✔ Abnormal placement/location of the placenta, which makes delivery difficult and potentially dangerous

✔ Ectopic pregnancy (the embryo starts growing in a site other than the uterus; almost all these pregnancies fail)

The risk of *stillbirth* (the death of an infant within the first hours of life) is significantly increased when the mother smokes. Also, some authorities estimate that up to 25 percent of Sudden Infant Death Syndrome (SIDS) is traceable to maternal tobacco use. (See the sidebar "Sudden Infant Death Syndrome" for more information.)

Developmental milestones

If you need additional reasons not to smoke while you're pregnant, think about your unborn child in terms of these milestones:

Weeks 9-12: The fetus is 2 to 3 inches long; nourishment and waste removal proceeds from the placenta via the umbilical cord.

Week 16: The fetus's face looks distinctly human.

Week 20: The fetus is 9.5 inches long and weighs ¾ pound.

Week 26: The fetus's eyes are open.

Week 28: The fetus is 12 inches long and weighs 1.5 pounds; the lungs became capable of breathing.

Week 38: The fetus is 18 inches long and weighs about 6 pounds.

If you smoke, now is the perfect time to quit. You have some choice over the kind of air you breathe. Your baby doesn't.

Quitting Smoking during Pregnancy

About one in eight women in the United States smokes during pregnancy. Shocking but true. Smoking during pregnancy puts both the mother's and the baby's health at risk. If no pregnant women smoked, the U.S. Public Health Service estimates that the number of infant deaths could drop by as much as 10 percent. Quitting now, even if you're already pregnant, lowers the risks to you and your baby.

Possible harm to the fetus seems to relate directly to the amount you smoke. The less you smoke, the better your baby's chances of being born healthy.

If you aren't a pregnant smoker but know someone who is, take note: More than any other group, pregnant smokers need strident, caring, and assertive encouragement to get them to quit. Many pregnant smokers have spouses or partners who smoke as well, increasing the temptation to have "just one" while trying to quit. Most of the women who are able to quit smoking while pregnant pick up again after pregnancy. You can see how many challenges there are.

See Chapter 18 for general information about helping someone kick the smoking habit. The following sections talk about the unique issues that arise when the quitter-to-be is also a mother-to-be.

Thinking about nicotine replacement therapy

Should you use the patch or some other form of nicotine replacement therapy, such as nicotine gum, nicotine aerosol spray, or the nicotine inhaler, during pregnancy? This issue is a complicated one that you should discuss with your doctor. Although these therapies will expose your unborn baby to nicotine, that nicotine may be less harmful than persistent heavy smoking, which exposes the fetus not only to nicotine but to other dangerous chemicals as well. You and your doctor can work out together what is safest for your developing baby.

Being aware of depression's role

Pregnant or soon-to-be-pregnant women beware: There is a well-established correlation between smoking and depression. Smokers are much more likely to have had serious depressions in their lifetimes than nonsmokers. If you are depressed, your chance of successfully quitting smoking decreases. Plus, it's easier to relapse if you're depressed, and withdrawal symptoms can be more severe than they are among nondepressed people.

Depression and anxiety can complicate your pregnancy as well.

If you are depressed, you tend to handle physical and emotional stress less than optimally. Depressed people can be either under- or overactive and may simply care less about things. Many depressed people feel hopeless and helpless. If you are depressed, you may wonder, "Why bother to do anything? Nothing's going to change." This is the wrong attitude to have when you're pregnant, because pregnancy is a time when you need to be especially aware of your body and your state of well-being. Pregnant moms need to feel emotionally connected with their babies and to provide the right psychological environment for the developing child.

Tell your doctor if you are depressed or having anxiety or other emotional symptoms.

In recent years, a great deal of research has been done on the safety of antidepressant medication during pregnancy. Although doctors are reluctant to prescribe any medication during the first trimester of pregnancy (when all the fetal organs are forming), there is substantial evidence that some antidepressants are safe and effective for women who need them during the latter part of pregnancy. See Chapter 14 for more on the treatment of depression.

Smoking and Breast Feeding

An issue that often comes up immediately following birth of a baby is whether to breast feed or bottle feed. The answer is: whatever's best for you and your child.

If you're a nursing mother, be aware that any drugs you take — including nicotine and other chemicals in tobacco smoke — are present in your breast milk and are passed along to your baby. Babies who breast feed from mothers who are heavy smokers (20 or more cigarettes a day) can develop nausea, vomiting, stomach problems, and diarrhea. Also, research has demonstrated that smoking may contribute to less-than-optimal breast milk production, which could make it difficult for you to breast feed your baby at all.

The next time you work in the garden, imagine embellishing your effort. Not only do you water the plants regularly and make sure that they get enough light, but you also drip potent toxins onto the soil. The poisons leaches through the earth and get into the roots of the plants and flowers and alter them in destructive and irreparable ways. This analogy may be a little extreme, but smoking and breast feeding at the same time is not unlike both caring for and poisoning your precious plants. For your baby's sake, don't smoke if you breast feed!

Maligning Marlboro Moms: The Long-Term Effects of Maternal Tobacco Use

Researchers are discovering all kinds of provocative and scary information about the effects of maternal smoking on children's development. For example, sons of mothers who smoke at least ten cigarettes a day during pregnancy are much more likely to develop conduct disorders than sons of nonsmoking mothers. (Conduct disorder may be the childhood and teenage precursor of what is known in adults as *antisocial personality disorder,* or sociopathy.) Kids with conduct disorder get involved in deviant and criminal behavior such as truancy, lying, physical aggression, and destruction of property.

When a pregnant woman smokes, not all the effects of smoking show up right away in the infant. Some of the effects of exposure to toxic compounds may appear later in the child's life — particularly behavioral ones. School performance problems and conduct disorder may not appear for years. Bear in mind that the concern about smoking mothers applies not only to tobacco but to *anything* you might smoke.

Sudden Infant Death Syndrome

Sudden Infant Death Syndrome (SIDS) is the unanticipated death of a baby who seemed to be in good health. The death remains unexplained even after extensive medical investigation. The scenario often involves a parent checking on a baby who is found not to be sleeping, but dead. SIDS, a horrible and tragic event in any family's life, is more common among children of parents who smoke.

You can take steps to minimize the risk of SIDS by making sure that your baby is well nourished, well rested, and checked regularly by a pediatrician. Sleeping arrangements for infants should include a firm surface. The baby should not be overwhelmed with too many clothes while asleep. Experts recommend that infants sleep on their backs. Avoid exposing the baby to people with colds and other kinds of infections that can be airborne. If you are pregnant, do not smoke, drink alcohol, or take any drugs unless they have been prescribed by your doctor.

Getting pregnant moms to stop smoking is way less expensive than dealing with the multiple and often devastating consequences of conduct disorder later on. Conclusions based on large-scale population surveys indicate that sons of smoking mothers are more likely to become criminals later in life. Speaking of behavioral problems, evidence suggests that children of mothers who smoke at least 14 cigarettes a day are more likely to develop attention deficit disorder, or ADD. ADD, which has come to public attention in recent years because of the increasing numbers of kids who are receiving medication for it, features a combination of hyperactivity, inattention, and easy distractibility.

Medical scientists speculate that behavioral problems like ADD among the offspring of smoking mothers could be due to the decreased oxygen levels that reach the developing fetus. Smoking mothers (and fathers and, for that matter, everyone) have increased levels of carboxyhemoglobin in their blood. Hemoglobin, which normally carries oxygen from the lungs to nourish the rest of the body, gets saturated with carbon monoxide from cigarette smoke and brings less oxygen to the baby and the mother's body.

Here are some other charming findings:

- Another large-scale study demonstrated that children of mothers who smoked at least a half pack a day were shorter and scored measurably lower on tests of math and reading.

- Infants of parents who smoke are twice as likely to suffer from serious respiratory infections than children of nonsmokers. Infants and children who are raised around cigarette smoke develop breathing problems, upper respiratory infections, and ear infections more often than children in smoke-free environments.

- The presence of tobacco smoke exacerbates allergies and asthma. Some estimates of the number of visits to pediatricians caused by exposure to secondhand smoke are quite high.

- Smoking during pregnancy may have implications for a child's long-term physical growth and intellectual development.

- Evidence suggests that smoking interferes with women's hormonal balance during pregnancy, and that this interference may have long-term consequences on the reproductive organs of her children.

- Offspring of pregnant female rats exposed to nicotine showed significant negative changes in brain structure. (Similar studies have not been done in humans because exposing pregnant women to cigarette smoke for the sake of a study is unethical.)

- Listening skills among children whose mothers smoked during pregnancy tested lower.

- Mothers rating children's school performance rated smoking moms' kids as having more behavior problems.

The dangers of asthma

Asthma is a serious illness. The *bronchi* and *bronchioles,* the airways that carry air to and from the lungs, become constricted. They get narrower during asthma attacks, and as a result breathing becomes more and more difficult. If you've ever had an asthma attack or seen someone else have one, you've witnessed the frightening struggle for air. Some people have asthma attacks when they breathe in particles of dust or other substances to which they have allergies. Other asthma attacks are brought on by stress or exertion.

There's no doubt that asthma can be precipitated by proximity to cigarette smoke. You can lower the risk of asthma spells in your child by keeping your home and cars smoke-free.

Chapter 17

Smoking and Teens

. . . .

In This Chapter

▶ Proving that prevention works

▶ Letting the steam out of peer pressure

▶ Tackling triggers

▶ Quitting as a family

. . . .

*T*oo many teenagers are still smoking these days. (Most people who smoke start early in life — the vast majority start before they are 18 years old.) Percentage-wise, many more young people smoke than older people. Fortunately, evidence proves that prevention and educational efforts work among young people. Demonstrating to teens that nicotine is a dangerous and addictive drug that leads to illness and to other addictions is what this chapter is all about. I also focus on ways to discuss these issues with teens and to ensure that they never start smoking in the first place. If your teen already smokes, this chapter explains how to help him quit.

Examining the Evidence

The good news is that in the past several years, the number of high school students who smoke has declined. This decline follows a rise in the number of high school smokers during the 1990s, which peaked around 1996-1997. The decline in the number of young people who smoke is due in part to cultural and social trends in recent years. Fewer people now consider smoking to be cool. Another part of the drop is due to education and preventive efforts. The more young people learn about the harmfulness of tobacco, the less likely they are to pick up cigarettes.

Fortunately, younger people respond to health information related to the consequences of smoking. The Centers for Disease Control (CDC) have established two survey programs to assist states in tobacco prevention and control: the National Youth Tobacco Survey and state Youth Tobacco Surveys. The surveys involve questioning large numbers of young people regarding their tobacco use. The information gained is then statistically matched with the respondents' age, gender, education level, and other demographic information.

The Hollywood influence

The palpable influence that Hollywood stars' smoking habits may have on youth raises justifiable anger and even outrage. Studies have shown that kids may be more likely to take up smoking if their film heroes do. One proposed remedy is to begin rating movies on the basis of whether the actors smoke on camera. If your favorite movie star smokes on screen, you may be more likely to have a positive attitude toward smoking yourself.

Macho screen and television actors swagger around with cigars the size of zeppelins hanging out of their mouths. And men aren't the only fashion victims when it comes to cigars. The media has popularized cigar smoking by women, particularly the glossy magazine *Cigar Aficionado*. Kids who see this may naturally conclude, "If it works for him, it'll work for me!"

Imagine if Kermit the Frog, Barney, or the Power Rangers smoked. What kind of message would that send to kids? Or how about Britney Spears? Young people need to hear about what really goes on in the lives of celebrities. Celebrities spend thousands of hours and dollars taking the best possible care of themselves they can. They train, watch their diet, get enough rest, work out . . . and for the most part don't smoke.

These surveys have helped the CDC define smoking behavior among teens and have revealed the following:

✔ Cigarettes are by far the most popular form of tobacco used by middle and high school students.

✔ After cigarettes, the second most popular form of tobacco among teenagers is cigars. Cigars, like cigarettes, are considered cool.

✔ The third most popular form of tobacco among teenagers is smokeless tobacco — chew, dip, and snuff. Bidis and *kreteks* (cigarettes containing a mixture of cloves and tobacco) are also quite popular among the younger set.

Enhance your credibility with the younger set. Know what bidis, kreteks, and other less-common tobacco products are and be prepared to explain the dangers of using them to your teen. Cigarettes aren't the only tobacco products that kids use. (See Chapter 2 for more on the various forms of tobacco.)

✔ About half of student smokers report that they smoke Marlboros.

✔ The most popular brand among African-American students is Newport.

✔ As many as 8 percent of middle school students first smoked a cigarette before they were 11 years old.

✔ Boys are more likely than girls to start smoking young.

✔ In many states, many stores do not card underage tobacco buyers.

✔ More than half of the students surveyed stated that they want to stop smoking.

✔ Most of the students — up to 90 percent — had been exposed to second-hand smoke during the week prior to being surveyed.

✔ Cigarette smoking among young people isn't necessarily concentrated among lower socioeconomic groups as it is among adults. Smoking rates in suburban and affluent youth are strikingly high. One theory is that the dramatic rise in teenage smoking during the 1990s was due in part to lower cigarette prices.

✔ Eight out of ten middle school students have seen actors puffing away in the movies. Up to a third of all middle schoolers report having smoked themselves.

Imitating What They See

Teens often begin smoking because their parents, their friends, and the movie and TV stars they idolize do. In their search for their own identity, young people often experiment by trying on different personalities. You can have a positive impact on young people's developing selves by pointing out examples of extremely successful, cool people who make a point of taking great care of their health — and by setting a good example yourself.

"Do what I say, not what I do"

One of the major culprits in adolescent smoking is the bad example set by parents and other adults. The number of moms and dads who ask their kids to do what they say and not what they do is off the charts. Presenting kids with mixed messages is a universal problem. Parents and other adults who smoke and then ask their children not to are asking younger people to conform to a standard that they themselves can't achieve. No fair! One of the great (and very serious) aspects of being young is that you expect people to play by the rules.

Kids expect their parents by and large to live by their own stated rules. If you don't want your child to smoke, don't let them know that it's really okay by smoking yourself!

Peer pressure and low self-esteem

Probably the most common reason that teenagers smoke is peer pressure. Adolescence is a time in life when the pressure to conform, to fit in, is unbelievably intense. For many kids, smoking is a passive form of compliance with the group. Adolescent users of smokeless tobacco are also far more likely than nonusers to have friends who partake.

Quitting smoking may need to involve quitting a particular social circle as well. Sometimes it isn't enough for a teenager to say no. Feeling like the odd kid out is a very negative, unpleasant experience for an adolescent. Teens whose friends are notorious smokers, drinkers, and partiers may need to choose new friends. It can be done!

Teenagers are trying to establish and declare their identities. Often, this effort involves attempts to define themselves as distinct from their parents and their parents' generation. In more extreme cases, kids become rebellious and defiant. For some teens, speaking out and being different is more important than being healthy or making realistic plans for the future — which can lead them to try things like smoking.

Preventing Your Teen from Picking Up the Habit

You may be wondering how to approach your teenager about not smoking. Some kids avoid cigarettes like the plague. Some have been on a crusade since childhood to get their parents — you! — to quit smoking. However, adolescence is the time of all kinds of new experiences. Many kids pick up a cigarette out of curiosity, because of peer pressure, or because they've been told not to smoke and they want to rebel.

The best way to prevent your teen from picking up the habit is not to smoke yourself — to set a good example.

Scare tactics, a form of "tough love," work for some teens. Scare tactics that have convinced many teens to shun smoking include seeing people with advanced pulmonary disease and seeing anatomical specimens of cancerous lungs. Granted, you may be challenged to find appropriate visual specimens, but if you search the Internet or call your county medical society, you're likely to find more than you bargained for! Departments of health may be happy to arrange school visits by experts who can tactfully discuss the dismal futures of those who keep smoking. The American Cancer Society and the American Lung Association also have a great deal of information that's accurate, up-to-date, and sobering.

Other teens relate better to a nonjudgmental approach. You might point out that

✔ Curiosity and wanting to try new things are normal for teens.

✔ Many people experiment with tobacco and other substances at some point in their lives.

✔ Many people have learned the truth about smoking the hard way — by getting sick or seeing someone else get a smoking-related illness.

✔ Peer pressure is difficult to face, but being your own person is far cooler than following the crowd and doing something that harms your health, like smoking. Smoking is not cool.

✔ Most of the celebrities and other role models whom people look up to take extra-good care of themselves.

✔ The future *always* comes. Living only for the moment comes with a high price. Perhaps your teen can come up with a number of examples where thinking about and planning for tomorrow has already paid off big, such as saving money for something she really wanted or studying for an important exam.

To show your kids that you aren't naïve, a self-righteous health nut, or a zealot, be real in your conversations with them. Although they may not act like they do, they want to know about your worries regarding tobacco.

Putting smoking in global terms

Try to get your kids to think about smoking in global terms. They may already know that the tobacco industry is a super-powerful behemoth with transnational claws. The tobacco industry wants as many people to smoke as possible. Although the tobacco companies have been forced to ease up on their aggressive advertising and marketing techniques in the U.S. and to give lip service to smoking prevention among the young, *that's not really where Big Tobacco is.* Big Tobacco would prefer it if all people of all ages were puffing away as often as possible. Think about it: children the world over lighting up and taking tobacco tars and other toxins into their otherwise healthy young bodies.

Sizing up your teen's attitudes and tendencies

Sit down and talk to your kids about smoking. You may even want to tell them about your own experience with tobacco. You can tell them about others who have tried to quit and struggled. You can explain how addiction works and describe some of the medical consequences of prolonged smoking. Why would anyone want to smoke when they can work out or do other things to make themselves look and feel better?

Asking questions is important, too. Ask your teenager:

- Have you ever tried cigarettes?
- Have you ever tried drinking?
- Do your friends or other people you know smoke?
- Does anyone you know drink or get high?
- What do you think about smoking? Do you think it's cool?
- Why are some people against cigarettes?

Questions about drinking and getting high are especially relevant because most teens who use alcohol and drugs also smoke. Substantial evidence shows that cigarettes are the gateway drug to alcohol, marijuana, and other mind-altering drugs. If your teen consistently denies that he and his friends smoke or drink, extend the conversation a little further. *How come* he's never tried a cigarette? Isn't he curious about what it's like? The idea is to get past denial and lip service to health and good habits.

Another key area to explore is self-esteem. One big reason that teens smoke is to pump up their self-esteem and self-confidence. How do your kids feel about themselves? Are they confident, are they assertive, and can they laugh at themselves in a healthy way? Do they have areas of accomplishment that help them feel good about themselves? Do they have many friends? To the extent that teenagers feel shaky about themselves and feel that they need to take extra measures to feel powerful, strong, and effective, they will be swayed by their friends who smoke and by advertising that sells cigarettes as passports to being cool.

Up to two-thirds of high schoolers have tried smoking.

Other areas to pursue include school and hangouts. Is your child's school a smoke-free zone? One way to find out is to walk or drive past the school at different times of day. Are there kids milling around outside smoking? What's the school's policy about smoking on school grounds? Finding out about the places where your child spends time after school and on weekends is also worthwhile.

Selfhood, not cigarettes

If you've ever seen a James Dean movie (*Rebel Without a Cause,* for example), you've seen a prime example of the angry — and smoking — young man. When Dean was hot, people reacted to him in intense ways. Many of his viewers thought he hit a point in swagger and bravado; many thought he spoke for teens as a group. The message was, "We're tired of being told what to do. We're tired of getting pushed around." Tragically, the gifted young actor lost his life in a motorcycle crash. Sometimes acting big and talking tough don't get you very far.

Another popular mouthpiece for teen angst is Holden Caulfield, the bleak young cynic from J. D. Salinger's *The Catcher in the Rye.* A generation of young readers related to Holden's endless questioning and defiant stance. When you go back to these books and films, what do you see? The defiance now seems stale, overplayed . . . *old.* See if your kids agree. Someone once said, "Living well is the best revenge." If you have an angry young thing living under your roof, try to convince your child that the best way to show defiance of authority is to succeed. Nothing succeeds like success.

You may be wondering when is the best time to broach the issue of smoking with your children. To a certain extent, each family and each adolescent is different. Kids of the same age may be at quite different levels emotionally. You need to gauge where your son or daughter is. Of course, if he or she is smoking already, the "when to discuss" issue is a nonissue. Get the subject out in the open as soon as possible. On the other hand, it's probably never too soon. Kids see people smoking and hear about smoking from their friends. Your kids will feel better to know that they can freely air the subject of tobacco at home anytime.

 Consider organizing a focus group of parents and/or kids to talk about smoking. Doing so will go a long way toward clearing the air about attitudes and facts on tobacco.

Getting across the gateway idea

The gateway idea — that tobacco use leads to use of other drugs, such as alcohol, marijuana, and even narcotics — is a controversial one. Some kids hear it as a blanket condemnation, as a parent's attempt to exert control and bend the facts. Getting the gateway concept across to kids is valuable, but emphasizing the downside of smoking *now* is just as important.

Aside from the evidence that many people who become addicted to alcohol and other drugs start out with cigarettes, plenty of other facts are worth bringing up:

- ✔ Many kids relate to information that exposes the brainwashing techniques used by cigarette advertisers. Once you raise their level of awareness, many kids understandably feel victimized by the tobacco industry's massive campaign to get them hooked.

- ✔ As glamorous as smoking may seem at times, most people who smoke regularly really are addicted to nicotine and can't stop readily. They may look cool, but when it comes to smoking, they don't have a choice!

- ✔ Most smokers start early in life. If your adolescent can avoid smoking now, he or she may never touch the stuff at all.

Teenage smoking is also the gateway to adult smoking. Experts report that whenever adolescent smoking increases, a corresponding increase in the number of adult smokers — and associated illness, lost workdays, and pain and suffering — becomes evident a few years down the road.

Another kind of gateway is worth mentioning: the gateway to health, energy, and good looks. This gateway opens up when you quit smoking (or never start).

Helping your teen realize that nicotine is a drug

In a world where crack cocaine and other hard drugs seem almost common, it's easy to think that cigarettes are pretty harmless by comparison. Teens especially may come to this conclusion. But they need to understand that nicotine is a drug that can do serious damage. It acts directly on the nervous system, causing stimulation, sedation, excitability, and agitation. There have been cases of nicotine fatalities — actual overdoses. Some researchers speculate that nicotine receptors and brain cell loops are involved in the onset of depression. It's not nice to fool with Mother Nature.

As Chapter 5 explains in detail, tobacco products can have devastating physical effects. For example, teenage girls who smoke increase their risk of developing breast cancer before they reach menopause. Smoking also may increase a person's chances of developing anxiety or a full-blown anxiety disorder. Everyone has experienced some level of moderate to severe anxiety at some point. Imagine feeling this way all the time! The best way to avoid breast cancer, lung disease, and other smoking-related illnesses is *prevention*. Don't smoke!

If your teens need further proof that nicotine is a powerful drug, get them to think and talk about what millions of people go through when they try to quit. Any drug that can cause such uncomfortable withdrawal symptoms must be powerful. It's far better to not smoke at all.

Forming healthy family attitudes toward smoking

Families define quality time in different ways, but common ingredients are fun, communication, and growth. When you and your kids get real with each other about the omnipresent lure and threat of tobacco, you can solidify as a family and respect one another's struggles to live well. Here are some ways to do so:

- Ask your teenager why more and more places are becoming smoke-free. Why is the law going in this direction? Share your experiences of being in a smoky restaurant or airplane.

- Sports are a great way to enjoy quality family time. When's the last time you saw a champion athlete take a smoke break?

- Notice how many Marlboro or Camel logos you see in the course of a day. Ask each other what the real price of this merchandise is. Take the money you save by quitting (or never smoking) and go shopping for logo-free goods.

- Dissect the influence that tobacco has had on your lives. The next time you go the movies, be sensitive to the use of cigarettes in the film. Be aware of the presence of secondhand smoke and learn more about the dangers of exposure to it.

- Talk about addiction. Many people who dismissed the addictive potential of tobacco are still smoking today. Up to a third of cancer cases relate directly or indirectly to the use of tobacco. Too many babies are born with severe problems, such as cleft palate, or more subtle ones, such as poor school performance, that were caused by in utero exposure to maternal smoking.

- Consider doing volunteer work as a family with the local American Cancer Society chapter or other community agencies.

- Some kids (and adults) like and actually prefer to live dangerously and take risks. Using tobacco products is one way to maintain a high-risk lifestyle. The downside is that when you're playing Russian (or Turkish or Virginian) roulette, one of the chambers of the gun actually contains a live bullet. If thrill-seeking and risk-taking are unshakable aspects of your teen's lifestyle (or yours), come up with creative alternatives to puffing on cancer sticks. Consider bungee jumping, whitewater rafting, mountain climbing, or aeronautics. There are many ways to gamble that are nowhere near as unhealthy or have such little long-term payoff as smoking.

We still have much to learn about preventing and reducing tobacco use among young people. Active family dialogue promotes both prevention and reduction of use on the grassroots level.

When discussing smoking with your children, researching the facts on tobacco can be a fun project. You could spend years digesting all the information that's out there. Take a look, for example, at these Web sites:

✔ Campaign for Tobacco-Free Kids: www.tobaccofreekids.org

✔ The American Cancer Society: www.cancer.org

✔ The American Lung Association: www.lungusa.org

✔ The American Medical Association: www.ama.org

Helping your teen say no to tobacco

Resisting peer pressure is difficult for any teen. The best way is to be prepared with answers before the question is asked so that when the time comes to say no, the right answer comes naturally. Teens can consider the following ways to say no:

✔ Thanks, but I'd rather live a full life.

✔ Thanks, but I'm allergic.

✔ I tried before and I didn't like it.

✔ I used to smoke but then I wised up.

✔ Ever seen the inside of a smoker's lung?

✔ No, thanks. Would you like a cup of battery acid?

✔ My cousin died of lung cancer.

✔ My grandfather has to suck on an oxygen tank because of smoking.

✔ No way! Do you know what's *in* that stuff?

✔ I'm in training. Count me out.

Several thousand young people start smoking each day. Over time, millions of cases of tragic, unnecessary illness and death will result. Is the warning box that appears on every pack of cigarettes, on every billboard, and in every magazine ad featuring smokes just an exercise in nagging? No. Is the involvement of the Food and Drug Administration, the American Medical Association, the American Heart Association, and the American Cancer Society just an exercise in pointless lobbying and hot air? No again.

Aiding Teens Who Smoke

If and when you find out that your teen has dabbled in tobacco use — or smokes regularly — the first thing you need to do is to have a heart-to-heart talk with your child and get the facts out in the open. Approach the subject gently but firmly. Reinforce the idea that being honest with each other is the best and only way to move forward. Find out how much your teen has been smoking, what he's been smoking, and with whom. When does your teen smoke? Is it a daily habit, or does he smoke only when his friends are around? After a short while, a pattern of use may emerge.

Your instinctual reaction may be a strong one, but you must stay in control. Quite often, authoritarian pronouncements have the opposite of the intended effect with kids. If you overreact, you run the risk of having your child continue to smoke just to assert himself.

Be clear about the extent of your teenager's habit. Ask him to map out his activities for one week. How many cigarette breaks appear on the schedule? Looking at how much and what kinds of time smoking occupies is highly instructive. People who go through this exercise learn a great deal about themselves and how they handle stress and empty time. (Empty time is stressful, too.)

Many teens are still in the experimental/curiosity stage, smoking only occasionally, so cutting cigarettes loose should be fairly easy. If you find that your teen smokes five or more cigarettes a day, quitting will be more difficult. Have your teen track carefully and methodically the times and places he smokes. Where is he most likely to smoke? Where is he least likely to smoke? Has he tried to quit before? What quitting methods has he tried? What has his experience been like? With this information, you can help your teen formulate a meaningful quit plan that takes triggers and lifestyle into account. Give him all the information you have available to you. See Chapter 8 for specific advice about putting together a quitting plan.

To give up a habit and a source of comfort that has been so accessible, your teen needs to replace tobacco with something that's equally gratifying. Maybe a family bank account that accumulates all the money saved from quitting will be an incentive to stay quit. A gift membership to a health club makes exercise a somewhat costly but often appreciated substitute for the smoking habit.

Use big guns in your effort to help your kid quit smoking. Access smoking-related support groups, Web sites, and other reading material. You may also want to consult with your child's doctor about the use of nicotine replacement therapies (NRTs) such as the patch. (See Chapter 9 for more on NRTs.)

Getting your teen to stop smoking involves commitment on everyone's part. People who spend time with him may be able to contribute in major ways to his recovery from the habit. If committed to quitting smoking, your teen may agree to have his friends and perhaps even people at school pitch in as cigarette chaperones. Sometimes having more than one pair of eyes watching — is he smoking or isn't he? — is helpful. If stopping smoking is forced upon him, the effort may not go over all that well. Kids in particular like to feel that they have some say over the decisions they make — especially a decision that has such far-ranging effects.

Triggers

Just like older people, and just like with other addicting substances such as alcohol, teenagers reach for smokes in response to triggers. The longer and more a person smokes, the more ingrained this trigger response becomes. Triggers come in all sizes, shapes, and varieties:

- Memories
- Places (the mall, the movies)
- Times of day (lunchtime, after school)
- Vacation time
- Parties
- Social cues (who's around?)
- An absence of authority figures

If your teenage son or daughter smokes, you need to find out the settings in which your child smokes and the triggers that make him or her reach for a cigarette. Once you understand this stimulus-response arc, you can begin to work on changing your teen's environment and lowering the frequency of these nicotine prompts.

Chapter 18

Helping Someone You Care About Quit

Quitting smoking isn't easy. Anyone making the attempt needs as much support as possible. That's where you come in.

If you are or ever were a smoker, you are intimately acquainted with the many struggles involved in quitting, which can include physical nicotine withdrawal symptoms, major lifestyle changes, and feelings of separation, loss, and grief. You can miss a habit such as smoking sorely once you give it up. People who stop smoking may even have to change their friends or at least part company with old familiar haunts where they were accustomed to lighting up. Proper diet and exercise often need to be included in a quit-smoking plan, especially for those for whom weight gain is a concern. Your effort to understand and support someone who's quitting needs to take all these complexities and struggles into account.

The strategies in this chapter equip you with the best and latest means of helping your significant other, sibling, friend, or anyone else cut this destructive habit loose.

Convincing Someone to Quit

You're reading this chapter because you're interested in finding out how to help someone quit smoking. You don't want to be among those who lose a spouse or friend to tobacco-related illness.

To help your loved one understand why quitting — *today* — is so important, try mentioning that smokers are more likely than nonsmokers to develop these medical problems:

- ✔ Acute necrotizing ulcerative gingivitis (gum disease)
- ✔ Cataracts
- ✔ Intestinal polyps
- ✔ Impotence
- ✔ Diminished fertility
- ✔ Heart disease
- ✔ Peripheral vascular disease
- ✔ Cancers of the lung, throat, stomach, and bladder
- ✔ Skin wrinkling

Don't let your loved one (or yourself) become just another statistic. If you need more evidence to convince your smoker to shed the habit, see Chapter 5 on the health-related consequences of smoking and Chapter 6 on its financial and social effects.

Finding Out Whether a Person Is Ready to Quit

You may be ready — long ready — for your loved one to quit smoking for good. The challenge is to find out whether you're both on the same page.

What happens when you talk to your loved one about smoking? Does he get defensive or attempt to change the subject? Does he sneak smokes? Other people are very direct and honest about their desire to quit, but may be intimidated by the process. If you've been through quitting yourself, you know how frustrating the process can be. Make sure that your loved one gets a chance to go over Chapter 13, which details the trials and tribulations of staying clean and clear of smoking relapse.

Most people who have quit and stayed quit tried many times before finally making it stick. Remind your loved one that any abstention from smoking, whether it lasts a day, a week, or a year or more, is a victory.

You may get a kind of nonverbal acknowledgment that your loved one is ready to give up the habit. She may throw you a significant look that tells you it's time to quit. She may even roll her eyes when lighting up, acknowledging how powerless she feels over this addiction. She may complain bitterly about the physical and psychological shackles in which she feels bound.

You can find out whether the person you care about is ready to quit in numerous ways. The following are common signs of readiness:

✔ Stop-start behavior: Lighting up and then crushing out cigarettes

✔ Expressing concern about health and the consequences of smoking

✔ Making doctors' appointments to check on health

✔ Asking others how they quit

✔ Attempting to cut back

✔ Having the first cigarette of the day later each day

✔ Asking you for help

If you've noticed one or more of these signs, follow through by asking about your loved one's concerns and plan. Make it abundantly clear that your concern arises out of love. Your intent is to support him, to help him get through. Ask him if he knows what kind of help is available. Does he know anyone else who has quit? Show him this book. Talk through his plan and take it to pencil and paper. (Turn to Chapter 8 for specific tips and strategies, such as choosing a quit day.)

Or maybe your loved one isn't as hungry for clean, fresh air as you are. Smoking may bother you more than it bothers her. If all you get in response to your suggestions is the cold shoulder or an angry, irritable reply, your next steps are to make sure that the common space you live or work in is smoke-free and to work on your own feelings. Your feelings about your loved one's smoking can clutter up your own head and life. Work on yourself and make a firm decision about how much you can influence the smoker in your life and how much you need to detach from that person's struggle.

Helping Someone Implement a Quitting Plan

Quitting smoking means taking stock and taking action. Like other major life decisions, the decision to quit can rock someone's world — unless that person has maximum support and ample resources. Your job as helper is to point out all the resources and tools you're aware of, to reasonably facilitate your loved one's decision to quit in whatever way you can, and to be there as a caring supporter regardless of the immediate outcome of the quit effort.

Although you can and should plan on being an integral part of your loved one's quitting strategy, don't feel that your involvement will make or break the attempt. Ultimately, she is quitting for herself and her own benefit (as well as yours). Equipping herself with as much information as possible, as well as a realistic action plan, is up to her.

I've seen people simply decide to quit *right now,* and in a few instances it actually works. For many people, however, quitting smoking is the kind of life decision that merits serious advance planning. Part of the benefit of formulating a strategy ahead of time is that you have time to collect and utilize resources. For example, does your wannabe quitter know about self-help groups, support groups, and classes that are available? Does he know about the role good food and exercise can play in making an attempt to quit smoking successful? Is he aware of the array of nicotine replacement therapies that are on the market, such as the patch, the inhaler, and nicotine gum, and how they work?

Suggest that he use a format like that in Table 18-1 to plan his first several quit days. He can map out the activities that he'll do to fill up each hour. Activities can include sleeping, eating, working, driving, socializing, exercising, and so on. Of course, one hour might involve several activities.

Table 18-1		Quit Day Calendar: Strategies for Liberation
Day	Time	Activity
#1	6:00 a.m.	
	7:00 a.m.	
	8:00 a.m.	
	9:00 a.m.	
	10:00 a.m.	
	11:00 a.m.	
	12:00 p.m.	

This is just a skeletal suggestion of where your smoker needs to be in terms of planning his time. The first quit day is the hardest for most people. The day before Quit Day 1 can be difficult, too, if the person spends a lot of time and mental energy dreading the experience to come. Realistically anticipating what the first day and subsequent days will be like is very useful.

The more specific and detailed the quitting plan is, the better. See Chapter 8 for information about how to put together a detailed plan.

Providing support

Some people describe how irritable they become when they stop smoking. Others simply feel tired for a few days. Your challenge is to support your significant other (or best friend or whoever) without becoming a pincushion. You can help by lending a patient ear when she feels like talking about her plans and concerns about quitting. If you are or have been a smoker, you can help by sharing your own quit experiences — and by not smoking yourself.

Another useful support is to remind your smoker that giving up something that has played such a big role in her life without substituting other rewarding or gratifying behaviors is difficult. Obviously, she doesn't want to exchange one addiction for another. Still, it's possible to find substitute pleasures that are healthful and rewarding in their own right. If she works out, she may want to exercise even more often. Drinking plenty of liquids or chewing gum for a few days works for many people. See Chapter 12 for more quitting strategies.

Being a quitting buddy

A *quitting buddy* is someone who has been through the struggle of quitting smoking himself, or at the very least appreciates the courage and stamina it takes to make it through. You don't want to patronize the quitter, but the first week — and especially the first few days — can be challenging. During this time, he deserves as many breaks as he can get, provided that you aren't being asked to do unreasonable things or make extreme exceptions for him.

Encouraging words and extra helpings of kindness and optimism can't hurt. Sometimes a pep talk goes a long way. If he needs help getting motivated to use his quit tools and resources, or if he needs extra encouragement to make it to a meeting or class, you can facilitate the effort. Direct him to the nearest Nicotine Anonymous meetings, for example. His quitting smoking will benefit not only him but everyone else around him.

Tell your loved one that millions of people have been through the process of quitting smoking — and have succeeded. Quitting smoking never killed anyone. It may make your loved one feel uncomfortable, act distressed and irritable, and want to climb the walls, but to be honest, the fear of quitting can be more unpleasant than quitting itself.

Remind the soon-to-be ex-smoker that whatever he goes through is worth it. If his number-one priority is quitting, whatever else happens in the first few quit days is okay (within reason). If he accomplishes absolutely nothing during the first 48 hours of stopping cigarettes, he still will have had two gloriously successful days. Appreciate his courage and self-discipline in making and sticking with the effort.

Gus's story

This story was told to me by one of my patients. (I've altered some of the details to obscure his identity.)

"My name is Gus. I am 58 years old, have four kids, and a sweet, loving wife. I grew up in Baltimore, where, after finishing high school, I started right away working in my uncle's car shop. The shop got a great reputation, and it wasn't long before we had more business than we could handle. Our specialty: foreign cars. Mercedes, Jags, Porsches, even some Lamborghinis. The owners would only let us fix these beauties.

"Now I'm in the hospital. They say I have lung cancer.

"It breaks my heart, thinking about how I've thrown away what could have been the best part of my life. Instead of being home, thinking about retiring in a few more years, I'm stuck here, with needles dripping medicine into my arms. The dials and monitors never stop. From my hospital window I watch children crossing the street, shouting to their moms or dads. My grandchildren come in to visit. When they ask, 'Grandpa, how do you feel?' I know not to be honest with them. I don't know if they know. I tell them what I think they want to hear.

"I feel worst about them. How could I do this to them? All these years (I smoked two packs a day, no filters), what was I thinking? I guess I thought I would never be the one to get sick. Never did take too many sick days. Except this last year, when I got this mean, low-level cough that wouldn't go away. At first the doctor wrote it off and wrote me a prescription for some medicine to clear it up. When it didn't go away, we took a closer look.

"The chest X-ray showed it clearly. There was a white patch where the picture was supposed to be dark. Something was growing in my lung. They gave me more tests, tubes down my throat. Meantime, the coughing never let up. Sometimes it got worse. Then the thing spread and I knew I was sick. I was tired all the time.

"I love my family. Don't let this happen to you."

Staying Ahead of a Stalemate: How to Rescue Yourself

Even if you've kicked the habit yourself, you're still in harm's way if the one you love and live with is still lighting up. Not only is all that secondhand smoke a proven danger to your health (see the following section for details), but resisting the temptation to take just one little puff will be that much harder for you. "One little puff" can do you a lot of harm.

Out of sight, out of mind should be your mantra. If your significant other isn't ready to quit, don't be shy about asking her to leave her butts at the door. Quitting is hard enough. If she loves you, she will support you in your effort not to smoke. Also keep in mind that your loved one may envy your resolve, especially if she's tried to quit and failed.

Don't think that you're acting like the Church Lady in asking her to abstain. Ask nicely. Confrontation and adversarial stances don't go nearly as far as calm, reasonable requests. Who knows — she may even want to give quitting another try. If she still won't stop when you're around, try to distract yourself when she lights up. When she reaches for a cigarette, reach for your sneakers and headphones and go out for a walk or run.

Sometimes nagging is a good thing. If you're a parent, you know how persuasive a child's nagging can be. You sometimes feel like you're at a war tribunal. You'll offer the kids limitless donuts and countless trips to their favorite amusement park if they'll just stop whining. Maybe you can use your own persuasive power to your advantage. If your loved one is smoking in a house where children live, start an all-out campaign to get her to quit. Cigarette smoke is unhealthy for children — and pets, too. Many people have stories about nagging *their* parents to the point of driving them crazy, all in order to get them to quit. Notes on the refrigerator, banging drums to the tune of "Quit for Us" . . . and guess what? Sometimes these underhanded tactics actually work!

Another ploy is to simply refuse to pick up a pack for them the next time you're at the market. You and your family can refuse to sit in the car while your loved one smokes. One woman who succeeded at nagging her father to quit recalls, "It wasn't only that he would have done anything for the drumming to stop. He realized how much he really meant to us, and how afraid we as children were that we would lose him to emphysema or lung cancer." (You don't actually have to go out and buy drums.)

Love can be the most powerful force in getting someone to quit. Ultimately, getting rid of cigarettes for good is Mom's or Dad's decision . . . but what little kid wants to cuddle up with someone who smells like an oil rig?

Identifying codependency

Codependency is a term that's bandied about frequently. The dictionary defines codependency as a condition of being controlled or manipulated by a person who has an addiction or other kind of problem behavior. Although it isn't a true medical or psychiatric disorder, it is a label that's used to describe people who live with or have to deal with others who have an addiction or exhibit other problem behaviors.

Many people who live with others who have problem behaviors are affected by the behavior themselves. Smoking is a great example. Not only do you have to smell the stuff on his clothes, in the house, and in the car, but some of it goes into your lungs and can harm your health. To the extent that his choices and lifestyle are worked out around the availability of a smoke, you may be adversely affected by his addiction. To the extent that you're in denial, or collusion, you may enable him to continue smoking because it's easier or more convenient than to argue about it.

Avoiding codependency

How do you react to your loved one's negative behavior? You watch her smoke; you may watch her hesitate or even try to fool herself before surrendering and lighting up. Watching another person self-destruct before your eyes can be devastating. *Self-destruct* may not be the first term that pops into your mind while you watch someone smoke. However, if you had a mental image of the person over the long haul, you would get a far clearer picture of the processes at work. Watching someone's future unfurl and deteriorate would be heartbreaking. If you've ever seen stop-motion photography of a rose blooming, this sequence would be the opposite. You would see the person getting wrinkled, having more and more trouble breathing, making more trips to the doctor, and finally succumbing to the wasteland of overpowering disease.

How do you react? Like most people, you probably have all kinds of strategies to turn off the stream of angry thoughts and worries that watching another person sucking on poison may provoke. If you are an ex-smoker, watching someone else smoke can be like watching pornography. Obscene. They say there's nothing worse than a reformed smoker or drinker.

It's easy to condemn someone for doing something that may have been second nature to you not too long ago.

Or you may recoil and think, "How could she do that to herself?" At the same time, you may be wondering, "How could she do that to *me?*" When people don't take care of themselves, the people around them often have to pay. When they claim that smoking is their decision, they're oversimplifying matters. If they get ill later on — and there's a good chance that they will — others will have to pay for their doctor visits, hospital stays, and medications. Health insurance companies may foot most of the bill, but the real costs are passed along to the rest of us who have to buy insurance. So the decision to smoke really isn't an individual one. It is a futureless one — as in, "Let someone else worry about this potential problem. Not me." Of course, I'm not being very generous by saying this. Most smokers have long lost the ability to choose whether to light up because they are addicted.

You need to figure out how to deal with the impact of the other person's addictive behavior on *you.* A big part of the codependency deal — the reactive formula (she acts, you react) — is taking the other person's behavior personally.

Letting go of the illusion that you can control another person's behavior is extremely difficult, but you have to do it. Otherwise, you'll drive yourself crazy trying. (Many people have actually made career choices, going into the therapy or psychiatry field, in pursuit of this phantom.) It is enough that you can control some decisions affecting your own life. Forget about telling others what to do. The best you can do is give your loved one information, show her that she has choices, and then step back and go on taking care of yourself. If you don't, no one else will.

This lesson is one of the big lessons of life. You may take great comfort in imaging that someone out there cares enough to make everything right, but that's wrong. You are the beginning and end when it comes to caring for yourself. You are it for you. The important thing is that you are fully aware of the choices that are available to you.

Dealing with Secondhand Smoke

If a person you live with and care about smokes, you have a double struggle: to get your loved one to quit smoking and to minimize, if not eliminate, your exposure to secondhand smoke. *Secondhand smoke* is smoke that's either exhaled from a pipe, cigar, or cigarette or results from the burning of a tobacco product; secondhand smoke can be inhaled unintentionally by other persons in the same space.

A cigarette burning in an ashtray delivers smoke to a room — and to your lungs — as surely as a freshly exhaled lungful.

Public health experts maintain that thousands of people die each year from illnesses related to secondhand smoke (see Chapter 6 for more information). If you are one of the people who puts up with toxic tobacco fumes on a regular basis, you can appreciate how pervasive and penetrating tobacco smoke really is. One time I had a few puffs of a cigar in my car, windows shut. The smell lingered for years. Smoke, which after all is nothing but a cloud of millions of vaporized tobacco particles, has a way of penetrating and clinging to clothing, furniture, and household materials.

There are a number of ways to deal with secondhand smoke:

✔ Learn as much as you can about it with a view toward sharing this information with your family member or friend who smokes.

✔ Talk to your loved one about your concern. Obviously, the conversation will be more challenging if this person has already been confronted about smoking. Diplomacy and a positive emphasis can go a log way toward getting your point across. You may want to describe all the benefits to all the occupants of the home that will follow when the smoke is better contained or eliminated.

✔ Insist that all smoking be done outside the home and the car.

✔ Find out about arrangements at your place of work for smokers. Are there designated areas for smokers? Are there designated smoke-free areas?

✔ Find out about municipal and state laws in your area that relate to smoking. You have a right to enjoy public spaces without inhaling someone else's smoke. Before making a reservation at a restaurant, find out what the smoking policy is.

Part V
The Part of Tens

The 5th Wave   By Rich Tennant

It'll be tough, but I'll see if they'll accept a non-smoking member.

In this part . . .

This part is made up of quick tips and tools to motivate you to quit smoking for good. You can take comfort in the fact that when it comes to quitting, you're never alone in your decision. Millions of people have been there before. In this section, I cover smoking rationalizations, signs that you want and need to quit, substitutes for smoking, and positive ways to spend the cash you'll save by not buying tobacco products.

Chapter 19

Ten Signs That You're Ready to Quit

. . . .

In This Chapter

▶ Knowing when you've reached your smoking limit

▶ Recognizing the social, financial, and personal signals to quit

▶ Fielding others' concerns about smoking

. . . .

*T*his chapter is a short list of signs that tell you when you're ready to quit smoking. If you surveyed a large number of people who have quit, you would likely come up with dozens, if not hundreds, of signs that made the difference for them in their decision to quit. You may be tired of the physical consequences of smoking. Smoking has real economic and psychological costs as well. You may find that it's not one issue alone, but a combination of several signals that gets you to quit.

Catching Your Breath

Once you start getting regular, persistent reminders that your lungs need a break — when you can no longer write off that cough or congestion to allergies or a cold — you may be ready to quit.

Understanding how your body works is a good launching point. The *trachea* (windpipe) branches out into *bronchi,* which further branch out into *bronchioles.* This complex set of expandable and collapsible tubes (think of it as an upside-down tree inside each of your lungs) is the air delivery system for your lungs. The entire network of tubes is lined with fine *cilia* — little hairs that wave and filter out foreign particles such as smoke and dust.

The breathing apparatus has other defenses as well. The lining of the respiratory tree secretes mucus to dilute and wash out inhaled toxic particles like smoke and tar (it washes out the particles by having you cough up the mucus). With chronic cigarette use, mucus production increases, the airway becomes more congested, and infection (bronchitis) may set in. The cilia may be overwhelmed — literally paralyzed — which worsens the situation with trapped toxins and airborne pollutant particles. The stuff just lies there in stagnant little pools, inviting infection. A sure sign of bronchitis is the presence of yellow or yellow-green mucus.

If you're experiencing any of these problems, consider it a sign that your body is ready to quit. How about the rest of you?

Watching Your Wallet

Being at the point where cigarettes are putting a major crimp in your budget is a very real, concrete indicator that the time to quit is now. Smoking is hitting you where it hurts: your wallet.

The price of a pack of cigarettes has risen steadily and dramatically over the past several years. For many, smoking has become a very expensive lifestyle choice that crowds out and replaces "luxury" items like food, shelter, and transportation. There's every reason to believe that the cost of cigarettes will continue to rise. Many smokers have switched from name brands to generics in an effort to hold down costs, but even these substitutes are quite pricey.

Even if you can still "afford" to smoke, the idea of all the money that you could either save or spend in better ways may pain you. When you find yourself digging ever deeper into your pockets to pay for a habit that brings you down in so many ways — spending more and enjoying it less — you're encountering yet another solid reason to quit.

Walking a Mile for a Camel

Ever feel like quitting smoking is just too much trouble? All the planning it takes, the self-denial, the self-control, the mental and behavioral strategies that you need to drum up — why bother? Dedicated smokers leave no stone unturned when it comes to staying supplied, however. Many hapless smokers have found themselves in desperate need of a smoke at inconvenient times (say, at 2 or 3 a.m.) or inconvenient places (camping in the Mojave Desert or in bear country). But even at times like these, no effort is too great to hunt down a stash.

Smokers frequently ask, "How do I know I'm hooked? When do I know I have a problem?" You know you're hooked when the habit makes problems for you — when smoking or procuring smokes uses up time that you'd ordinarily devote to healthful pursuits like work, sleep, and family activities. Sure, you'd walk a mile for a Camel. But how far would you go to lock in a lifestyle and future of clear breathing and robust health? When you're sick and tired of making epic journeys for a smoke, it's high time to quit.

Feeling Like a Social Misfit

I see them all the time: the people at work who huddle outside the building in all weather, at all times of day. They have a signature look, an aura of guilt, of turning the other way when they're seen. Each one clutches a little tube of rolled tobacco. They inhale furtively, greedily, intent on taking in enough nicotine to last them until their next smoke break in two or three hours.

Nicotine, whether in cigarettes, cigars, pipes, or chew, is not cocaine, but it's still a mind-altering drug. Society puts up with the habit for a number of reasons, but you will notice a tremendous variation in attitude and tolerance among people you know. Sometimes even smokers can't or won't tolerate breathing secondhand smoke! Others' attitudes vary from knowing indulgence to self-righteous indignation. The point is, each time you smoke around others, you run the risk of being criticized, stigmatized, pitied — even abhorred.

"Who cares what others think?" you may say. But quite often, you read disapproval and belittling in the eyes of others when in fact it originates from you. Knowingly maintaining a habit or behavior that's self-destructive is difficult. Each time you light up, you have to expend mental energy putting away thoughts of consequences and self-worth. You may be thinking each time you smoke, "Why would I do this if I really cared about myself?" From there, it's easy to see how you could assume that others readily reach similar conclusions about you when they see or "catch" you smoking.

Speaking of being caught: Talk about excess baggage! All the time and energy that you put into getting smoking supplies and masking telltale odors, burns, and stains . . . who needs it? Wouldn't it be great to feel healthy and attractive rather than secretive and smelly?

Being Unable to _____ (Fill in the Blank) without a Smoke

At my peak, I was smoking a pack a day. I eventually got to the point where almost any activity that required concentration and extended mental effort meant — you guessed it — cigarettes. Whether it was studying, writing, or making calls, the occasion always called for a smoke. When the mental gears wouldn't turn, I would reach for a cigarette. I would make a little progress, and then five or ten minutes later I would get stuck again, so once again I lit up.

After the second or third cigarette, my insides were in such a state of commotion that concentrating had become physically impossible. I was too wired! It didn't take too long for me to realize that I was trapped in a vicious cycle of tobacco-fueled anxiety.

Once I quit smoking, I substituted other oral gratifications when I needed them: a glass of water, an apple (or three), a pencil eraser. When I finally got to the point where I could work for extended periods without smoking, I felt much more in control of my energy and my life.

Extend your imagination to encompass the galaxy of activities beyond mere working to include the entire universe of human activity. There probably isn't a single human endeavor, from gardening to clock-making to dropping bombs, that hasn't been accompanied by a compulsive "need" to smoke. After you've gotten used to lighting up along with a particular activity, the act of smoking becomes a reflex, as in, "I can't have dinner without having a cigarette or cigar afterward," or, "I can't get out of bed in the morning without having my first cigarette of the day."

This is slavery in its most abject and primary form. If you're concerned about how much you "need" a smoke when you _____ (fill in the blank), you're near quitting time.

Catching Criticism from Others

This book is not intended as criticism. It's meant to be a meaningful resource that you can use at any time, repeatedly, until you internalize its lessons and don't need it any longer. You'll get plenty of criticism from other sources. Your family, your kids, and your school or work mates probably have a lot to say about your smoking. If you're like most smokers, you've already gotten more lectures than you can stand.

The remarks range from "How can you do this to yourself?" to expressions of outright disgust — "What a revolting habit!" — to plaintive, guilt-inspiring pleas to spare your life and the future suffering of your family. Don't minimize the accumulated impact of these statements on your well-being and your self-regard. No one likes to be told again and again that you're making bad choices. People don't like to be lectured or harangued. Quite often, the direct result of being told what to do (or admonished) is to do the opposite. Sometimes defiance or rebellion — making a statement about freedom of choice — becomes more important than one's health or personal safety.

Don't underestimate how great you'll feel once you've thrown off the burden of all this negative commentary. You simply don't need this tremendous weight of guilt and defensiveness. You have enough issues and conflicts in your life; you don't need additional ones. Besides, who wants to be answering to and scrutinized by others all the time? Of course, this criticism — at least as far as smoking is concerned — is valid. Smoking is costly, makes you and your surroundings smell bad, ages you prematurely, and eventually will ruin your health.

You need to get behind the decision to quit. Although many people around you will benefit from your quitting, you need to quit primarily for yourself. Otherwise, you may resent having to radically alter your behavior to please others. But one of the many perks of quitting is that you end up pleasing plenty of other people while you please yourself.

Smoking More and Enjoying It Less

Finding that you're smoking more and enjoying it less? In the universe of smokers, you are not alone. As with so many other "pleasures," smoking has a window of maximum enjoyment. Too few cigarettes and you find yourself craving more. Too many and nicotine poisoning sets in.

Have you ever simply had too much to smoke? It's an experience you're not likely to forget. Too much nicotine results in classic symptoms that are really sickening. Your heart beats rapidly, your head pounds as though jackhammers were strapped to your temples, and you feel dizzy, lurching in and out of normal consciousness from lack of oxygen (along with nicotine, you've inhaled too much carbon monoxide, which crowds out the oxygen in your bloodstream). Worst of all, you experience a gut-wrenching nausea that can lead to vomiting.

Charming! Why would anyone put themselves through these extremes?

Tobacco toxicity aside, many smokers find that it's all downhill after the first hit of the day. Somehow, the 200 or so puffs that follow the day's first don't compare in taste or impact. The alerting or calming effect of successive cigarettes lessens as the day progresses. When you consider the downsides — the cough, the acrid taste, the yellow fingers, the ever-mounting health debit that smokers try to ignore — it's only reasonable that those who smoke more get less and less out of it as time goes on.

This phenomenon has a physiological basis. The longer you wait between cigarettes, the greater your level of nicotine abstinence (withdrawal). Your first smoke of the day is essentially a detox smoke, easing you down from hours of smoke-free sleep. Conversely, if you smoke excessively, you're simply piling on toxic effects without the "gain" of eliminating or reducing withdrawal symptoms.

Reacting to Comments from Others

The first 10 or 20 negative comments from family, friends, and other concerned people may roll off your back, unheard and unheeded. But after a while, these remarks start to become guilt-provoking and bothersome to the extreme.

Your reactions to hearing someone say, "You really should quit, you know," or, "It's time to cut down," may vary from mild annoyance to soul-wrenching embarrassment. When you think about it, you are (if you want to be!) accountable not only to yourself but to those you love and care for. The responsibility is enormous. When friends and family members question you about your smoking, part of what's troublesome is that they're showing more concern about your health and future than you are.

Many smokers find comments from their children particularly vexing. I remember how I was constantly at my mother when I was a child, begging her to stop smoking. The news about cigarettes and lung cancer was out, and, like millions of other children, I was deeply frightened that I might lose my parent. If and when you have a smoker's cough, if and when you're hacking up gobs of discolored mucus, and if and when your fingertips are stained brown, your addiction is lit up for others like a blinking neon sign.

What begins as a covert habit all too often turns into a medical or social concern. Part of the controversy surrounding the tobacco industry is who should pay for the billions of dollars in lost work and healthcare costs that invariably follow years of smoking — the tobacco industry, the healthcare industry, or the taxpayers? Ultimately, the average citizen foots the bill because of the increased cost of health insurance. Insurance companies have no problem passing along the increased costs of healthcare to everyone, including nonsmokers.

Missing Your Senses of Smell and Taste

Your senses — taste, touch, smell, hearing, and sight — are a complex and finely tuned instrument capable of detecting minute levels of sensory input. Your smell receptors, located in your nose, are able to differentiate among particles on the molecular level. Your palate is likewise composed of an array of extraordinarily high-tech receptors on the tongue, grouped according to taste type.

With practice, you can hone your senses of smell and taste. Food and wine connoisseurs can pick up subtle distinctions in flavor and distinguish between vintages of a wine; they can tell how long a roast has been marinated and in what kind of sauce.

You can also *de*volve these senses. Continued exposure to toxic chemicals such as tar, nicotine, and the other constituents of tobacco erodes the sense of smell and taste over the course of years. The good news is that after you quit smoking, your sensitivity and receptivity make a comeback. Your awareness of the world of odors around you rebounds. This may seem like a small matter, but once you get a hint of the banquet of fragrances and flavors that you may have let slip over the years, you're likely to want more.

Smell is our primal connection to life. Biologists believe that the so-called "smell brain" is the oldest part of the brain, a part of the nervous system that we share with insects, lizards, and mammals that has evolved over millions of years. It's one of the gateways to intense attraction (or repulsion). Our bodies are tightly cued in to the presence of friendly, hostile, or sexy odors. Regaining your awareness of this cornucopia of sensations is a major reason to abandon those butts.

Wanting a Healthier Future

Many people live from day to day, or even from moment to moment, rather than plan for the future. If you're one of these people, remember that not making a decision is the equivalent of making one. Not making a decision is a decision to let things continue as they are.

How do you see your future? Does it involve a Stairmaster . . . or a portable oxygen tank? Do you see yourself getting fitter, healthier, more energetic, and more resilient with the passage of time, or becoming increasingly wrinkled, tired, and dependent on tobacco and possibly medications and medical equipment?

To some extent, the choice is yours. Granted, everyone inherits a genetic program for illness or health (usually a combination of the two). In the course of a lifetime, this program expresses itself as traits, predispositions, and even outright strengths or disease. But ultimately, what happens to you is the consequence of *both* inheritance and your environment. You do have some control over your surroundings, your body, and your fate.

Achieving excellent self-care is an exciting challenge. You can play a significant role in your outcome, for good or for ill. You don't have complete control over your life, but at the end of the day, being able to say that you fought the good fight and did as much as you could to improve your life (and, by extension, the lives of those around you) feels a lot better than the alternative. Waking up in the morning and thinking back to the day before, unmarked by the pollution of smoke, feels great. Likewise, anticipating an uninterrupted string of days that feature clear breathing, clear thinking, and healthful living is terrific. Enlarge the scope of your goals. Quitting smoking is not just about tossing out the cigarettes — it's about taking care of your priceless vehicle, your body.

Chapter 20

Ten Rationalizations That Keep You Hooked

*R*ationalization — the fine art of talking yourself into doing something that's not in your best interest — is a skill that you have developed over the years. Smokers are great at coming up with reasonable-sounding explanations and justifications for their behavior. This chapter gives you a short list of some of the more popular and successful strategies used to fool yourself into continuing to smoke. Note how many of these rationalizations have "worked" for you when you've reached for a smoke. You may never want to fool yourself again!

I'll Quit When I'm on Vacation

This rationalization is a perfect example of how people wind themselves up in arguments that are irrational and convoluted — yet somehow convincing. The idea is that quitting is such an arduous, stressful exercise that it's best put off until a later date. Preferably a much later date. Preferably to a time when you're enjoying perfect calm and maximum relaxation.

There are at least two major problems with this rationalization (although some people do succeed in quitting while on vacation!). One is the notion of putting off the decision until later. Although quitting smoking is a huge decision that requires mobilizing all kinds of support — quitting may not last if it's done impulsively — you don't want to put it off indefinitely. "On vacation" is a vague date that may never arrive. A better approach is to choose a specific quit date and work toward it, mustering all the resources and tools you can between now and then.

The other problem with this argument has to do human nature. Vacation is a time you set aside to pamper and indulge yourself — to kick back and have fun. By most smokers' definitions, smoking is part of all that. (Beach, sunglasses, tall tropical drink, pack of cigarettes or cigar — you get the picture.) The last thing you want to deal with on vacation is the stress of nicotine withdrawal and the sudden absence of your combustible friend.

Then again, it's all about how you define *vacation*. Many ex-smokers consider the cessation of smoking — the termination of that toxic contact between the body and the storehouse of poisons known as a cigarette — a real vacation. If you think of clear and easy breathing, minus tobacco, as a health holiday, you may start to feel differently about quitting . . . and about vacation.

The more specific your plan for your vacation, the more specific your approach to keeping away from tobacco can be.

Rationalizations are funny. They highlight the ease with which we fool ourselves. Saying you'll quit when you're on vacation is like jogging faster just so you can finish and have a smoke. Why not quit next week? Why mar a vacation with the additional pressure of forced abstention? The first few days of quitting are the hardest, and you probably don't want to spoil your bliss on a beautiful Caribbean island at a time like that.

I'm Not on Vacation

This rationalization is the flip side of the coin that the preceding rationalization represents. "I'm not on vacation" is an example of the kind of double-talk that smokers use: They say, "I'm on vacation, so I'll smoke," and then they say, "I'm not on vacation, so I'll smoke."

Most of the time available to you to quit is non-vacation time. Quitting smoking is a time-consuming effort accomplished one day at a time. The effort is a protracted one, exerted over many days — you can't just take a few days off and think you can quit for good in such a short time. Quitting smoking is a life goal that, once achieved, is a gift you give to yourself over the course of weeks, months, and years.

Here's another way to look at it. The gift of your life at work or school and at home is ample reason to quit. When you're caught up in your day-to-day life, you're busy, distracted, and engaged. I hope that your work/school and family activities are creative and fulfilling enough that they take your mind away from craving cigarettes and keep you on task. You might dedicate your quitting to improving your career, your schoolwork, or your family life. These endeavors will benefit directly from quitting.

The benefits may not be immediately evident. Things will get a little worse from time to time, and you may feel sluggish or wired (or both) the first few days of quitting, but you'll get through. When you come out at the other end, you'll no longer be throwing away time, energy, and money in the pursuit of a smoke. It's great to be able to keep on doing whatever it is you're doing without experiencing cravings. It's liberating not to have to walk outside or go to the car or otherwise excuse yourself to light up. Quitting smoking is an empowering experience. You'll have much more control over your time and your life; this heightened sense of self-mastery will have many positive spin-offs in other areas of your life.

While you're busy working or taking care of your family, assemble a set of rewards (other than smoking). Smoking is a bonus people give themselves in the course of the work or school day to keep themselves primed, energized, and motivated. What five *positive* reinforcements can you come up with to reward yourself during the day? For some, it is the completion of a task. For others, it is a ten-minute stretch or even a quarter-hour's worth of meditation with the office door shut. Having a snack or beverage is a reasonable alternative to a smoke.

The first few days are the toughest. If you snack more or fill up on liquids during this time, it's okay. It's temporary. You can lose a few pounds, but diseased lungs can be forever. Reward yourself for quitting by planning a terrific (and smoke-free) vacation!

My Life Is Too Stressful

Many people experience moderate to severe anxiety and/or depression over the course of a lifetime. Many more go through less intense but nonetheless painful and uncomfortable episodes of "nerves," "the blues," panic attacks, and feeling overwhelmed. Stress is a fact of life. You may not have control over many of the adversarial or difficult aspects of the world you live in, but you definitely have control over your reactions. You can choose how to handle challenging situations.

The first step is to critically examine the statement "My life is too stressful." Is it? Which part of your life is the most stressful? What do you mean by *stressful*, anyway? Some people actually thrive on stress. Each person has an optimal amount of activity and challenge. Have you exceeded yours? What can you do about it? Can you take active steps to reduce the amount of stress that life is throwing at you? If not, are there psychological or emotional steps you can take so that your internal world is a safer and more comfortable place?

Don't forget that having an expensive, health-ruining habit that makes you feel guilty and out of control is stressful in and of itself. The energy that goes into rationalizing continued smoking is significant. Denial of the facts, of the life-snuffing potential of every puff you take, costs you energy. Your energy is far better directed toward tasks that will improve your life and will open rather than close the future.

The next time you consider quitting and then decide not to because your life is too stressful, consider that part of this stress results from loss of control over self-destructive behavior. If you couldn't stop yourself from saying hurtful things to people you cared about, or did anything that was overtly harmful that seemed out of your control, it would be extremely stressful. The same holds true for tobacco use.

Smoking Helps Me Eat Less

There's no denying that smoking helps you eat less. Many people freely substitute cigarettes for food, particularly when they're busy running around taking care of things. Lighting up may be easier than switching gears and having a snack or a meal. For the calorie conscious, having something that gives you an extra charge *and* burns up energy is highly appealing.

If you were severely ill or in traction, you might eat less, too!

This is a great opportunity to reframe your thinking. Eating can be an ally — it keeps you alive. Eating is not the same as overeating, although, like so many other things, it can be done to excess. The challenge is to make food a friend. It is possible to think of food rewards that won't lead to weight gain.

For example, have you ever had the opportunity to relish the smell of fresh vegetables or spices harvested straight from the garden? How often do you get to enjoy a special meal either at home or at a restaurant? Activities such as going to a favorite restaurant can be great rewards for not smoking. Your reward at the end of Quit Day 1 can differ from the goodies you promise yourself at the ends of successive quit days.

Activities other than smoking help you eat less. Prominent among them is exercise. One of the many rewards of quitting is being able to enjoy a really good workout. Aerobic exercise kicks off the release of endorphins, the body's pleasure molecules.

Smoking Calms Me Down

Anxiety and stress are endemic. Pandemic. People everywhere talk about the level of tension in their lives. People talk about conflicts, chronic problems, and issues that won't go away.

A great approach is to get a perspective on what's really stressing you out. Is it related to work? Is it a relationship problem? Is the problem a thorny dynamic between you and yourself? Chances are the factors that stress you change from day to day, hour to hour. Although understanding and resolving the major issues in your life are beyond the scope of this book, it's worthwhile to list the top three stressors in your life. Once you've set them down on paper, you can begin working on them.

Here's a related question: Do you consider the lack of calm in your life to be normal, or is stress so pervasive and intense that it literally rocks your world? If you have jarring, disruptive, or even cataclysmic levels of anxiety or lack of calm, you can take steps to turn things around.

Talking to a friend can be enormously helpful. It's surprising how internal conversations can accumulate and amplify to the point where it seems like nothing will help. Turning to another person to vent can make a world of difference. You may be pleasantly surprised at how much another person can relate to your experience.

Another level of therapeutic venting is counseling. Many people find that getting professional help turns things around big time. Getting a different perspective can turn an earth-shattering problem into a finite, resolvable issue.

Smoking Gives Me More Energy

Quitting smoking is your number-one priority. One response to this rationalization is that any level of energy is enough in a day without smokes. In other words, any day without tobacco is a successful day, even if it means dragging yourself around for a short time.

Your body and brain will re-establish an energy equilibrium once you quit. Although you may be tired and/or wired in the first few days, you'll find, as millions of others have, that cutting cigarettes loose for good results in enormous gains in vitality. Plus, it's okay to be laid back on occasion. Not every moment has to be action packed.

The kind of energy that smoking gives is fool's gold. You borrow it for a very short time and then have to pay it back many times over. Most drugs, including nicotine, involve a rebound effect. If the drug gives you a lift, it brings you down later. If a drug initially relaxes you, you can expect to feel restless, hyper, and wired when it wears off.

What pursuits other than smoking give you energy? Try to partake in these activities so as to maximize your energy level without needing to resort to cigarettes.

All My Friends Smoke

Many people begin smoking because a friend, family member, or boyfriend or girlfriend smokes. It seemed like the right thing to do at the time. I remember how I fell into it. I was 17, away at college, and thought I had fallen in love. The object of my affection was a sultry, hip girl. She dressed cool, thought about things in interesting ways, and smoked. I even liked the way she held her cigarettes. I thought, "I can do that." And so I did. Many hundreds of packs later, I found myself craving the things at all hours. I found heaps of discarded butts, cigarettes crushed out on the floor of our apartment, tar- and lipstick-stained ends that were the first and last word in toxicity and filth.

You may be married to a smoker. Having a husband or wife (or roommate) who smokes makes picking up a cigarette the easiest thing in the world to do — and makes it incredibly difficult to abstain.

Kids smoke for many reasons, chief among which is to fit in with the crowd and to look cool. Isn't it ironic how the code of behavior among kids, emphasizing rebellion, is ultimately conformist?

It's curious, too, that social trends have pretty much reversed themselves, at least as far as smoking goes. Now it's the odd man out who smokes. More and more restaurants and other public places either set aside segregated areas for smokers or ban smoking outright. Smokers are increasingly seen as outsiders who have to secret themselves to a not-too-public place to get their fix.

Smoking ads have been banned from television, but smoking ads in magazines portray young, sexy people having a great time. The idea is that if you smoke you can be young and sexy, too. That's called hype. If you smoke, you're actually barring yourself from certain social circles and drawing attention to yourself as someone who has a nasty habit that can't be kept under wraps.

Smoking Is Cool

Really! What if you reengineered your concept of cool? Bear in mind that the general idea of what's cool or attractive varies widely from decade to decade, and even from year to year. In the 1950s, for example, the stylish look involved pillbox hats, cashmere sweaters, lots of makeup (for women), and big hair. Where has all that gone? Similarly, popular magazines in the 1940s promoted cigarettes as healthful, as adding zip to your day. Everyone knows where that idea has gone.

In the hippie heyday of the 1960s, musicians and other celebrities tried to outdo each other in the flagrant self-abuse category. Drinking more, smoking more, and running themselves down (yet managing to continue to perform) became a form of heroism. Unfortunately, this lifestyle led to the deaths of a number of stars. Even more unfortunate, some naive and adulating fans, particularly younger ones, started emulating these self-destructive lifestyles. Yet much of the bravado and showmanship of that time was hype. The performers who stuck with their art, who have lived to tell their stories and continue their craft, have for the most part taken *extra* pains to nurture their bodies. The stars of today have personal trainers, not drug dealers.

Evolution and growth are cool. Taking the higher road is cool. Doing right by yourself is cool. If you care about being cool, hold yourself to the highest standard of all: your own. Taking care of yourself and your body is one of the coolest things you can do.

No One Has Proven that Smoking Is Dangerous

That rationalization is wrong — dead wrong. The tobacco industry has spent decades and hundreds of millions of dollars on research and advertising to convince people that tobacco is harmless. The industry simply can't do it. The undeniable consensus of thousands of clinical trials, the unwavering if not unanimous tally of countless demographic and statistical surveys, is that tobacco is harmful in the extreme.

Although nicotine by itself doesn't cause cancer or lung disease, the only way to get pure, uncontaminated nicotine is to use a nicotine replacement therapy, such as the patch, inhaler, or gum. Every other form of nicotine delivery system, including chewing tobacco, snuff, pipe tobacco, cigars, and cigarettes, is loaded with additives and complex chemicals that accompany nicotine hand in hand. Some of these chemical delights are created as a result of combustion. Burning the tobacco leaves volatilizes the chemical compounds and changes them into smoke so that the tobacco can be absorbed that much more readily into your lungs.

Some scientists and other experts and consultants (especially those bankrolled by the tobacco companies!) have objected that the research findings are based on extreme conditions that don't mirror ordinary life. These naysayers point out that some of the research results derive from laboratory situations in which experimental animals such as guinea pigs and mice are given doses of tobacco compounds hundreds and even thousands of times more potent than you get from a cigarette.

Are you willing to put your health and your life on the line because of this kind of reasoning? If a chance exists that these toxic substances will harm you, why take the risk? Besides, we now know that lung cancer is the most prevalent and preventable cause of death among American males. Put that in your pipe and smoke it.

Tomorrow Never Comes

Too many people live by this philosophy. Whether you're talking about gambling, overeating, smoking, or excessive drinking, this attitude works by means of tunnel vision. Many New Age and holistic-type philosophies place a heavy emphasis on living in the here and now, but you *can* have too much of a good thing. If you live *exclusively* in the here and now, without a thought or care for tomorrow, you rob yourself of one of the most important tools you own: the ability to plan.

Without planning, things don't get done. As obvious as it sounds, you'd be amazed at how often people fail to put it into practice. Living as though tomorrow will never come is an indulgence, a beautiful fantasy that children enjoy. That's because grown-ups are looking ahead for them. As an adult, you must take the bull by the horns and believe in the future if you're going to not only survive but thrive.

Time is real and, as the song says, waits for no one. If you keep putting off the quit decision, tobacco poisons will continue to accumulate in your body. Your body doesn't know about "tomorrow never comes." For the body, tomorrow *always* comes. If you're taking good care of your body, this can be a good thing. If you eat right, get adequate rest, and exercise, your body should be an ever-evolving work in progress, continually surprising you with new and pleasant sensations and capabilities.

Dogs bury bones to retrieve later, beavers build dams . . . so what's up with you? Even if you have a hard time believing in the future, act as though tomorrow *will* arrive. This attitude really pays off when you're first quitting. When you think ahead to the next morning and visualize how you'll feel after waking and remembering that you didn't smoke, you'll feel spectacularly proud of yourself.

Chapter 21

Ten Great Smoking Substitutes

*Y*ou've probably heard the saying that if you give up a habit, you need to replace it with another habit — preferably a healthy one! Smoking is no different.

If you are to succeed at quitting smoking — if you are to give up a "friend" that has stuck with you through thick and thin, a friend that's always there by your side (and in your handbag, in the glove compartment of your car, on the night table, and so on) — you need to replace the habit with something else.

Substituting alternate rewards and gratifications for tobacco is a matter of harm reduction: You want to replace the cigarette habit with a different one, provided that the replacement habit is supportable and less harmful than cigarettes — and hopefully not harmful at all. In this chapter, I give you ten ideas of good habits that you can substitute for the bad habit of smoking.

Working Out

If you find yourself feeling jittery or stressed as you quit smoking, you may want to give exercise a try. Not only is a workout such as jogging, tennis, or walking good for almost anybody, but it's also a great way to calm your nerves and feel centered thanks to the *endorphins* (the brain's feel-good molecules) that exercise triggers. You feel healthy, bright, and clean after a good workout.

Exercise comes in many forms. Even if you have breathing problems or physical limitations such as arthritic knees, you can still work out, provided that you follow your doctor's advice.

One form of exercise that's available to everyone practically anywhere is *isometric* exercise, which involves pitting one muscle against another without any bending or stretching. You can do isometrics exercises at home, in the office, or at school. The best thing is that they require only a few minutes at a time.

Another effective form of exercise is weight training. Like many other activities, this one can be habit-forming. You can usually pick out the dedicated weightlifters at the gym. If you enjoy lifting weights, chances are that you're doing it more to tone up and to tighten sagging or flabby areas. As you watch yourself transform your body over the course of weeks, you not only enjoy looking better, but you feel better as well.

For my money, the most enjoyable form of exercise is *aerobic,* which includes jogging, running on a treadmill, or taking kickboxing, aerobics, or even certain types of yoga classes. Aerobic workouts make you sweat. If you're new to this type of exercise, you may find yourself struggling to get over the so-called wall — the physical point during exercise at which you're so tired, so utterly not enjoying it, that every muscle and nerve in your body cries out, "Enough! Stop!" This point, of course, is the exact moment at which to persevere. Once you hit the wall and then make it over, you'll probably get the endorphin rush — the physical and mental payoff that keeps runners running and tread-millers treadmilling.

Taking Extra Leisure Time

Time is one of the most precious commodities around. Everyone complains that the day doesn't have enough time in it and fantasizes at one point or another about having more time. So what would you do with an extra five hours of free, uncommitted time a week?

Chances are, if you've given up smoking, you have that extra time. Think about it. How much time did you spend each week getting and then smoking cigarettes? Five, ten hours? What did you have to show for that time?

Perhaps you've been putting off a personal pursuit or hobby because of a lack of time. Undoubtedly, you can come up with dozens of incentives and positive reinforcements to reward yourself. You may be the type of person who will use any spare time to do extra work, such as completing projects, home repairs, or unfinished business at the office. Or you may be like me and throw yourself headfirst at the nearest available sofa or bed to catch some *zzzs*. Relaxation is a good thing. Taking time out from the slings and arrows of day-to-day life is an essential part of self-care — as important as food and shelter.

Many newly quit smokers notice that they feel tired and can't escape the feeling that they're dragging themselves around. That's fine. Your body is rebounding from the thousands of mini super-charges and jolts it got each time you puffed. Your batteries need to recharge. If quitting is your number-one priority, then having two or three days where you're not at your peak is okay. A few unproductive days is a reasonable price to pay for the increased vitality, energy, and self-regard that nonsmokers (that's you!) enjoy.

Drinking Lots of Fluids

Drinking lots of fluids actually promotes your attempt to quit. Increased amounts of fluids literally help wash out some of the toxins and pollutants that have accumulated in your body as a result of using tobacco.

Stock up on orange juice. Some evidence suggests that cigarettes burn up ascorbic acid, or vitamin C, in the body, so replenishing your body's stores of vitamin C either with citrus juices or with tablets (100 to 500 mg a day) is a good idea.

Let's not mince words. Tobacco use — whether you're talking about cigarettes, a pipe, or cigars — is a very *oral* habit. The act of putting a pipe stem or cigarette between your lips and inhaling hot, stimulating smoke many times a day is highly gratifying and extremely reinforcing. The more you do it, the more you want to do it — and the more you miss it when you stop doing it.

Ever seen a guy with a big fat cigar hanging out of his mouth and imagined that instead of a cigar, it was a pacifier or baby bottle? This doesn't require a great leap of the imagination. Many people have so-called oral fixations and spend much of their time eating, smoking, chewing gum, biting their nails, or talking. The lips and mouth are richly supplied with nerve endings, and the more these nerve endings are stimulated, the more they want to be stimulated. If you've seen the ragged chewed end of a pen or pencil or the cracked and mottled fingernails of a habitual nail biter, you know exactly what I mean.

Having plenty of liquids provides a refreshing and healthy oral substitute for cigarettes. Water, juice, and low-calorie beverages are good choices. You'll find that as time passes and your cravings for nicotine diminish, your reliance on fluids and/or other oral gratifications will probably subside as well.

Meditating

Meditation is one of the most powerful and gratifying tools you have available to you. The beauty of meditation is that it's easy to learn and extremely portable. You can meditate anywhere and at almost any time.

To meditate, start by taking a deep breath and visualizing the inrushing air as cool, cleansing, and filling every part of your body with clarity, peace, and calm. Continue your deep, regular breathing. Use a slow, measured count of four for the inhalation, four for the held breath, four for the exhalation, and four for the pause before restarting. Feel the oxygen expanding into the furthest reaches of your body. Starting with your toes and then working up, alternately clench and relax each body part, spending as much time as necessary to instill a poise, a kind of relaxed alertness, in each limb and muscle. As you proceed, keep visualizing the incoming breaths as cleansing, wiping out the day's thoughts and cares. You're aiming for stillness, for awareness that's not clouded or distracted by errand lists, snatches of a song, or thoughts of "I."

When you first start to meditate, you may grow impatient and distracted with the process. A kink in the back, a minor leg cramp, the sound of your children playing downstairs — each of these distractions can work to pull you away from your task. As you become more practiced, finding the zone of tranquility, of deep inner focus that can remain unbroken, becomes easier. The time will come when the state of mind becomes so primary that you literally lose track of time and the events of the world.

For more information about meditation, see *Meditation For Dummies* by Stephan Bodian (Wiley Publishing).

Focusing Your Energy Outward

Focusing your mental energy, your perceptions, and your immediate responses to the world outward is a great strategy for quitting success and for success in general.

Many people who are burdened with too much anxiety or too many thoughts, reactions, or worries find that the location of this unrest is *inner*. The feeling that you have to have a smoke, for example, originates from somewhere within your mind, body, and brain. The satisfaction of this craving also takes place inside your body — in your mouth and lungs. If you're depressed or worried, it's likely that you're preoccupied with yourself, your future, your past, or the way your body and mind feel.

Try taking your focus outside yourself. Force yourself to look actively at the world around you, to notice the sky and the trees, and to take in the faces and movements of other people. Gather a highly detailed collection of mental snapshots and mental audiotapes of the world around you. Ever really notice all the subtle sounds and smells that make up a winter or spring day? The more you see, the more you find to see.

When every fiber of your being is crying out for a smoke, you can resist by turning your attention outward from your body to something else. The person standing next to you at the bus stop — what does she look like? What happens if you say hello to her? What is she wearing? Do you think she's going to a safe, pleasant place, or does she have her own inner struggles that she has only partly succeeded in masking from the rest of the world?

This strategy is unbelievably effective and helps not only with quitting smoking but with many other personal challenges as well. Directing your focus to all the things in the world around you is also a terrific antidote to anxiety and is a principal method for making a powerfully positive impression on other people.

If you're in the process of quitting smoking, you're probably having constant impulses, longings, and cravings for a smoke. It may help to think of these cravings as originating from *within* you. Placing your cravings inside you means that there's another place — namely, outside of you — where the cravings don't go. You're uncomfortable to the extent that you allow these cravings, which are temporary, to rule your thoughts. Instead, try to let the sights, smells, and sounds around you rule your thoughts and feelings.

Are you a person whose primary or most relied upon sensation is visual? If that's the case, make a point of spending as much quality time as possible taking in the brushstrokes of the painting on display in the corridor at the office or the colors that the sun percolates through the clouds as it sets beneath the skyline.

Some people have other dominant sensory modalities. If you're a sound-oriented person, use this time to refine your aural sensibility. When you listen to sounds, make it an active process of hearing, of teasing apart the aural strands that make up the voices of the crowd, the song, or the television news announcer.

Paying close attention to things not only distracts you from the transient discomfort of quitting smoking, but also sharpens your senses and offers an immediate payoff. Whether you like it or not, this world is a material one, and the more you notice, the more detailed and spectacular it seems. Take your attention and open things up further. Long after you've cut tobacco loose, you'll still be enjoying and learning new ways to experience the world in greater and more delicious detail.

Using Nicotine Replacement Therapies

Chapter 9 gives you a comprehensive review of everything you need to know about nicotine replacement therapies. The purpose of mentioning them in this chapter is twofold:

✔ The first is to remind you of the wealth of tobacco alternatives and substitutes that exist, including the patch, nicotine gum, nicotine aerosol, inhaler, and Zyban. Your eventual goal is to free yourself from nicotine entirely, but getting the nicotine your body craves without the accompanying toxins contained in cigarette smoke is a much better alternative.

✔ The second is broader. Life and the things that arouse your excitement and curiosity are the real nicotine replacement therapies. People are nicotine replacement therapy. Work and creation are nicotine replacement therapy. After all, what is therapy? It's any activity that promotes health and healing.

Based on my experience, and upon that of many others I've spoken with, worked with, and treated, I can confidently guarantee that whatever you do that's important to you — whether it's house painting or designing aircraft carriers or doing origami — will come together better, smoother, and faster without cigarettes. Health concerns aside, taking tobacco in any form is a massive waste of time. The thousands of moments of distraction that cigarettes provide are dead time (in more than one sense of the word). When you're tired or out of ideas or patience, you're better off simply to get up, take a walk, or run some water over your hands. Things go better when you pay attention.

I'm sure you've seen people who multitask their distractions — people who chew gum, smoke cigarettes, and carry on phone conversations at the same time. The most effective and impressive folks in the world are those who are able to concentrate intensely on the moment, whether they're having fun, working on a sculpture, or giving up cigarettes.

Falling for Fruits and Vegetables

I have to admit that at first blush, "falling for fruits and vegetables" doesn't sound like a terribly exciting or gratifying adventure. Here I am trying to point out the exciting, life-renewing, and vitalizing possibilities of quitting smoking, and what do I offer you as a replacement? Produce. And nuts and juices, too.

The launching point for this radical perspective is your attitude and way of thinking. When you decide to quit smoking, you need to unload a lot of the baggage that accompanies the habit — specifically the habit of thinking of smoking as a good thing.

Don't minimize the tremendous attachment you have to smoking. Along with the logical and rational conclusions you've drawn for yourself about tobacco, you probably have just as many positive thoughts, associations, fond memories, and otherwise pleasant regards for the habit. Along with the negativity, with the health and financial and other concerns, you think of smoking in affectionate, tender, and longing ways. Part of you thinks that smoking — the taste of the fumes, the ritual of lighting up, the heft of the unopened pack in your hand — is a mighty good thing.

It's time for a radical attitude adjustment. Hot, acrid vapors that constrict your blood vessels and coat your insides with sticky, cancer-causing tars are bad. Rethinking many of your tastes and preferences is a fundamental aspect of quitting smoking. You need to learn to appreciate and value totally different tastes and sensations.

Think about celery — the cleanness of it. Or spinach — can you smell it? Can you taste the difference between romaine, Boston, and iceberg lettuce? How do you feel about a cold, luscious peach on a hot summer day? Constant exposure to chemicals like nicotine dumbs down your palate. You achieve the opposite result of refining and upgrading your taste buds when you stop tampering with the delicate symphony of taste and smell.

Healthy foods are not boring. Self-abuse ultimately is. Take the time and promote the health and sensitivity required to stop and smell the roses.

Visualizing Health

The visualization thing is quite interesting. It's a double-edged sword. On the one hand, it's important to appreciate the impact that seeing things the way you want them to be has on your life and feelings. On the other hand, it's also important not to blame yourself inappropriately for the bad things that come your way. In other words, visualization is powerful — but not all-powerful.

Although definitive scientific evidence doesn't prove that intense visualization of your desires brings them into being, it makes sense that it would work that way. If you harness your energy and dedicate greater and greater amounts of your mental time to ever more specific pictures of what you want, you can easily imagine that the people, places, and things around you will, to a certain extent, sort themselves out around these intensely visualized desires.

If you're thinking hard and passionately about that new BMW you want with every fiber of your being, chances are you're going to notice every BMW that passes you by. You're going to spend ever greater amounts of time thinking about how to save up enough money to buy one. In just the same way, if you visualize a life without smokes — and I mean visualize in every sense how you'll look and feel, how food and air and the inside of your mouth will taste, and how an autumn breeze will smell — this continual effort will boost your intention to the point where you're taking more and more opportunities to think about things other than cigarettes.

Visualization is the step between desire and actualization. When you deeply and creatively imagine something to the point where you can almost feel, taste, and hold it, it's practically yours.

Changing Your Priorities

As a smoker, you have specific priorities. These priorities include making sure that you always have enough cigarettes on hand, that you bring them with you wherever you go, that you always have matches or a lighter, and that you have sufficient opportunities to light up at home, at work, and on the road. Smokers' priorities also include having that first cigarette of the day, as well as self-medicating throughout the day so that their nicotine levels (and thus their mood and energy level) never run too low. Having a cigarette with a cup of coffee, after a meal or after sex, and when you get in or out of your car — by now, these well-worn rituals have probably become ingrained priorities in your life. You feel uncomfortable jettisoning them for others.

I can suggest alternate priorities, some of which may be obvious to you if you've already decided to quit smoking. One is committing to the future. Rather than gratifying the cravings and needs of today, let yourself imagine what the future will bring. Another priority is quashing the guilt, shame, and embarrassment that usually accompany a self-destructive habit like smoking. When living without these feelings becomes sufficiently important to you, you'll do what it takes to leave them behind.

Yet another new priority is living in and feeling your body as it is at the moment, without having to jump in right away and alter it. Notice how you're breathing. Is your pulse moving along at a steady rate, or is it jumping and throbbing erratically? Is your skin cool and dry, or is it moist and sweaty? How about your facial muscles — are they relaxed, poised for whatever sights and sounds are to come your way this day, or are they already tense, vigilant, and alert to negative possibility and stress?

Calm, resilient awareness that simultaneously enables you to enjoy what the day brings and be sufficiently alert to mobilize for situations that require quick handling, is the way to go. You can achieve this state more fully and authentically without smokes.

Change your priorities. Decide to be a hero. Actively decide to live in and enjoy the body you were given rather than be a sleight-of-hand guy who's always trying to manage moods and stress and all the vicissitudes of life with smoke (and cigarettes) and mirrors.

Redesigning Your Interior

Interior redesign sounds funny, I guess. When you think about it, though, the effort to make yourself over begins inside. It flows outward from the heart and mind and feelings. It *is* interior redesign.

What does the inside of your mental home look like now? Is it gracious, full of light, comfortable, and spacious, or is it a "carpenter's dream," begging to be renovated? To the extent that you do things that you know are bad for you — things that at least part of you doesn't want to do — your inner world is in disarray. You have angry factions constantly at war with each other — kind of like an inner battle of Hatfields and McCoys.

The way you want to be is solid, consistent, and steady. You decide what you want in life, and then you mobilize what it takes to get it. The way you *don't* want to be is fragmented and chaotic inside, wanting one thing and going for another. Smoking is a perfect example of the latter. You know that smoking is bad, yet you reach for the cigarette anyway. This action involves suppressing those parts of you that are opposed to smoking, which means that you're actively discounting or silencing important parts of yourself. You're throwing drapes over some of the most important and beautiful rooms in your inner house.

Try to make it so that the "rooms" of your inner house can recognize each other and be on good terms. You don't want a family of angry, needy nicotine addicts in one wing of the house and a family of peace- and health-loving do-gooders in the other. It's your body. How do you want it to look and run? Should you be the one making the major decorating decisions, or should they be made by Brown and Williamson or the American Tobacco Company?

Chapter 22

Ten Things You Can Do with the Money You Save

In This Chapter

▶ Rewarding yourself for quitting

▶ Helping others with your saved money

*W*ith the money you save from quitting smoking, you can buy an entire library of works on tobacco, enjoy ten gourmet meals, or send a child to camp. And that's just a few ideas of ways to spend the money you save from not buying cigarettes.

If you smoke a pack a day at $4 a pack, you spend a total of $1,460 a year. If, instead, you put this money in the bank and earn a conservative (not to say paltry) 4 percent annual dividend, you end up with $1,518.40 after one year. Happy spending!

Buy This Book for Your Friends

Suggesting that you buy more copies of my book sounds pretty self-serving, I guess. Nonetheless, purchasing additional copies of this book and giving them to friends as gifts is a far better way to go than to buy another pack of cigarettes. In simple economic terms, you can purchase this book for the price of four to five packs of cigarettes. You can buy this book with the money you would spend on *one* expensive Cuban cigar.

Take my word for it: Reallocating your resources toward healthful, positive purposes is a great feeling. Taking the high road really does feel good. Even if you don't have specific people in mind who might benefit from this book's information, support, and pep talks, you can still donate a copy of *Quitting Smoking For Dummies* to your local library. After all, almost 50 million Americans still smoke. That's a lot of people who need to learn more about how to quit.

Donate to the American Cancer Society

Few charities do more life-saving, life-changing work than the American Cancer Society (ACS). The ACS has been supporting research and clinical and educational efforts to combat cancer for decades. The mission of the agency, comprised of more than 3,400 local units, is to eliminate cancer through prevention, advocacy, education, and service. At least a million people in the United States get cancer each year, with most of these cancers occurring in those over the age of 55. Lung cancer is the most frequently diagnosed cancer and makes up 14 percent of all cancers and 28 percent of total cancer deaths.

More than 2 million volunteers are directly involved in helping promote the society's goal of wiping out cancer. The ACS has provided almost $2.5 billion in research funds and has further distinguished itself by giving grant monies to 32 Nobel Prize winners early on in their scientific careers. Prevention projects of the ACS include tobacco control and health education activities in schools. Workshops and massive mailings of society publications to healthcare professionals and to the public aid in the crusade against lung and other kinds of cancer. The American Cancer Society also promotes vigorous political efforts on behalf of research funding and national and state-level efforts to reduce smoking among minors.

The ACS Web site, www.cancer.org, is a comprehensive guide for patients, families of patients, professionals, and everyone else who wants to find out more about preventing and treating cancer. Sections of the Web site are devoted to finding out who is at risk, and to prevention and detection efforts as well.

Not buying tobacco and tobacco products not only may save or extend your life, but you can use the money you save from quitting to help others. Cancer is one of the enemies of the human race. Taking money from the tobacco companies and donating all or part of it to those who crusade for health and life is one of the most gratifying substitutions you can make.

Take a Terrific Vacation

Whether it's to the beach or your backyard, a vacation is a terrific way to reward yourself for good work. You know, either from personal experience or from reading this book, that quitting smoking is hard work. Giving up the habit is so challenging that most people fail their first time around. When you finally hit your stride and quit smoking for good, you have an occasion to celebrate!

Ideally, when you're on vacation, you have no responsibilities aside from kicking back, relaxing, having fun, and rejuvenating. Without deadlines to meet, papers to write, or people to manage, you should be able to retreat into whatever personal space you need to stop smoking.

One of the main strategies for quitting involves shaking things up — upsetting your ordinary expectations of what happens or is supposed to happen during the course of the day.

Take a vacation devoted to rest, exercise, clean air, and good food. A vacation with a physical activity theme may be just what you need. I know many people who actually enjoy going out into the wild, into the forest, or up into the mountains to rediscover themselves among nature. While you're out there, you can rediscover your lungs in the fresh, clean, open air.

The wisdom of thousands of years of accumulated practice in yoga teaches that physical and mental energy is fueled by air. The way you breathe may have a wide-ranging impact on your overall energy level and your sense of well-being.

If you're a stay-at-home person who enjoys nothing more than the world seen from the perimeter of your apartment or backyard, a vacation is still the opportune time to live out your newfound priorities. You can do everything you enjoy doing with more focus and perhaps even better results without the tobacco distraction.

Go ahead, live out that whitewater rafting or mountain climbing or southern France fantasy you've been secretly nurturing for years. It's your life: Use it, live it, enjoy it to the hilt. It'd be a pity to let it go up in smoke.

Get a New Wardrobe

New clothes are a luxury you may only dream about. If you're like me, new clothes are fun to think about but certainly not something you're actually going to go out and buy unless the need is pressing and you're down to your last pair of shoes.

The money you save on tobacco will be substantial. Major. Six months of abstaining from a pack of cigarettes a day nets you about $700, assuming that a pack costs $4. Granted, this is the price of just one Armani blouse, but if you shop at a reasonable place and choose items that are somewhat more downscale than the Italian designer stuff straight from the couturier, you can do quite well.

Another reason to refurbish your clothing supply is that the nasty odor of tobacco smoke lingers long after you quit smoking. As your sense of smell improves, you begin to notice the different fragrances that new and fresh fabrics (as well as everything else in the world!) have. Getting a fresh start on your appearance — on the package of self that you present to the world each day — doesn't have to be a pipe dream. You can have those new duds with the extra money you'll have on hand. I suggest that on your first quit day, you reward yourself with a not-too-extravagant present and repeat the process as your success extends. (Do not buy a smoking jacket!)

Enjoy Ten Gourmet Meals

If you enjoy eating, having dinner at a fine restaurant is a great reward for cutting cigarettes loose. You may be wondering, ten gourmet meals? Isn't that expensive? Obviously, it is. But once you go out and spend the money on fine fare, you'll realize how much your cigarette habit has cost. You can get a fine meal at many high-end restaurants for the price of a carton of smokes.

I'm not suggesting that you stop smoking and start putting away as many calories as possible. In fact, one of the main reasons you're probably quitting is for the sake of your health. If you discover that you're substituting eating for smoking, try raw vegetables, such as carrot or celery sticks, or sugarless gum. Also try drinking plenty of fluids.

Generalizations about quitting and weight gain are based on the population at large, not on particular individuals. Many people who quit smoking revel in their new healthy lifestyle and do not put on weight. Some use quitting smoking as a launching point for getting more exercise, getting more rest, and improving their appearance. It's possible to lose weight after quitting as well. Substituting quality meals for fast food and snacks is the way to go.

Open a Savings Account or Mutual Fund

If you've calculated the amount of cash you'll begin to accumulate the moment you quit smoking, you can start comparing investment tools and do even more exciting calculations about the potential extra income your savings can bring you.

If you save about $1,500 a year and invest this money in a conservative, slow-moving savings account that yields an annual rate of 3 percent, you'll have a minimum of $1,545 after one year. I say a minimum because many banks compound interest daily or quarterly, so the amount you'll see at year's end is actually greater than $1,545. And that's just the first year!

If you're interested in potentially higher-yield investments, such as stocks, bonds, and mutual funds, you have a seemingly endless array of investment opportunities to choose from. You can find out more about financial vehicles that make your money grow with time at your bank or credit union, online, or in the financial pages of the newspaper. Entire magazines are dedicated to the world of investment and finance. If you don't have the stomach for truly high-risk ventures, an investment portfolio based on index funds, which essentially parallel the progress of the stock market at large, is said to be a safer but potentially good-yielding instrument over time.

Money is time is life. If you had all the money you ever wanted, what would you do with it? Would you use it to make more time for the things you love to do? Smoking in a sense is the opposite of money. It depletes you of cash and of time.

Join a Health Club

If you don't already work out at a gym or club, you may have reservations about starting. Part of the reluctance to give it a try may be the expense. However, many facilities are willing to let potential new members have a trial workout or pay for the use of the club one day at a time. Some people, particularly if they're overweight or self-conscious about their appearance, are hesitant to go into a health club where seemingly perfect specimens in spandex and Lycra effortlessly crunch hundreds of pounds. But not all health clubs are like that. Take advantage of those free trials to find a place where you feel comfortable.

Everyone starts somewhere. Even the Greek god striking poses before the gym mirror started out weak, flabby, and insecure.

If you're really shaky about showing up at the gym, visit during an off-peak time of day or night. Many facilities are large enough that you can find a corner or niche where you feel reasonably comfortable and secluded and avoid prying eyes. Another option, probably the best of all if you can afford it, is to work one or more times with a personal trainer at the club. The personal trainer acts as your sponsor, your personal champion, and he or she can give you a tour of the place and help you determine your optimal workout.

If, for whatever reason, you really don't want to join a health club, you can take the money you save on tobacco and invest in a treadmill or a set of weights, which you can probably set up at home without much difficulty. Having your own equipment gives you virtually unlimited access to exercise without leaving the house.

Working out is one of the best things you can do for yourself. Strenuous exercise, particularly aerobic exercise, is good for your heart, your lungs, your circulation, your muscles, and your head. Exercise can be addicting. And it's an addiction you can be proud to have.

Hire a Personal Trainer

Wouldn't it be great if you could rent a personal quitting trainer? I know of a few cases where extravagantly wealthy types have hired personal psychologists or physicians. Maybe a personal Quit Mentor is a professional whose time will come! You *can* hire a personal physical trainer to evaluate your fitness needs and shepherd you through the paces at the gym, the pool, the tennis club, or the track. Fitness takes many forms, and what works best for someone else may not be to your liking at all. If you prefer yoga or more spiritually focused activities such as meditation, you can find guides who will train and monitor your progress through the various levels of these disciplines.

Personal training is widely open to interpretation and can refer to personal growth and advancement on any or all of the following planes: physical, mental, emotional, financial, and spiritual. Some combination of these areas is preferable to one pursuit alone. As you know, advancement in one area at the expense of the others sometimes creates an exaggerated or even grotesque character. Balance, the golden mean, is the most healthful and sensible goal to pursue. (For example, imagine if you succeeded at quitting cigarettes but dropped everything else in your life.) Growth should be concentric; as your muscles tighten and your breathing and perceptions open up, so should your heart.

A personal trainer can help you choose your goals in a way that assures that you reach them.

Send a Child to Summer Camp

The list of great ways to spend your quit-smoking funds is pretty much endless. The suggestions I list in this chapter are not so much arbitrary as selective, along the lines of getting the most bang for the buck. Turning around an addiction and not only saving yourself but also giving a kid a wonderful experience promotes the joy and well-being of at least two people. Perhaps you have a child and you've been on the fence about whether to send him or her to camp this summer. Here's your chance. The money you save on tobacco can pay for some or most of your child's sleep-away or day camp experience. Each time you consider picking up a cigarette and don't, you can think about how your decision is adding to the quality of your child's life.

If you don't have a child, don't know of a child who could use some help getting to camp this summer, or otherwise are not taken by the idea, send yourself to camp instead!

Build a Web Site

Building a Web site may be a project that you've been contemplating for some time. Not everyone is computer savvy, but a surprisingly large number of people have jumped on board this still relatively new medium to promote themselves, their idea, or their business.

Quitting smoking means letting go of a habit: a time-, energy-, and spirit-consuming activity that has meant a lot to you — maybe more than you realize. To the extent that you can replace smoking with a substitute gratification, you've succeeded in detaching your focus from one major pursuit. Now you can focus your efforts elsewhere.

Even if you aren't another Bill Gates, and even if you aren't the world's quickest study when it comes to Web design, now is a great time to throw yourself into the burgeoning world of the information superhighway. Every day, the Internet grows in complexity and size. Most every interest, every arcane byway of human curiosity and knowledge, is finding a niche on the Web. If you know nothing about computers, you can turn the hair-pulling white-knuckled angst of quitting (I hope it's not *that* bad!) into a fresh pursuit of information, experiences, and even new friends on the Internet.

Index

• *O* •

• *P* •

• **Z** •

Notes

Notes

Notes

Notes

Notes

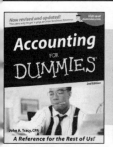

FOR DUMMIES®

A world of resources to help you grow

HOME, GARDEN & HOBBIES

0-7645-5295-3

0-7645-5130-2

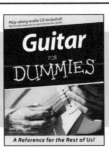

0-7645-5106-X

Also available:

Auto Repair For Dummies
(0-7645-5089-6)

Chess For Dummies
(0-7645-5003-9)

Home Maintenance For
Dummies
(0-7645-5215-5)

Organizing For Dummies
(0-7645-5300-3)

Piano For Dummies
(0-7645-5105-1)

Poker For Dummies
(0-7645-5232-5)

Quilting For Dummies
(0-7645-5118-3)

Rock Guitar For Dummies
(0-7645-5356-9)

Roses For Dummies
(0-7645-5202-3)

Sewing For Dummies
(0-7645-5137-X)

FOOD & WINE

0-7645-5250-3

0-7645-5390-9

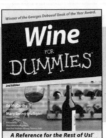

0-7645-5114-0

Also available:

Bartending For Dummies
(0-7645-5051-9)

Chinese Cooking For
Dummies
(0-7645-5247-3)

Christmas Cooking For
Dummies
(0-7645-5407-7)

Diabetes Cookbook For
Dummies
(0-7645-5230-9)

Grilling For Dummies
(0-7645-5076-4)

Low-Fat Cooking For
Dummies
(0-7645-5035-7)

Slow Cookers For Dummies
(0-7645-5240-6)

TRAVEL

0-7645-5453-0

0-7645-5438-7

0-7645-5448-4

Also available:

America's National Parks For
Dummies
(0-7645-6204-5)

Caribbean For Dummies
(0-7645-5445-X)

Cruise Vacations For
Dummies 2003
(0-7645-5459-X)

Europe For Dummies
(0-7645-5456-5)

Ireland For Dummies
(0-7645-6199-5)

France For Dummies
(0-7645-6292-4)

London For Dummies
(0-7645-5416-6)

Mexico's Beach Resorts For
Dummies
(0-7645-6262-2)

Paris For Dummies
(0-7645-5494-8)

RV Vacations For Dummies
(0-7645-5443-3)

Walt Disney World & Orlando
For Dummies
(0-7645-5444-1)

Available wherever books are sold. Go to www.dummies.com or call 1-877-762-2974 to order direct.

FOR DUMMIES®

Plain-English solutions for everyday challenges

COMPUTER BASICS

0-7645-0838-5

0-7645-1663-9

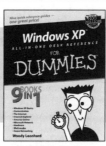

0-7645-1548-9

Also available:

PCs All-in-One Desk Reference For Dummies (0-7645-0791-5)

Pocket PC For Dummies (0-7645-1640-X)

Treo and Visor For Dummies (0-7645-1673-6)

Troubleshooting Your PC For Dummies (0-7645-1669-8)

Upgrading & Fixing PCs For Dummies (0-7645-1665-5)

Windows XP For Dummies (0-7645-0893-8)

Windows XP For Dummies Quick Reference (0-7645-0897-0)

BUSINESS SOFTWARE

0-7645-0822-9

0-7645-0839-3

0-7645-0819-9

Also available:

Excel Data Analysis For Dummies (0-7645-1661-2)

Excel 2002 All-in-One Desk Reference For Dummies (0-7645-1794-5)

Excel 2002 For Dummies Quick Reference (0-7645-0829-6)

GoldMine "X" For Dummies (0-7645-0845-8)

Microsoft CRM For Dummies (0-7645-1698-1)

Microsoft Project 2002 For Dummies (0-7645-1628-0)

Office XP For Dummies (0-7645-0830-X)

Outlook 2002 For Dummies (0-7645-0828-8)

Get smart! Visit www.dummies.com

- **Find listings of even more** *For Dummies* **titles**

- **Browse online articles**

- **Sign up for Dummies eTips™**

- **Check out** *For Dummies* **fitness videos and other products**

- **Order from our online bookstore**

Available wherever books are sold. Go to www.dummies.com or call 1-877-762-2974 to order direct.

FOR DUMMIES®

Helping you expand your horizons and realize your potential

INTERNET

0-7645-0894-6

0-7645-1659-0

0-7645-1642-6

Also available:

America Online 7.0 For Dummies
(0-7645-1624-8)

Genealogy Online For Dummies
(0-7645-0807-5)

The Internet All-in-One Desk Reference For Dummies
(0-7645-1659-0)

Internet Explorer 6 For Dummies
(0-7645-1344-3)

The Internet For Dummies Quick Reference
(0-7645-1645-0)

Internet Privacy For Dummies
(0-7645-0846-6)

Researching Online For Dummies
(0-7645-0546-7)

Starting an Online Business For Dummies
(0-7645-1655-8)

DIGITAL MEDIA

0-7645-1664-7

0-7645-1675-2

0-7645-0806-7

Also available:

CD and DVD Recording For Dummies
(0-7645-1627-2)

Digital Photography All-in-One Desk Reference For Dummies
(0-7645-1800-3)

Digital Photography For Dummies Quick Reference
(0-7645-0750-8)

Home Recording for Musicians For Dummies
(0-7645-1634-5)

MP3 For Dummies
(0-7645-0858-X)

Paint Shop Pro "X" For Dummies
(0-7645-2440-2)

Photo Retouching & Restoration For Dummies
(0-7645-1662-0)

Scanners For Dummies
(0-7645-0783-4)

GRAPHICS

0-7645-0817-2

0-7645-1651-5

0-7645-0895-4

Also available:

Adobe Acrobat 5 PDF For Dummies
(0-7645-1652-3)

Fireworks 4 For Dummies
(0-7645-0804-0)

Illustrator 10 For Dummies
(0-7645-3636-2)

QuarkXPress 5 For Dummies
(0-7645-0643-9)

Visio 2000 For Dummies
(0-7645-0635-8)

Available wherever books are sold. Go to www.dummies.com or call 1-877-762-2974 to order direct.

FOR DUMMIES®

The advice and explanations you need to succeed

SELF-HELP, SPIRITUALITY & RELIGION

Sex
0-7645-5302-X

Parenting
0-7645-5418-2

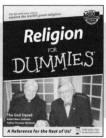

Religion
0-7645-5264-3

Also available:

The Bible For Dummies
(0-7645-5296-1)

Buddhism For Dummies
(0-7645-5359-3)

Christian Prayer For Dummies
(0-7645-5500-6)

Dating For Dummies
(0-7645-5072-1)

Judaism For Dummies
(0-7645-5299-6)

Potty Training For Dummies
(0-7645-5417-4)

Pregnancy For Dummies
(0-7645-5074-8)

Rekindling Romance For Dummies
(0-7645-5303-8)

Spirituality For Dummies
(0-7645-5298-8)

Weddings For Dummies
(0-7645-5055-1)

PETS

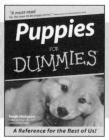

Puppies
0-7645-5255-4

Dog Training
0-7645-5286-4

Cats
0-7645-5275-9

Also available:

Labrador Retrievers For Dummies
(0-7645-5281-3)

Aquariums For Dummies
(0-7645-5156-6)

Birds For Dummies
(0-7645-5139-6)

Dogs For Dummies
(0-7645-5274-0)

Ferrets For Dummies
(0-7645-5259-7)

German Shepherds For Dummies
(0-7645-5280-5)

Golden Retrievers For Dummies
(0-7645-5267-8)

Horses For Dummies
(0-7645-5138-8)

Jack Russell Terriers For Dummies
(0-7645-5268-6)

Puppies Raising & Training Diary For Dummies
(0-7645-0876-8)

EDUCATION & TEST PREPARATION

Spanish
0-7645-5194-9

Algebra
0-7645-5325-9

The ACT
0-7645-5210-4

Also available:

Chemistry For Dummies
(0-7645-5430-1)

English Grammar For Dummies
(0-7645-5322-4)

French For Dummies
(0-7645-5193-0)

The GMAT For Dummies
(0-7645-5251-1)

Inglés Para Dummies
(0-7645-5427-1)

Italian For Dummies
(0-7645-5196-5)

Research Papers For Dummies
(0-7645-5426-3)

The SAT I For Dummies
(0-7645-5472-7)

U.S. History For Dummies
(0-7645-5249-X)

World History For Dummies
(0-7645-5242-2)

Available wherever books are sold. Go to www.dummies.com or call 1-877-762-2974 to order direct.

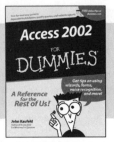